Pricing Policy and Price Controls in Developing Countries

Pricing Policy and Price Controls in Developing Countries

K. D. Saksena

Frances Pinter (Publishers), London
Lynne Rienner Publishers Inc., Boulder

© K. D. Saksena 1986

First published in Great Britain in 1986 by
Frances Pinter (Publishers) Limited
25 Floral Street, London WC2E 9DS

First published in the United States of America by
Lynne Rienner Publishers Inc.
948 North Street
Boulder, Colorado 80302

British Library Cataloguing in Publication Data
Saksena, K. D.
   Pricing policy and price controls in developing
   countries.
   1. Price regulation — India
   I. Title
   338.5'26'0954   HB236.I/

ISBN 0–86187–622–9

Library of Congress Cataloging-in-Publication Data
Saksena, K.D.
   Pricing policy and price controls in developing
countries.

   Includes index.
   1. Price regulation — Developing countries.   2. Price
regulations — India.   I. Title.
HB236.D44S25   1986   338.5'26'091724   86–3287
ISBN 0–931477–85–9 (U.S.)

Typeset by Folio Photosetting, Bristol
Printed by Biddles of Guildford Ltd.

Contents

Preface	ix
1. The case for price controls and pricing policy	1
2. The nature and objectives of pricing policy	17
3. Theory of price control	33
4. Some general issues relating to pricing policy	44
5. Some problems and issues relating to the determination of controlled prices	64
6. Marginal cost pricing versus average cost pricing	92
7. The problem of rate of return in relation to price-controlled industries	102
8. Dual pricing	121
9. Some aspects of price controls and pricing policy in India	140
10. Growth, performance and pricing of public enterprises in India	174
11. Price control: some conclusions	208
Appendix	223
Index	225

To my mother

Preface

Although 'pricing policy and price controls' had been the subject of my interest, it was during my nine months' stay at Oxford as a Visiting Fellow at Queen Elizabeth House that I got an opportunity of thinking and working on it in a somewhat sustained and systematic manner that enabled me to write this small book. The book attempts to analyse some of the basic theoretical and practical issues which arise in the formulation and implementation of pricing policy and of a system of price controls, particularly with reference to developing economies like India's. It deals mainly with matters of general interest to all market economies: only two chapters are devoted entirely to India — one discussing the salient features of the price controls as they have been operating in India, and the other the issues relating to pricing policy in the context of public enterprises in India.

I must record my deep sense of gratitude to Dr Francis Seton of Nuffield College and Dr Frances Stewart, Fellow of Somerville College, under whose supervision this work was done at Oxford; and also to Mr Arthur Hazlewood, Warden of Queen Elizabeth House, and Mr Neville Maxwell, the programme co-ordinator who constantly helped and encouraged me in my work. I am indebted to Dr C.H. Hanumantha Rao and Dr Raja J. Chelliah (both presently Members of the Planning Commission, Government of India) with whom I have had several useful discussions on various issues prior to my visit to Oxford. I also gratefully acknowledge the help I received from Dr P.S. Sharma, Mr Kewal Ram, Mr Ishwar Das and Mr Chaman Lal (my colleagues in the Economic Administration Reforms Commission, Government of India) while in India during the preliminary stages of this work. I am also grateful to my wife Madhu, who was a source of constant inspiration, encouragement and help to me in writing this book.

I may mention that the present work does not in any way reflect the thinking or the views of the Government of India, but my own ideas on the various issues discussed, based on my own thinking and analysis of facts and empirical data, in my personal capacity as a student and researcher at Oxford.

1 The case for price controls and pricing policy

The term 'pricing policy' has gained currency among economists, administrators and politicians alike. The term implies some kind of control or regulation of prices or interference with the free play of market forces by an external agency to achieve certain objectives which may otherwise not be achieved. The external agency is invariably a central authority or the government which decides not only the objectives to be achieved, but also whether the need for intervention in the functioning of the market mechanism has arisen; the form or mode of intervention; as well as its timing and duration. The government has to, so to say, formulate a policy or guidelines for action and also evolve suitable legal, institutional and administrative frameworks for implementing and monitoring that policy. Pricing policy is thus not synonymous or co-extensive with price control — it is a much wider term which covers, *inter alia*, the following:

(a) the objectives sought to be achieved by price controls;
(b) the various forms which the interference with the market mechanism may take, ranging from a mere exhortation, advice or suggestion to the manufacturers or suppliers to total control of prices and quantities of the goods produced and their distribution;
(c) the laws enacted or the executive directions issued to the producers/sellers/distributors and the institutions set up, statutorily or otherwise, or administrative arrangements made or procedures evolved to enforce them and to monitor the progress and effects of all action relating thereto; and
(d) above all, a set of basic principles covering (a) (b) and (c) above.

The principles referred to in (d) above are not always economic principles but generally value judgements regarding what ought to be done, for whom and in what manner. These principles may reflect the basic philosophy, aspirations, ideals or ethical values, or sometimes even considerations of political or administrative expediency, which may form the basis of all economic policies, including pricing policy: they reflect essentially the kind of economic and social order and quality of life which might be the ultimate goal of all social and economic policies and endeavours, and may differ in both content and emphasis in different economies.

Economies are generally categorized as 'capitalist', 'socialist' and 'mixed' economies. In fact, both the purely capitalist and the purely socialist economies are only conceptual models, and in the real world all economies are mixed, having some features of both. Even the so-called 'socialist' economies have certain elements of capitalism as the free play of market forces is allowed to determine prices and production in some part of the consumer goods sector and a certain degree of competitiveness is often sought to be introduced in certain spheres to promote efficiency. The capitalist economies similarly have a large and expanding public sector, nationalized industries or industrial units which operate under competitive or oligopolistic conditions, and sometimes as virtually state monopolies. The distinction between the socialist and the capitalist systems, though sometimes somewhat blurred since both have public and private sectors and elements of both competition and monopoly, is still quite significant.

In the socialist economic system, the market mechanism is sought to be superseded or supplanted by the allocation of all economic resources through a central authority according to the principles and priorities decided by it, and is temporarily tolerated and grudgingly suffered in certain other sectors for achieving the objectives of the central plan. In a capitalist economy, while the government may intervene in the free functioning of the market mechanism in pursuance of various objectives, the endeavour is to work through the market and not to interfere with it as a system. The basic premise of the capitalist system is that the market mechanism, if allowed to work freely, would cause an optimum allocation of resources and create conditions for continuous growth in output and employment, and needs to be interfered with only to even out short-run fluctuations or to correct the imbalances or inequities which may sometimes arise due to its imperfect functioning or due to abnormal conditions created by exogenous factors like, for instance, war. The socialist system, on the other hand, while tolerating the market mechanism and even trying to make use of it in the transitional phase, aims at ultimately achieving a marketless, moneyless and stateless era of prosperity and plenty. The theory of scientific socialism, however, does not attempt to explain or establish how the working of the socialist system would usher in such a millenium: it only explains how the inherent contradictions of the capitalist system would cause its destruction, giving way to socialism where all means of production would be socially owned and operated. Markets, prices and some kind of price regulation are thus ubiquitous phenomena found in all economies irrespective of their ideologies or the nature of their economic organization.

The concept of pricing policy, which necessarily implies interference with the market mechanism or determination of prices by the free play of the market forces of demand and supply, is irrelevant in an economy where conditions of perfect competition prevail. In such an economy, the buyers and sellers of any commodity are so numerous and its quantity demanded or supplied by each one of them forms such an infinitesimally small portion of the total quantity demanded or supplied that no individual buyer or seller could possibly, by his own action, in any way influence the price of that commodity. Both the buyers and the sellers are thus price takers, and each seller has a perfectly elastic demand curve for his product at the prevailing market price and can sell any quantity at that price. Both also have perfect knowledge of the market conditions. Each product is perfectly homogeneous and perfectly divisible and the factors of production too are perfectly divisible and perfectly mobile. Each individual behaves rationally. If he is a consumer he maximizes his utility or satisfaction, given his scale of preferences, his income level and the market prices. Similarly, each producer or seller maximizes his profits given the technological conditions of production and the prevailing market prices of inputs and finished products. Consumers are governed by the Law of Diminishing Utility and producers by the Law of Diminishing Returns, so that each consumer is able to reach an equilibrium where he maximizes his utility, and each producer also reaches an equilibrium position where he maximizes his profits. These equilibrium positions are reached by 'trial and error', and the entire economy attains a position of 'general equilibrium' of prices and production. This is not due to any conscious co-ordination and planning by any visible agency, but is the result of unconscious co-ordination through the market mechanism. The system demonstrates a harmony of interests between society and the individual so that each individual, while 'he intends his own gain' is 'led by an invisible hand to promote an end which was not part of his intention';[1] and the activities of all the self-seeking individuals, each pursuing his own interest, result not in chaos and anarchy, but in an economic order which promotes the interest simultaneously of both society and the individual.

This economic order is a kind of economic democracy characterized by what is called 'consumers' sovereignty', where consumers ultimately decide what goods are to be produced and in what quantities, by casting their money votes in the form of prices they would be prepared to pay for various quantities of goods, which provide necessary signals to the producers and sellers of those goods. These price signals determine the direction in which economic resources flow, and also the factor prices, factor shares or reward which each factor of production would get, and move the entire system on to an equilibrium position of optimum allocation of resources. This is a position where 'welfare' is maximized: the welfare of each individual who maximizes his utility as well as that of the community in the sense of 'the sum of the utilities of the individual households in the community'.[2] From the producers' angle, this is a position where total profits are maximized under given technological conditions of production. This is an optimum position as any deviation from it or any reallocation of resources would reduce the total welfare of the consumers and the total profits earned by the producers, and also the level of efficiency of production. The conditions of this optimum, generally known as 'marginal conditions', have been carefully formulated by many economists and we need not go into them for the purposes of our analysis.

The need and relevance of pricing policy arises because no capitalist economy characterized by private ownership of the means of production and a freely functioning market mechanism actually corresponds to the model of a perfectly competitive economy. In this model, the price signals determine the allocation of resources and the resultant volume and composition of output, pattern of employment, factor shares and distribution of income. If the price signals operated properly, they would cause an optimum allocation of resources and should obviate the need for any interference with the market mechanism. The case for price control and pricing policy thus rests essentially on the failure of the price signals to operate in the desired manner.

For any kind of signals to operate properly and efficiently, it is necessary that they function independently of those who are to be guided by them, and that the latter are not able to manipulate them in any way; otherwise the signals lose all meaning. In the model of a perfectly competitive economy, the price signals do function in this manner because both the buyers and the sellers are so numerous that they cannot, by their individual action, affect the market price; and the possibility of their combining or joining together is also ruled out. They are thus price takers and not price givers. Such a situation does not exist anywhere in reality. Even if we assume that it did exist sometime in the past, it could have been expected to develop, and has in fact developed, into a situation where the suppliers or sellers do not always take the market price as given, and successfully influence it to their advantage. The competitive character of the perfectly competitive model itself creates conditions where competition does not remain perfect, and the producers acquire a certain degree of control over the market price. For if the market price is to be taken as given, the only way a producer or manufacturer can increase his profit is by technological improvements which reduce his costs and increase his profit margin. Technological changes are imperative in a competitive economy, and these have several major effects. Firstly, they tend to increase the size of the individual industrial units to suit the changing technology. Bigger industrial units using improved technology enjoy economies of scale and increasing returns or decreasing costs over considerable ranges of output. Secondly, the products do not remain homogeneous, and there emerges a wide range in each product consisting of several differentiated products. Thirdly, the factors of production or inputs do not remain perfectly divisible, as large, indivisible units of plant and machinery have to be installed; and the capital investment required for their acquisition and installation becomes 'lumpy' and cannot be varied in small quantities. Fourthly, the producers and sellers do not remain passive agents so far as the marketing of their products is concerned. In a world where no product is homogeneous and every product has a range and a variety of differentiated products, the only way to sell one's 'product' is by creating an impression in the consumer's mind that it is different from the similar products of other producers and in some way superior to them. Because of the availability of several similar competing, though differentiated, products, no producer can sell any quantity of his product at the current market price, and the demand for his product is not perfectly elastic at that price, even if we assume that he cannot influence that price by his own action alone. This leads to advertising and sales promotion drives, which are inconceivable in the competitive model which assumes perfect knowledge and homogeneous products.

Fifthly, the theory of harmony of interests of the individual and soiety breaks down. Changes in the quality, quantity and variety of goods, both over space and time, are taking place very rapidly and consumers have very imperfect knowledge about them, which sellers exploit to their own advantage. Moreover, because of external economies and external diseconomies arising in the process of production, there occur divergences between what are called 'marginal social benefits' and 'marginal private benefits' on the one hand (due to external economies) and 'marginal social costs' and 'marginal private costs' (due to external diseconomies) on the other. Sixthly, in a competitive situation characterized by continuous technological change, increasing size of industrial and business units and the scale of their operations, indivisibilities and lumpiness of investments, the basic premise of the perfectly competitive model ceases to hold good. The number of producers and suppliers generally tends to get progressively reduced as small producers are not able to survive in the competitive struggle (unless they combine to form a viable group or are given state protection in some form), and digopolies and monopolies emerge which manipulate production and prices in a manner which may not be in the interest of the economy or in the interest of certain sections of society, which may need protection against their activities. Seventhly, the so-called consumers' sovereignty of economic democracy may operate to the detriment of society or of large sections of the consumer public. Consumers' sovereignty may in actual practice mean not the sovereignty of the mass of consumers, but that of relatively few affluent individuals who have the largest number of money votes, and whose votes may actually decide the allocation of resources and the pattern of production. Even the bulk of consumers may not be able to exercise their money votes properly owing to sheer ignorance or to having been misguided by advertisements. This may result in an allocation of resources and a composition of national output which may not be in the interest of the consumers themselves, or it may result in the diversion of scarce economic resources to socially undesirable channels. In any case, consumers' sovereignty loses its meaning and significance when the producers or sellers, through product differentiation and aggressive advertising, create consumer preferences for goods which might not otherwise have been consumed, and change the demand pattern to correspond to the pattern of consumer goods which they find commercially advantageous to produce.

The so-called 'welfare economics', by using the model of perfect competition and the tools of marginal analysis, postulates a set of 'marginal conditions' which a perfectly competitive economic system tends to achieve. The achievement of these conditions implies maximization of welfare. Welfare is a normative concept involving value judgement. Welfare economics assumes that 'welfare' consists in people getting what they want in quantities corresponding to their scale of preferences and their capacity to buy as determined by their incomes and the prevailing market prices, which each individual by himself is powerless to alter. As we know, individuals need not necessarily be the best judges of their own interest, and may want things which may not always be desirable from their own or from society's point of view. An economic system guided solely by consumer preferences may, therefore, produce goods which may be ethically or socially undesirable. The concept of welfare optimum also implies that one allocation of resources and the resultant composition of output is as good as any other so long as it is in accordance with consumer preferences. It further assumes that an individual's welfare depends on his own consumption and is entirely unaffected by what others consume. Another unrealistic assumption underlying this concept is that the distribution of income has nothing to do with maximization of welfare, and 'the sum of utilities of the individual households in the community' (which is the concept of welfare adopted) is not affected by redistribution of income. In other words, it is assumed that the marginal utility of money is the same and remains constant for all individuals irrespective of the quantum of their money income, so that income distribution is not a variable affecting total welfare of the community, which is maximized. The concept of an equitable distribution of income is irrelevant in this scheme of things. All these are highly questionable assumptions which render the formulation of the marginal conditions for optimizing welfare a futile and meaningless exercise based on a basically wrong value judgement regarding what constitutes 'welfare', as well as wrong notions about the factors which determine the quantum of welfare which a perfectly competitive system is supposed to tend to maximize.

Although the theory of perfect competition and welfare maximization on which the case for *laissez-faire* or non-intervention with the free play of market forces rests represents a high degree of sophisticated scientific reasoning and analysis, it has limited practical significance because it assumes away almost all the complicating factors and involves a basic value judgement regarding the concept of welfare itself. This theory shows an obsession with concepts like optimum allocation of resources, maximization of welfare and efficiency of production and equilibrium under static conditions where consumer tastes and production technology do not change. Under such conditions, and further assuming perfectly divisible and homogeneous inputs and outputs in a world characterized by perfect knowledge and perfect mobility, the free play of market forces operating through price signals would result in the most efficient allocation of resources which would not only maximize production and productive efficiency of given resources, but would also maximize 'welfare' in a certain sense. Such a system would also attain an equilibrium in the sense that the entire system as well as the individual consumers and producers comprising it would reach their maximum positions. The entire model is so simple, is based on such simplistic assumptions, has so few economic variables, and is so devoid of complications, that it could be, and has in fact been, reduced to neat mathematical formulations. The basic questions which need to be answered in regard to this model and its policy conclusion of *laissez-faire* could be stated as follows:

(a) Do the assumptions of perfect competition hold good in the real world, and if not, do they not destroy the case for non-interference with the operation of price signals?
(b) Does the optimum allocation of resources under conditions of perfect competition also imply full employment of economic resources?
(c) Is the concept of 'welfare' which is said to be maximized in the perfectly competitive model valid?
(d) What is the significance and relevance of the concept of equilibrium in a dynamic setting and what are its policy implications?
(e) Is the attainment of equilibrium at a level where resources are optimally allocated the basic economic problem, or does that problem itself need to be restated? If so, how and what are the policy implications of that restatement?

As discussed earlier, the assumptions of perfect competition do not hold good in the real world. The imperfections of competition may also give rise to several distortions in the production pattern and to inequities in the distribution of income. Market imperfections may further cause inefficient use of scarce resources or their deliberate underutilization, quantitative restriction of output and its qualitative deterioration. These imperfections may necessitate interference with the market mechanism, including direct price controls. In certain cases it may become necessary to ignore the price signals because they might have been given by a tiny minority of consumers having a very large number of money votes or by wrongly motivated, ignorant or misguided consumers. Sometimes it may be considered necessary to produce certain goods for which there may be no demand and for whose production the market may have given no signal at all. For instance, in an underdeveloped country with a large agricultural population barely surviving at subsistence level owing to low yields in agriculture, there may be no demand for fertilizers in the initial stages of development due to the ignorance of farmers about their usefulness, but it may still be considered necessary to put up fertilizer plants at considerable cost and induce demand for fertilizers through publicity and extension methods. Such a country may also be lacking in the basic infrastructure, the market mechanism may never give any signals for its creation, and it may remain condemned to a sub-human level of existence unless investments are made in creating the infrastructure of rail and road transport, power plants, dams for irrigation and flood control, steel/cement/fertilizer plants, etc. In fact, the traditional theory of a market economy loses practical relevance in a backward economy embarking on a programme to initiate a process of self-sustaining economic growth for which the direct commandeering of scarce economic resources by the state may sometimes become a practical necessity.

The obsession with optimum allocation of given economic resources to maximize 'welfare' seems to be a hangover of the inebriation which had lulled the economists into the belief that all income is automatically spent either on consumer or on investment goods; that supply creates its own demand so that there could be no general excess or deficiency of demand causing glut or unemployment; that any short-run gap between saving and investment is eliminated by changes in the rate of interest, leaving the levels of income and employment unaffected; that there is stable equilibrium at full employment and any position of less than full employment is necessarily a temporary, transitional stage where economic forces constantly urge the system on to a position of full employment and this could not be an equilibrium position. Having deluded themselves with the idea of living in such an unbelievably blessed world, they further persuaded themselves to believe, by a seemingly clever use of the tools of marginal analysis (which were subsequently developed and perfected), that left to itself the system would not only ensure full employment of all economic resources, but also their optimum allocation, maximizing welfare and efficiency. There is, however, no reason to believe that the level of the 'welfare optimum' will always be the level at which all resources will be fully employed. The point where given resources are allocated optimally may very well be a point where all available resources may not be fully employed due to lack of effective demand, or due to 'specificity' and 'complementarity' of resources,[3] which may necessitate not only a certain level but also a certain composition of output to ensure their full employment. If 'full employment' is considered to be a desirable social and economic objective, the economy cannot be left to be guided solely by the price signals of a market economy, and state intervention in the free functioning of such an economy by undertaking investments in the lines not indicated by the price signals, or direct manipulation of price signals to make resources flow in the desired directions or away from those not desired, may be resorted to as a matter of conscious policy.

Another basic question, namely, whether the concept of 'welfare' implicit in the theory of 'welfare optimum' is itself valid, has to be answered in the negative. The concept is obviously normative in character, involving value judgement; and both the notions underlying it, viz. that the individual himself is the best judge of his own welfare and his welfare consists in getting things which he desires according to his scale of preferences, and that his 'welfare' in this sense is independent of what others desire or consume and is unaffected by the consumption or possessions of others, are questionable. As we know too well, in several cases individuals may have (or may be persuaded to have through misleading advertisements) mistaken ideas about what they really want; and what they want may not always be in their best interest. Similarly, welfare, being a state of mind, may, in many cases, be affected by the level and the standards of consumption enjoyed by others around and not merely by one's own consumption. A more serious objection to this concept of welfare is that it assumes that society's welfare is maximized when each individual comprising it maximizes his own utility or welfare, and that there is a basic harmony or identity of interest between the individual and society. This is an unrealistic assumption since the volume and the pattern of the output and the distribution of income in an economy guided solely by price signals given by consumers maximizing their welfare or utility, individually and collectively, may not be found to be socially desirable, equitable, just or conducive to the health or the growth of the economy. A modern 'welfare state' which undertakes the responsibility for providing a certain minimum level of income and essential services (for example, health and education) to everyone, and social security to those who need it, cannot leave it to the price system to provide for the basic needs and make equal opportunities for development available to the economically weaker sections of the community. The practical problem is not the maximization of an imaginary 'welfare', but the provision of certain basic facilities and the meeting of certain minimum requirements for all, particularly those who would otherwise not be able to do so, the solution of which may only lie in the interference with the market mechanism and in not heeding the price signals in all cases or correcting these signals by direct manipulation and control.

The concept of equilibrium is germane and vital to the theory of perfect competition and welfare optimum. All the economic variables (for example demand, supply, saving, investment, income, employment, utility, profit, efficiency) reach a state of 'general equilibrium' in this scheme of things where everyone, individually and collectively, reaches his maximum or optimum position. The policy conclusion is that the market mechanism or the price system which makes the attainment of this state of bliss possible need not be interfered with. However, even under static conditions, 'equilibrium' is only a conceptual and not a real phenomenon, which only helps us to understand how economic variables tend to behave under certain given conditions. It may have little practical significance since the system may, in fact, never attain an equilibrium position in practice; and even if it did, there may be no means of ascertaining or verifying it.

There are so many disequilibrating factors constantly in operation that even if by chance the system ever reached a level of equilibrium, it might not remain there for any appreciable length of time. In a dynamic world, the system may continuously move towards higher and higher (or, possibly, lower and lower) levels of general equilibrium, depending on several self-propelling, self-sustaining and often self-accelerating forces generated in the process of growth by the system itself or else autonomously by an external agency, without ever actually reaching an equilibrium level. The concept of general equilibrium under static conditions becomes largely irrelevant in dealing with the problems of a real economy which is growing and not stationary at any particular level. In a changing economy, interference with market forces and the price system may be considered to be a practical necessity for initiating or accelerating certain growth processes or for preventing, arresting or regulating certain observed tendencies which may be taking the system away from the path of desired economic progress. The path of growth or progress is through continuous disequilibrium, and the disequilibrating factors may also be the causal factors for growth. The state of equilibrium is purely conceptual, and its significance lies not in the system ever reaching it, or, having reached it, remaining on it, but in the identification of the disequilibrating factors which need to be controlled to achieve growth with stability; and in helping in the formulation of economic policies for achieving this objective. In reality, the number of variables is so large, their interrelationships so complex, and the disequilibrating factors so numerous that no mathematical model or formulation could possibly reflect any real economic situation and indicate the policy imperatives to achieve the objective of growth with stability. The fundamental economic problem in a growing economy where consumption pattern, technology, population, income distribution and rates of saving and investment are constantly changing is not one of optimum allocation of given resources under static conditions. The problem is threefold:

(a) how to employ all available economic resources, particularly human resources, fully and most efficiently;
(b) how to constantly augment these resources, particularly capital, and increase their productivity; and
(c) how to distribute the output and the income in the most equitable manner consistent with the objective of growth with stability.

The basic problem, as stated above, may not, in concrete terms, be the same for all economies: its formulation in operational terms necessarily involves value judgements regarding various matters, such as the desirability of the full employment of all available resources, particularly human resources, the desired rate of growth of output and incomes and the period over which it should be achieved, the extent of sacrifice of present consumption for a higher level of consumption in future considered feasible, the minimum level of income to be ensured for everyone and the manner in which the national income and the increases in it should be distributed among those different categories of people who generate them. These are obviously questions, the answer to which cannot always be left to the market mechanism or the price system, since the questions belong to the realm of economic policy and not economic theory. These are vital matters which no country and no government can possibly leave to be tackled by price signals alone; and every country and government, irrespective of its political or economic ideology, has in fact been, to a greater or lesser degree, interfering with and sometimes even ignoring price signals in formulating and implementing a set of economic policies designed to achieve the objectives (which may not all be strictly economic) it has set itself (for considerations which may also not be strictly economic). In any case, practically speaking, the basic economic problem has never been that of maximizing consumer welfare or consumer surpluses of all individuals and the productive efficiency of given resources under given conditions, which the market system, left to itself, may do under perfectly competitive conditions. The basic problem is, and has perhaps always been, that of fully utilizing all available resources in the most efficient manner under fast-changing conditions to continuously maximize the national income and output of the desired composition over a period of time and to ensure the sharing of that national income and output in accordance with the considerations of equity and social justice which may not be the same everywhere. There is no simple or unique solution to this extremely difficult and complex problem which any system of formal economic reasoning or body of economic theory could provide. Here we are necessarily in the realm of economic policy, involving control and regulation directed towards given ends.

To sum up, a strong case for interference of some kind in the market mechanism or price control exists for the following reasons:

(a) The assumptions of perfect competition do not hold good in real life.
(b) Even if perfectly competitive conditions are assumed to exist for the sake of argument, they would not necessarily result in full

employment of available resources or an equitable distribution of income.

(c) The model of perfect competition only explains how the system would reach an equilibrium position under static conditions, and has, therefore, no relevance for any real world situation where conditions are constantly changing and equilibrium is perhaps never reached due to the continuous operation of several disequilibrating factors, which still take the economy to higher and higher levels of national income and output; and where the basic economic problem is how to achieve the desired rate of growth with the least instability.

(d) The concept of 'welfare optimum' arrived at by use of the tools of the marginal analysis is based essentially on a questionable normative concept of 'welfare' involving value judgement, and on several equally questionable assumptions, and has practically no relevance for economic policy. The real economic problem in a dynamic world from a practical angle is not that of maximization of any such 'welfare', but of controlling the behaviour of strategic economic variables like saving, investment, employment, volume and composition of national output and income and its distribution, and of efficiency of resource utilization for the achievement of certain objectives decided independently on considerations, many of which may not be economic, involving value judgements; and economic policies have to be formulated and implemented accordingly for the achievement of those objectives through policy instruments such as price controls, credit control, taxation and public expenditure.

(e) Even if it is assumed, for the sake of argument, that 'welfare optimum' is a theoretically sound and practically feasible proposition, and such a position could in fact be achieved in any real life situation, it cannot be argued that the corresponding distribution of income would be equitable or socially most desirable. If distribution of income is recognized as an important variable affecting the total welfare of the community, and if it is conceded that a more equitable distribution of income could increase it, price control has to be recognized as an instrument for increasing it by augmenting the real incomes of the categories of consumers and the money income of the classes of producers (for example in the case of support price operations for agricultural produce), for whose protection it is resorted to, relative to the incomes of other categories/classes.

Notes

1 Adam Smith, *An Inquiry into the Nature and Causes of the Wealth of Nations*, New York, Modern Library, 1937, p. 423.
2. A. Bergson, *Essays in Normative Economics*, Cambridge, Mass., The Belknap Press at Harvard University Press, 1966, pp. 194–5.
3. See N. Kaldor, 'Stability and Full Employment', *Economic Journal*, **48**, December 1938.

2 The nature and objectives of pricing policy

The term 'pricing policy' implies several things. Firstly, it implies some form of control of market prices and interference in the free functioning of the market mechanism. Secondly, it presupposes the existence of certain conditions which necessitate price regulation. Thirdly, it means a set of measures directly influencing the level of certain prices with a view to changing those conditions in order to achieve certain objectives. Here we are in the realm of value judgements or 'normative economics', as the objectives reflect the economic, political and social philosophies and ideals that a country might have adopted or might have been pursuing, which would naturally not be the same everywhere. Fourthly, it also implies that it is not the only policy. There may also be other policies that it may have to further and be consistent with, or which reinforce it. In any case, it is part of the economic policy, which is a comprehensive expression for the entire set of principles and measures governing the management of the economy; and it has to be formulated and implemented within the broad framework of the general economic policy being pursued, and not work at cross purposes with it.

The price mechanism under conditions of perfect competition achieves two things: maximum efficiency for each individual production unit and maximum utility or welfare for each individual consumer. It also achieves equilibrium for individual producers and consumers as well as 'general equilibrium' for the economy as a whole. These are not objectives consciously pursued and achieved but the results of the free functioning of the system under certain given conditions without any conscious co-ordination, planning or direction by anyone. However, as explained in the previous chapter, the conditions of perfect competition do not exist in practice and the ecnmic system in fact works in a manner which creates several imperfections. Competition itself brings about technological advances which make the industrial units grow in size. The elimination of a large number of relatively inefficient units in the competitive struggle leaves fewer and fewer units producing a larger and larger proportion of the total output and thereby gaining greater and greater power to influence prices and production to their commercial advantage, to the detriment of consumers.

Market imperfections and the emergence of oligopolies and monopolies may result in the restriction of output and deterioration in the quality of goods produced. The pattern of production or the composition of output may be distorted in the sense that it may not correspond to the actual needs of consumers or of the economy, and may result in a structure of relative prices which may distort the income distribution, the relative factor shares or the relative incomes of different categories of producers (for example those engaged in agriculture *vis-à-vis* those producing industrial goods or those providing services). The self-seeking, uncoordinated and unplanned activities of the producers and consumers under such conditions might result in underemployment of human resources, underutilization of existing industrial capacity side by side with large unsatisfied demand, an inflationary rise in the general price level with conditions of depression, stagnation and sickness in certain vital sectors or industrial units, and the creation and accentuation of income disparities giving rise to social and political unrest. Thus free functioning of the market mechanism may create conditions necessitating conscious control of the price system for achieving certain desired objectives.

The free market economies fall into two broad categories, the developed and the developing, the latter also being referred to as the 'Third World' countries. In some of the developed capitalist countries, price controls have been used extensively during wartime for 'resource mobilization' and 'price stabilization'. In normal times also these controls have come to stay as an anti-inflationary measure for ensuring the supply of essential consumer goods to the consumers and essential inputs to the industry at reasonable prices. They have also been used to provide protection to agriculturalists by guaranteeing a certain minimum price for their produce. On the whole, price controls in developed capitalist countries could achieve the following objectives:

(a) Resource mobilization in times of war by direct control and commandeering of economic resources in order to divert them to the production of essential supplies for the armed forces and also essential commodities for the civilian population at reasonable prices.
(b) Price stabilization to ensure that wartime pressures on the limited real resources do not push the general price level up unduly high, and in normal times the prices of wage goods do not rise so as to set a wage price spiral into motion.
(c) Ensuring that the free play of market forces does not result in misallocation of resources and consequent distortion of the relative price structure and the composition of national output which may not be consistent with national priorities or cause undue hardship to the bulk of consumers or retard the growth of the economy and investment flows in the desired direction in the required measure.
(d) Ensuring that the oligopolistic and monopolistic forces do not unduly restrict output or deteriorate the quality of the goods produced or mislead consumers by aggressive advertising, thereby causing underutilization of installed industrial capacity or underemployment of economic resources and production of substandard goods, which may even be harmful to consumers.
(e) Maintaining a minimum agricultural price level *vis-à-vis* prices of manufactures to protect the farmers against the relative fall in their income and to preserve and provide incentive for greater agricultural production and productivity.

The objectives stated above could possibly be summed up under six headings, namely, Efficiency, Welfare, Full Employment, Equity, Growth and Stability. The free play of market forces under perfectly competitive conditions could achieve the objectives of maximization of efficiency and welfare under static conditions without any regard to the other four objectives, which are vital under dynamic or changing conditions. Both efficiency and welfare are maximized in the perfectly competitive model by the activities of individual consumers and producers, each acting rationally, motivated by their own self-interest of utility or profit maximization, as the case may be. The entire picture changes in the real world where market imperfections make the attainment of this 'welfare optimum' impossible if each individual is allowed to pursue his own self-interest. Maximization of efficiency of resource utilization and maximization of welfare become policy objectives to be achieved by conscious co-ordination and control of the behaviour of producers and consumers. While efficiency remains an objective and statistically measurable variable which individual production units could achieve if they were properly motivated, 'welfare', which is essentially a subjective concept, being ultimately a state of mind, is no longer considered to be the subjective satisfaction of the individuals alone, as they may have imperfect knowledge and could be misinformed or misguided. To a large extent, the state or society decides, according to its own independent judgement, what is the consumer's interest and how it is to be protected and promoted. Consumer welfare becomes a policy objective to be actively pursued by the modern 'welfare state', but the concept of maximization of their welfare loses all practical significance, as theoretically and operationally the concept of welfare itself undergoes rapid changes in line with the changing values of society. The other four objectives, of Equity, Full Employment, Growth and Stability, which are more or less assumed away in the perfectly competitive model, are in practice very important in any economy, and are pursued as major policy objectives. Here again, it is primarily value judgement rather than economic reasoning or considerations which determines what is an equitable income distribution and which sections of society require protection and to what extent; the way in which human and other resources are to be utilized and what the pattern of their utilization, employment and remuneration should be; what the desirable patterns and rates of growth are and how much instability or fluctuation the system can bear; and economic policies, including pricing policy, are framed and implemented accordingly.

While the basic objectives of pricing policy, as outlined above, would be more or less the same in all types of economies, there may be variations of approach and emphasis. There is, however, one major difference between pricing policy in a capitalist economy and that in a socialist economy. Whereas a capitalist economy believes in the efficacy of the market mechanism, and interference in its free functioning is resorted to because of its imperfections, giving rise to several distortions necessitating direct control over prices and production in some sectors to achieve certain objectives; and the pricing policy aims at some kind of price reform and even trying to reinforce individual action and initiative to the greatest extent possible; the socialist system, though implicitly accepting the role of prices in the rational allocation of resources, attempts to control prices in almost the entire capital goods sector (and generally, in part of the consumer goods sector as well), permitting minimum possible freedom to the competitive forces in the market to provide incentives and promote or reward efficiency. The entire exercise in a socialist system is directed towards evolving a set of prices of capital goods which may correctly reflect their relative scarcities so that they may be allocated rationally and utilized most economically and efficiently, arriving at a structure of relative prices of all goods and services which is consistent with and conducive to the achievement of the objectives of the central plan in accordance with the principles and priorities embodied therein. The socialist system's ultimate aim is to reach a stage of plenty where money, prices, planning, etc. will become superfluous and the state itself will wither away, though socialist theory does not indicate how exactly such a golden age could ever be ushered in. On the whole, the socialist system seeks to control the prices, production and distribution of all goods and services to achieve the objectives of the central plan; and these objectives are more or less the same as in a capitalist economy in spite of variations in their operational content and emphasis and the priority assigned to each objective due to differences in their economic and social philosophy and the value judgements based thereon.

The underdeveloped or developing countries comprising the Third World have free market economies. These countries are generally in a 'vicious circle of poverty' because of low incomes, low savings, poor capacity to invest and consequent low incomes and mass poverty. Shortage of capital, inadequate infrastructural facilities for industrial growth, the predominance of agriculture and large disparities in income distribution (due to the somewhat feudalistic structure of their agrarian economies which consist of a few large landowners and a vast majority of landless agricultural labourers and farmers owning tiny uneconomic holdings in the rural sector, and a relatively small number of industrialists and traders and a large number of low-paid workers in the urban industrial sector) are some of the salient features of these economies. The free play of market forces in such economies may only tend to perpetuate poverty; and a process of planned development has to be initiated by the government to husband limited capital resources to create the necessary infrastructure and utilize the available manpower and natural resources to help the economy 'take off' on the path of self-generating and self-sustaining economic growth. In these countries, the government has to control directly the allocation of scarce economic resources and prices and the production of essential consumer goods and vital inputs for industrial production, as well as the levels of industrial and agricultural wages according to certain principles and priorities decided generally through the democratic process.

The most important objectives of economic policy in these countries are growth with stability and equity or economic justice. In the initial stages of planned development, large investments are made in many development projects which generate income and demand for consumer goods in the short run far in excess of supplies currently available which fail to keep pace with the growing demand due to the inelasticity of these supplies. Supply inelasticities may be due to several factors, such as low agricultural productivity and a low level of responsiveness of agricultural production to price increases, due in turn to uneconomic holdings and outdated technology, long gestation periods for development projects and the allocation of lesser resources to quick-maturing projects or the production of consumer goods. This results in a rise in the price of essential consumer goods, a fall in the real incomes of the poorer or weaker sections of the community, and a generally inflationary situation, which might disrupt the process of economic growth itself. Direct control of production, prices and distribution of essential consumer goods, and sometimes of essential industrial inputs may, under such conditions, become necessary to correct the inequities caused by the rise in the general price level and changes in the structure of relative prices. The term equity may have a wider meaning in the context of developing economies as it may mean not only an equitable distribution of income among different economic classes, but also among different geographical or economic regions, some of which may be economically more backward than others and may need special protection to help them catch up with the others or at least not lag too far behind. It may also mean ensuring that agricultural prices do not fall to unremunerative levels through support price operations, in order to maintain a certain parity between agricultural and non-agricultural incomes.

Besides the macro-economic objectives of controlling inflationary pressures which inevitably arise in the initial stages of planned economic development largely owing to short-run inelasticities of supplies; maintaining real incomes of the weaker sections at a certain minimum level; ensuring the availability of essential industrial inputs at reasonable prices to prevent distortions in the structure of industrial costs and prices; promoting balanced regional development; and preventing a fall in agricultural incomes *vis-à-vis* non-agricultural incomes, another very important objective of pricing policy from the viewpoint of developing economies is resource mobilization. Lack of capital being the greatest bottleneck to economic growth in these countries, pricing policy can also be used as a non-tax device for raising the level of savings in the economy. Pricing policy can stimulate aggregate savings and mobilize resources for growth in three ways, namely, by reducing consumption, generation of larger surpluses in industrial enterprises and the redistribution of income. In addition to rationing, consumer demand for price-controlled goods can be kept at a low level by deliberately keeping their price sufficiently high. The prices fixed for such products also determine the profitability of the industries producing them and their capacity to generate internal resources out of which reserves are built up for investment and dividends are paid to the shareholders. Pricing policy can thus significantly affect the volume of business savings as well as savings by individuals receiving dividend payments. To the extent that fixed prices augment the real incomes of the vulnerable sections of the community, and prevent the prices of essential inputs and intermediate products from rising steeply, the capacity to save of both consumers and producers is thereby increased. Moreover, pricing policy can also be used to augment government revenue. Higher prices for the products of state-owned or nationalized enterprises in a monopolistic position (which could sometimes be used as an alternative to higher taxation) may yield higher revenue to the government. Similarly, if prices of price-controlled products are fixed at sufficiently high levels and are adequately remunerative, it may prevent the emergence of a black market and the generation of black money, thereby bringing larger sums into the tax net. Operationally, therefore, restricting consumption, stimulating business savings and savings by individuals, increasing government revenue and preventing the generation of black money may be the objectives of pricing policy in a developing economy as part of the broad objective of resource mobilization and increasing the rates of aggregate savings and investment.

As regards the objective of full employment, pricing policy may not be a very effective instrument, since it can only operate by changing the relative price structure in order to make unemployed or underemployed resources, in terms of both men and materials, more fully employed. Pricing policy may not directly affect the level of aggregate demand, but it may affect the allocation of resources, the structure of relative prices and the consequent volume and composition of national output, thereby indirectly affecting both the volume and the pattern of employment. In underdeveloped countries, however, where a large proportion of the total population is engaged in eking out a living by working on very small, uneconomic agricultural holdings and the pressure of population on limited cultivable land is excessively high, there exists an altogether different kind of unemployment. While everyone is apparently employed, so many people are working on such small pieces of land that a large number of them could be withdrawn without any reduction in the total agricultural output. Pricing policy could not possibly remove this kind of 'disguised unemployment', caused primarily by diminishing returns to labour on a given area of agricultural land reducing the marginal productivity of labour to zero. Such a situation could be tackled by other economic policies designed to achieve structural change, shifting the surplus agricultural population by providing them with gainful employment in industrial projects elsewhere, and thereby utilizing the 'saving potential' concealed in disguised unemployment for capital formation.

The above analysis of the objectives of pricing policy and the variations in approach and emphasis in regard to those objectives in different economies also bring out the following points, regarding the nature of pricing policy and its objectives:

(a) What have been discussed above as objectives of pricing policy could as well be said to be the objectives of economic policy as such. Pricing policy is essentially a part or an aspect of a comprehensive economic policy or a set of measures which may be adopted to achieve substantially the same set of objectives. There is a good deal of overlapping or complementarity in the objectives and effects of different economic policies; and all economic policies have to be so conceived, formulated and implemented that they support, supplement and reinforce each other for the achievement of the same or similar objectives. What combination of monetary, fiscal and other measures — including direct control of production, prices and distribution — needs to be adopted in any particular situation will depend basically upon the judgement of the policy-makers, which may in turn depend on, or be conditioned by, so many factors and considerations, some of which may not be strictly economic in nature.

(b) Whereas other policies, for example monetary and fiscal policies, try to control the behaviour of economic variables such as savings, investment, employment, income and output largely indirectly by creating incentives and disincentives so that the individuals or the institutions affected thereby find it profitable or in their interests to act in a particular manner and/or to refrain from acting in a particular manner, pricing policy directly controls the levels of prices (and sometimes even production, by fixing quotas of production or production targets and their distribution). Thus, while other economic policies expect the free functioning of the market mechanism itself to achieve the desired objectives under the influence of a set of incentives and disincentives, pricing policy directly interferes in the market mechanism and with the consumers' sovereignty, and decides the prices, and sometimes also the quantities to be produced and the manner of their distribution. Such direct control may become necessary in certain circumstances to protect the weaker sections of the community against a fall in their real incomes caused by a steep rise in the prices of essential consumer goods.

Monetary and fiscal measures may not be feasible or effective in providing relief or protection in such cases. For instance, fiscal measures such as subsidies may not be feasible, owing to government's limited financial resources; and tax concessions on such goods may not always be passed on to consumers in the form of lower prices. Monetary measures, by which the level of effective demand and the flow of financial resources could be regulated, may also not be a suitable instrument in such a situation.

(c) Price controls need not always be resorted to to curb profiteering or the making of excessive profits in any particular industry. Higher profits may mean greater internal resource generation and also more revenue for the government, which may sometimes be conducive to the growth of the industry and the economy. Excessive profits, arising from temporary scarcities, could possibly be mopped up by suitable adjustments in excise levies. The need to control prices arises essentially when it is considered necessary on grounds of equity, growth or allocation of resources according to national priorities. The free functioning of the market mechanism may sometimes create scarcities, real or artificial, of certain essential goods by diversion of resources to the production of non-essential goods, the deliberate restriction of output and the underutilization of installed capacities, hoarding or holding back of stocks and similar other monopolistic practices. Direct control of prices, production and distribution may become necessary in such circumstances. For the success of pricing policy, however, it would be necessary to identify the causal factors giving rise to scarcities and undue price increases in particular sectors and adopt a package of economic policies which may, while supporting and reinforcing the pricing policy in protecting vulnerable sections against price increases, also remove the root causes of shortages by encouraging growth of output and preventing misallocation of resources. The package of policies to be adopted to deal with such a situation has to provide incentives for cost reduction or efficiency of production, greater managerial efficiency, etc., so that the conditions for restoration of the free functioning of the price mechanism are created as quickly as possible. Price control is not an end in itself, but only a means to achieve certain ends. The enforcement of price control measures involves both administrative and financial burdens for the government. It is, therefore, necessary that a suitable package of measures be adopted to remove the causes necessitating resort to price control so that conditions are created where price control is no longer necessary and could be lifted.

(d) The objectives of pricing policy, as set out above, may not always be in harmony with each other. There is, for instance, an obvious conflict between the objectives of economic growth and equity. A relative price structure which protects the vulnerable sections of the community, maintains a certain parity between agricultural and non-agricultural incomes and reduces income disparities and inter-regional disparities in development may not be consistent with a high rate of economic growth. To achieve a high rate of economic growth, the prices fixed should be such as generate greater internal resources to augment the investible funds required for the modernization and expansion of industrial units. But a price which is sufficiently high to generate adequate profits for growth may be too high for the class of consumers seeking to be protected by price control to afford. For a high rate of economic growth, greater sacrifices in present consumption or tightening of the belt may be necessary, which may not be found to be practically feasible or politically desirable. Yet another area of conflict is stability and growth. The process of planned development in a developing economy lacking in the basic infrastructure for economic growth involves large-scale mobilization of resources into channels which, while immediately generating large spendable incomes, does not result in the production of sufficient quantities of consumer goods in the short run to match the massive increase in their demand, thus creating conditions of inflationary price rises and instability. If pricing policy is used for directly stepping up the production of consumer goods by allocating greater resources to the industries producing them, the availability of resources for investment in other projects, which may be vital for economic growth, is correspondingly reduced, at least in the short run. Some sort of compromise has, therefore, to be struck between various objectives by the policy-makers who may be guided by considerations which may not all be economic in nature.

(e) Although price control may generally be resorted to in an inflationary situation when prices have been rising steeply owing to real shortages (created by heavy demands on limited supplies during abnormal conditions like war, or the generation of large incomes creating additional demands for consumer goods during initial stages of development when supplies remain inelastic in the short term) or to artificial shortages (created by market imperfections, causing the restriction of output, underutilization of capacity, hoarding or holding back of stocks, etc.), it is not an anti-inflationary measure as such, as it may only conceal or repress inflationary pressures and not directly remove the cause of inflation. The cause of inflation — an excess of aggregate demand over aggregate supply — could be removed by either reducing aggregate demand through monetary and fiscal measures or by making supplies more elastic in the short run, or a combination of both, as the case may be. Under inflationary conditions, price control generally takes the form of fixing prices or price ceilings at levels which are lower than the prevailing market prices or the price levels which would have prevailed had there been no control of prices. This pushes up demand further or generates greater excess demand. The objective of price control in such a situation is not to bring about an equilibrium between demand and supply, which the price mechanism in a market economy, however imperfect it might be, tends to achieve: the objective is to ensure that free market prices (which might be equilibrium prices) are lowered to levels where a large body of consumers/users can afford to buy them to meet their essential minimum needs.

In the case of essential industrial or agricultural inputs, the objective of price control may be to bring them down to levels where they do not unduly distort the cost structure of the industries using them, inhibit their growth or depress their production levels. Thus, in an inflationary situation the basic objective of price control is to ensure an equitable distribution of real incomes which permits certain minimum levels of consumption of essential consumer goods by everyone, and to achieve a production pattern which corresponds more to actual needs, particularly those of the vulnerable sections of the community in preference to an alternative pattern which would otherwise have emerged, corresponding not to the real needs of the bulk of the consumers, but to the capacity to pay of the relatively fewer affluent ones. Price control, *per se*, may therefore not be conducive to the growth of the industry whose product prices are controlled unless controlled prices are fixed at remunerative levels or subsidized by the state to the required extent so as to leave sufficient margin of profits to the producers to preserve their incentive to produce more and also more efficiently and to provide them with the necessary funds internally to do so. Price control in an industry may, however, sometimes give a fillip to other industries, depending on the price-controlled industry for the supply of essential inputs, if that supply is maintained at a sufficiently high level to match the demand. Price controls may have to be accompanied by the following measures (besides support for and reinforcement by other economic measures) to achieve the twin objectives of growth and equity:

(i) demand management by rationing and distribution control coupled with effective enforcement measures to prevent the emergence of black markets which may arise because the controlled prices are lower than the prices which would have otherwise prevailed; and

(ii) supply management in the price-controlled and other related industries by identifying the causes of low production and productivity (for example, financial bottlenecks, technological constraints, etc.), with a view to taking measures to remove them.

Both (i) and (ii) generally require not only direct control of prices but also some degree of control over production and distribution as well, and also support for and reinforcement of these direct measures of control by indirect controls through monetary and fiscal measures.

(f) Pricing policy may be a more suitable instrument of economic policy in areas where monetary and fiscal measures may generally not be effective in achieving the desired objectives.

Monetary measures may not work in a primarily agricultural economy consisting mostly of rural areas not covered by banks and financial institutions. Similarly, neither reliefs in direct taxation nor concessions in commodity taxes would give any benefit to the vast majority of the agricultural population in a country like India where the latter are outside the net of direct taxation and generally do not consume most of the taxable goods produced in the industrial sector in the urban areas. The only way to maintain the real incomes of an agricultural population such as this at a certain minimum level, and also some kind of parity between agricultural and non-agricultural incomes on considerations of equity and economic justice, may be by fixing minimum or floor prices for agricultural produce below which they are not allowed to fall (as the government undertakes and arranges to buy any quantity at those prices), commonly known as support price operations.

(g) Pricing policy has to keep the perspective of the entire structure of input and output prices in view while regulating the prices of individual commodities. All prices are interrelated, the degree of interrelationship varying from commodity to commodity. Control of the price of any commodity affects the relative price structure. These interrelationships, therefore, have to be borne in mind, and the effect of any price regulation on the entire integrated price system considered so as to prevent avoidable distortions. For instance, an attempt to control the price of a final product without regulating the price of the inputs, or vice versa, might create distortions. If the price of the inputs or intermediate products are kept low, and the prices of the final products are not controlled simultaneously, the result may be a decline in the profitability and production of the inputs or intermediate products and a rise in the profitability of the finished products; and a situation may arise where shortage of inputs/intermediate products may inhibit the growth of the industries producing the final product in spite of the low prices of inputs. Similarly, if the prices of final products are controlled while those of inputs/intermediate products required for their production are not, the profitability of the industries producing the final products may be lowered, thus inhibiting production, and stocks of unsold inputs/intermediate goods may pile up. Sometimes, the regulation of the price of a commodity may affect the demand and supply of a substitute using the same raw material. Price regulation of sugar, for instance, may divert sugar-cane to the production of *khandsari* and *gur*, thereby increasing their availability and lowering their prices, also causing an increase in their demand, which may have the effect of reducing both the quantities produced and those demanded in the case of sugar.

The degree of ease or difficulty with which the price of any commodity can be regulated depends largely on the significance of that commodity in terms of its interrelationships or linkages with other prices, and the extent to which changes in its price would affect the relative price structure. Linkages could be in the form of the price-controlled product being an input for some other products or a finished product using certain inputs or a substitute for any input or finished product. The fewer the linkages, the lesser the importance of the product in the relative price structure, the easier it is to work out the impact of a price change for such a product on other prices. In controlling the price of any product, not only the effect on profitability of its production — which may determine its supply and availability — but also its effect on the profitability and supply position of the inputs required for its production, its substitutes and other related products are to be kept in view. In fact, proper price control may require consideration of its effect on the entire price system or the structure of prices. This does not, however, mean that the price controlling authority has to achieve some kind of 'general equilibrium' of all prices. General equilibrium is only a conceptual model which may help in understanding the processes which urge the system towards it: it may never be attained in practice (at least we have no way of ascertaining or verifying whether such a position has been reached), owing to several disequilibrating factors being in constant operation. Practically speaking, only a broad internal consistency in the structure of relative prices could be attempted, so that the very purpose of the control is not defeated owing to unwanted or unintended effects on other prices.

(h) The price-controlling authority has to evolve an effective and efficient system of monitoring the behaviour of production, costs and prices of all commodities considered vital from the viewpoint of the objectives sought by pricing policy and also the effects of any price control measure on the structure of relative prices to determine what other measures need to be taken, when, and whether the measures taken are having the desired effect, so that timely corrective action can be taken.

3 Theory of price control

A theory is an explanation of a phenomenon in terms of cause and effect. It is an attempt to identify and analyse the factors, fixed as well as variable, which, by their action or interaction, cause the occurrence of a phenomenon or prevent its occurrence or recurrence. Theorizing consists of formulating a set of generalizations or hypotheses regarding the behaviour of particular variables under given conditions, which could be tested by logic or reasoning and also practical experiments wherever feasible, or historical or empirical evidence, wherever available. Since the causal factors in any phenomenon concerning human behaviour are too many and their interrelationships too complex, any theory explaining such phenomena has to abstract from certain factors or assume them to be constant; and the validity of the theory may depend largely on the effect of such assumptions on that phenomenon, and on how realistic those assumptions are. Theory enables us to predict the behaviour of the variables causing a phenomenon under given conditions, and, therefore, gives the power to control that behaviour to achieve certain ends. We have a 'price theory' in this sense, which not only helps us in understanding the phenomenon of price under different market conditions, but also gives clues regarding the possible ways in which prices could be controlled to achieve certain objectives. Price theory thus includes the theory of price control, and no separate theory is necessary to explain the phenomenon of price control. However, there have been attempts to develop some kind of separate theory of price control. It is proposed to discuss two such theories of price control here: the one propounded by Von Mises in his *Theory of Price Control (Theorie der Preistaxen)*,[1] and the other subsequently by J.K. Galbraith in his book entitled *A Theory of Price Control*.[2]

For analytical convenience, Von Mises's theory of price control could be stated in the form of the following propositions:

(a) A distinction needs to be drawn between 'true control' and 'false control'. There is 'true control' if the fixed price deviates substantially from the equilibrium price in a state of perfect competition. If the fixed price is the same as the equilibrium price, it is a false control which only confirms the functioning of the market mechanism.

(b) In the case of monopoly of supply, 'the intervention of the authority has available the whole margin lying between the highest monopoly price and the lowest competitive price'. Setting the controlled price at the level of the competitive price prevents the exploitation of consumers on the one hand, and eliminates the motive to reduce production by charging a higher price and thereby improves the supply position.

(c) The controlled price could be either above the equilibrium price or below it. If a minimum price is fixed which is above the equilibrium price, the supply exceeds demand at that price, and the excess supply creates a tendency to sell below the controlled price. Since increasing the demand to match the increased supply may be practically difficult, the supply is generally reduced. There are secondary effects too since the demand 'which is unwilling or unable to pay the higher price for the product invades other markets, on which it generates price increases and/or an extension of production'.[2] To avoid such effects, state intervention may have to be extended to all prices and quantities. Similarly, in the event of setting a maximum price below the equilibrium price, demand would exceed supply, which may result in the creation of black markets; and to

> eliminate this phenomenon, supply must be increased by constraint, or demand must be restrained by rationing. The rationing of a product liberates an effective demand which turns to other markets where it generates price increases and/or increased production. The desire to prevent such secondary effects may here again lead to State control of all prices and quantities of goods offered.

(d) From the position stated at (c) above, it follows that true controls 'are not consistent with the objective, since they are always introduced at the cost of those whom they are designed to protect or benefit'. A controlled price higher than the equilibrium price creates a situation of excess supply, while the one lower than it creates excess demand. The former does not benefit the producers or the suppliers as they are not able to sell their entire output, and the latter does no service to consumers as supplies are reduced and a large part of the consumer demand remains unsatisfied. It further follows that true controls result in escalation of government intervention to avoid the secondary effects of price control in both situations: 'price controls, forced sales, rationing, forced production, and finally taking over by the State of the planned direction of all production and distribution'. The inevitable conclusion is that price controls are not consistent with a capitalist system, and that there are only two mutually exclusive systems, namely Capitalism and Socialism, and there can be no middle way, as any price control creates conditions necessitating complete take-over or direction of all production and distribution by the state.

Von Mises's theory of price control is, in effect, a theoretical defence of the free functioning of the market mechanism by trying to demonstrate that any price fixed by an external agency at any level other than the one determined by the free play of market forces will create conditions either of excess demand or excess supply, thereby defeating the purpose of price control; and would further have secondary effects necessitating escalation of price controls so as to cover all production and distribution. The theory is based on the assumption that there is an equilibrium price for every commodity in a free market, any substantial deviation from which in order to benefit buyers or sellers would be self-defeating, as it would not only fail to achieve its purpose, but also cause the breakdown of the entire market mechanism and its replacement by another system involving comprehensive state control of all economic activity.

The equilibrium price to which Von Mises has referred is the equilibrium price under conditions of perfect competition. Firstly, perfect competition is a purely conceptual model since competition is nowhere perfect in the real world. Secondly, the concept of an equilibrium price in the sense of a price where the forces of demand and supply have come to rest, and neither the buyers have any desire to buy more than what is supplied nor the sellers to supply more than what is demanded, is also purely conceptual, and it may not actually obtain anywhere in the real world. An equilibrium price is a market-clearing price, and there is no way of finding out in any real-life situation whether the prevailing market price is an equilibrium price or not. The concept of equilibrium price is useful since it provides an insight into the process of price formation under any market conditions (not necessarily those of perfect competition). There is a tendency for movement towards an equilibrium price or movement away from it, depending on the conditions of demand and supply (for example under dynamic conditions in the case of certain commodities to which the 'cobweb theorem' applies, there would be movement towards equilibrium only where the demand was more elastic than supply over a price range, and a movement away from it where the supply was more elastic than demand). But the concept of an equilibrium price under perfect competition is totally irrelevant to price control, as the controlled price cannot be fixed with reference to it for the simple reason that perfect competition exists nowhere, and no one knows what the equilibrium price is and whether the price actually prevailing in the market at any time is an equilibrium price in the sense that it is a market-clearing price. In fact, market conditions may be changing so rapidly that no equilibrium price may ever be established; and there may be no question of the controlled price being fixed above or below it.

The need for price control arises because the prevailing market price (which may or may not be an equilibrium or market-clearing price) is considered to be unfair to a section of consumers or producers and to be creating certain distortions in the structure of production and relative prices and causing misallocation of resources. The prevailing price of a commodity may be so high that a large number of consumers who are in great need of it cannot afford to buy it at that price, or so low that a large number of producers find it unremunerative. These high and low prices may need to be regulated in the interests of consumers or producers, as the case may be, and also in the interests of the economy. There is no such thing as 'true' or 'false' control, and price control is resorted to when, in the judgement of the policy-makers, the price determined by the free play of market forces (irrespective of whether it is an equilibrium price or not) is either too high (which makes it unaffordable for a large section of the community) or too low (which is unremunerative and likely to unduly depress the relative incomes of those producing that commodity). Price control is, in effect, a declaration of lack of faith in the power of the market mechanism, due to several imperfections and disequilibrating factors under dynamic conditions, to allocate scarce economic resources and create a pattern of prices, production and distribution which may be in the best interests of the community and the individuals comprising it, or consistent with the social and economic philosophy, principles, priorities and programmes adopted and being pursued as principal policy parameters. This is the philosophy of price control: there is perhaps no theory to it. In any case, no price control can conceivably confirm the market mechanism in the sense of trying to achieve what the market mechanism is already achieving.

In drawing the distinction between true and false control, Von Mises seems to think that price control consists in fixing the controlled price alone. Actually, price control is a comprehensive expression covering all measures which monitor the behaviour of production, costs and prices of all commodities considered to be essential consumer goods or industrial inputs, with a view to deciding which needs to be brought under some kind of price discipline, the nature and timing of the price control and the enforcement and other measures needed to effectively implement and reinforce it.

The proposition that in the case of monopoly of supply the controlled price could be fixed anywhere between the highest monopoly price and the lowest competitive price is neither theoretically valid nor operationally practicable. The highest monopoly price of a product is the price which maximizes the monopolist's profit, which in any concrete situation could perhaps be theoretically determined if the cost and the demand functions were known; but, even theoretically, there would be no way of determining the competitive price for such a product as it would be purely hypothetical. Moreover, competition, under dynamic conditions, may introduce so many factors and imponderables that it may not be practicable to determine even hypothetically what the competitive price would be. In any case, it would be a meaningless exercise so far as determination of the controlled price is concerned. The controlled price is generally fixed, not with reference to an imaginary or hypothetical highest or lowest price, but at a level which, while covering the average costs fully according to certain norms, also leaves an adequate margin of profit to the producer, and is not so high that the bulk of consumers cannot afford it.

It is true that setting the controlled price at a level which is lower than the prevailing market price immediately before the imposition of price control creates excess demand because a large number of consumers then find it affordable. In such a situation, there might also be many consumers willing to pay a higher price for it than the controlled price, which might cause the emergence of a black market. A large part of the demand may, however, be met by ensuring fuller utilization of existing capacities in the industrial units, wherever underutilized capacities exist (these do in fact exist under monopolistic or oligopolistic conditions), and by the state providing incentives for the creation of new capacities, and if need be, directly regulating production and distribution. Excess demand at the controlled price need not invade other markets, creating shortages there and causing escalation of price and production controls, if price control is properly conceived and implemented. In any case, excess demand could possibly only spill over to the markets of the substitutes, and the secondary effects referred to by Von Mises may depend on the degree of substitutability of the price-controlled product and the availability of substitutes at an affordable price. While it is true that effective enforcement of price control measures may necessitate demand management by rationing and distribution control and also supply management to ensure adequate production, there is no reason to believe that such measures would escalate to all areas of production and distribution and cover the entire economy. In fact, price control could be implemented by adopting a suitable package of measures so as to remove the shortage which necessitated it, and create conditions where it could be withdrawn and free functioning of the market mechanism restored.

Setting a controlled price at a level higher than the prevalent market price or the price likely to prevail in the market is generally carried out in the case of agricultural produce when a steep fall in agricultural prices is expected due to a rush to the market immediately following the harvest, because of the seasonal character of agriculture and the immediate cash needs and low holding capacity of farmers. There is no question of there being an excess supply under such conditions, as the supply of agricultural produce in any particular season is more or less fixed. The object of fixing a minimum or support price above the ruling market price or the price which would have prevailed had there been no price control is to ensure a reasonable return on investment in agriculture, and an equitable distribution of income between those engaged in agriculture and those in non-agricultural vocations. There may be no secondary effects escalating price controls and extending the area of state intervention in such a situation.

From the above discussion, it is evident that Von Mises's theory (if it can be called one) is based on wrong premises and assumptions, misrepresents the nature of price controls as they are actually conceived and operated and does not explain the phenomenon of price control as it actually exists in the real world. Both his conclusions, namely that price control cannot achieve its object of benefiting either consumers or producers, and that it is bound to escalate to other areas, eventually resulting in total control of all economic activity by the state (and that there can be no middle way), are neither valid theoretically nor borne out historically by actual experience. Specific price controls have successfully been used by the advanced capitalist countries which have also developed free market economies without the secondary effects envisaged by Von Mises. In a purely socialist economy where all means of production are owned by the state, the term 'price control' becomes a misnomer since there are no free market prices to be controlled. But even in socialist economies there are prices, in whatever manner determined, which need some sort of regulation. There are also certain sectors where limited competition and price formation by free market forces may sometimes be permitted as a matter of conscious policy. A purely capitalist and a purely socialist economy are only theoretical models, and in practice all economies have features of both capitalism and socialism and elements of both competition and monopoly to varying degrees. In reality we generally find a 'middle way', with neither pure capitalism nor pure socialism anywhere. With the emergence of the concept of the modern welfare state, the paramount policy parameter in most states is the promotion of the public 'welfare' in whatever manner conceived, all other considerations being secondary. Most states have, therefore, been pursuing policies designed to achieve certain objectives in accordance with their national values, priorities and aspirations, without any doctrinaire adherence to the ideologies of capitalism or socialism, and without eschewing measures termed either 'capitalist' or 'socialist', if they are found to be necessary in order to achieve those objectives.

Von Mises has thus not developed any theory of price control, but has only tried to argue that price control would tend to operate in a manner which would defeat the very purpose for which it was used, and would escalate the area of state intervention to such an extent that a free market economy would be converted into a totally state controlled socialist economy. Galbraith has similarly not developed any theory of price control in his book *A Theory of Price Control*, but has only given an interpretation of how price controls were actually conceived and operated in some countries during World War II. In the process, Galbraith has attempted some generalizations and made some observations based thereon which seem to provide the rationale for those price controls and also to suggest a framework of economic policies which needs to be followed to make them work and achieve certain objectives. As has rightly been observed, 'the book is less a theory of price control than it is an interpretation that blends history with *ad hoc* reasoning'.[3] The main propositions which emerge from Galbraith's analysis could briefly be stated as follows:

(a) Generally there are imperfect markets of an oligopolistic nature due to which price controls may not always necessitate control of the volume of production. In an oligopolistic situation, suppliers may have reserve or unutilized production capacities, fuller utilization of which may meet the excess demand generated by price control. Sellers under such conditions also exercise an informal control over demand since buyers and sellers do not act anonymously, as in a perfectly competitive situation, but are identifiable by each other. In such imperfect markets, therefore, 'price control *qua* price control is a workable instrument of economic policy, at least in the short run'.[4]

(b) Price control had been used during World War II, particularly in the United States, mainly for the mobilization of resources and 'to attain maximum resource employment of the greatest possible efficiency, to get a militarily optimal allocation of resouces between military and civilian use . . ..'[5] Subsequently, 'price control has been employed with the primary objective of stabilizing prices', when the economy was under inflationary pressure due to heavy military expenditure.

(c) During World War II, the United States and other major belligerents, except Russia and China, adopted an economic organization which Galbraith calls the Disequilibrium System, characterized by '(1) a more or less comprehensive system of direct control over the employment of economic resources (2) a nearly universal control over prices, and (3) an aggregate of money demand substantially in excess of the available supply of goods and services', and also 'the use of an effective system of rationing to reinforce price control in those markets that approximate conditions of pure competition'.[6]

(d) Price control creates an excess demand which, if not managed properly, may make that price control unworkable. There is a 'margin of tolerance' defined as 'the volume of demand in excess of current supply that added to, or is consistent with, additions to aggregate output . . ..'[7] The excess demand has to be balanced by an equivalent volume of current saving or additional production to keep the 'disequilibrium system' within the 'margin of tolerance' and achieve the twin objectives of resource mobilization and price stabilization. 'Control of wages and prices of wage goods is central to the strategy of price control in the disequilibrium system',[8] to prevent an 'inflationary spiral' from being put in motion and to keep the system within the 'margin of tolerance'. In more or less purely competitive markets, e.g. the markets for 'two important classes of wage goods, food and clothing',[9] formal rationing becomes indispensable as 'the necessary reinforcement to price control'.[10]

The propositions stated above do not constitute a theory of price control, but merely explain how price control actually operated during the war period, and how it could be made workable and used as an effective instrument of resource mobilization and price stabilization during wartime. Galbraith has analysed not only the implications of price control, but of a set of economic measures including price control adopted during World War II and thereafter by certain belligerent countries, which he describes as the 'disequilibrium system', with a view to indicating the conditions under which that system could work and the supplementary measures necessary to reinforce price control in order to make it work successfully. The broad policy conclusion drawn is that the system has to be kept within the 'margin of tolerance' by not allowing excess demand to exceed the additional output to be produced by both stepping up production and restricting demand by rationing in the case of wage goods or other suitable measures. Another policy conclusion is that while state control of the volume of production and demand may not be necessary in the case of goods produced under oligopolistic conditions since producers or sellers under such market conditions may themselves adequately regulate both, formal rationing (and perhaps both demand and supply management by the state) may become necessary in the case of goods produced under competitive conditions (particularly wage goods like food and clothing) in order to prevent wages and prices of wage goods from chasing each other, giving rise to an inflationary spiral which may make the 'disequilibrium system' unworkable.

The basic question which arises is whether we can, or need, have a theory of price control, the answer to which may be in the negative. Existing price theory itself explains the factors and compulsions which under certain circumstances give rise to the need for price control, the distortions and inequities which may be created owing to various market imperfections necessitating some kind of discipline of the free market price to achieve certain ends. The existing theory also enables us to understand and analyse any concrete situation with a view to deciding whether price control is called for and also to evolve a suitable set of economic policies or package of economic measures to deal with such a situation and to make price control work successfully. There does not appear to be any gap in our theoretical knowledge which needs to be bridged by developing a separate theory. In fact, both Von Mises and Galbraith have only interpreted the phenomenon of price control in the light of existing price theory and drawn certain conclusions. Whereas Von Mises has concluded that price control is bound to be self-defeating and will ultimately convert a capitalist system into a socialist system with total state control and direction of production and distribution in all spheres, Galbraith's conclusion is that it can be made to work successfully and achieve its objectives under certain conditions. Neither have developed any theory as such, and their analyses only confirm that no separate theory of price control is needed or could possibly be developed. When we talk of price control, we are essentially in the realm of economic policy or applied economics. Whether the price of any commodity needs to be controlled, and if so, why, when and how, are basically questions which cannot be answered by economic reasoning alone, and the answers to them essentially depend on judgements based on various considerations, all of which may not be economic in nature. What can at best be attempted is not a general theory of price control, but some kind of practical hints regarding the stage at which price control could be introduced, the objectives to be achieved, the manner in which it needs to be enforced and reinforced by other economic measures, and the time at which it could be withdrawn as no longer necessary. Such hints need not, and perhaps cannot, be formalized into a separate theory of price control; they would in fact be based on the application of the existing theory to concrete situations and might be in the nature of practical precepts to suit particular conditions.

Notes

1. See 'The Effects of National Price Controls in the European Economic Community', Research Report by Horst Westphal, Hamburg, EEC, 1968, pp. 76–8.
2. J.K. Galbraith, *Theory of Price Control*, 2nd edn, Cambridge, Mass., Harvard University Press, 1980.
3. *American Economic Review* (review of Galbraith's book by G.H. Hildebrand), **42**, 1952, pp. 986–90.
4. J.K. Galbraith, *A Theory of Price Control*, op. cit., p. 25.
5. Ibid., p. 29.
6. Ibid., p. 29.
7. Ibid., p. 35.
8. Ibid., p. 43.
9. Ibid., p. 49.
10. Ibid.

4 Some general issues relating to pricing policy

Although price control largely originated as an emergency measure during wartime, it has now come to stay and has become more or less a permanent feature of all capitalist economies characterized by an otherwise freely functioning market mechanism. It has become so mainly because in the developed market economies it is found to be a powerful instrument for ensuring that market imperfections do not distort the structure of relative prices and the pattern of production and income distribution, and create conditions of instability which may impede the process of economic growth itself, and also avoidable social and political tensions. The underdeveloped or developing economies comprising the Third World have found it essential to embark on a programme of planned development, direct control of prices, production and distribution in certain vital sectors for the allocation of scarce national resources according to plan priorities, maximum resource mobilization and control of inflationary pressures which inevitably arise in the initial stages of economic growth. There are some basic policy issues which arise in the course of the formulation and implementation of pricing policy in all market economies, which could be stated as follows:-

(a) When should price control be resorted to?
(b) Which commodities need to be brought under some kind of price discipline, or what should the criteria for selection of commodities for price control be?
(c) Should price control necessarily also be accompanied by control of volume of production and distribution?
(d) Does price control need to be supplemented and reinforced by other measures?
(e) How long should price control last?
(f) What should be the nature or the form of price control?
(g) Whether price control in the case of any commodity need

necessarily extend to the control of the prices of the inputs required for its production and also of its available substitutes?
(h) Whether it is necessary to have a legal or statutory basis for price control?
(i) What the institutional arrangements necessary for the formulation, implementation and monitoring of price control are?

As observed earlier, price control is to some degree a corrective measure to remove the distortions which the free functioning of the market mechanism may sometimes give rise to owing to the various imperfections in its working. It may also be a necessary adjunct to the direct commandeering or large-scale mobilization of economic resources called for during a war or in the initial stages of planned development in a developing economy. Since market imperfections are universal phenomena, conditions of perfect competition being non-existent in the real world, they cannot by themselves justify or be used as a pretext for price control. It is only when the imperfect functioning of the market mechanism tends to create a number of conditions which are not considered to be consistent with or conducive to the achievement of some basic social and economic objectives (e.g. the objective of an equitable income distribution or of achieving the desired rate and pattern of economic growth), or causes limited economic resources to flow into low priority sectors or even undesirable ventures, and when the situation cannot possibly be wholly remedied other than by direct intervention by the state that the need for price control can be said to have arisen. Similarly, an extraordinary situation (e.g. during a war or when an underdeveloped economy launches an ambitious programme involving massive investment to create the infrastructure required for industrial growth) does not by itself provide adequate justification for price control, unless it is considered that other economic measures, which essentially operate through the market mechanism (e.g. monetary and fiscal measures), would not alone deliver the goods. Just when a situation calling for price control has arisen is basically a question of economic judgement for which no hard and fast rule can possibly be laid down.

The distortions referred to above relate to the allocation of economic resources and production/provision of goods/services and their distribution and the distribution of real income which may not always be amenable to monetary and fiscal or other economic measures alone; and may, therefore, necessitate price control. Some of these distortions, for instance, could be as follows:

(a) Creation of real scarcities of essential consumer goods and industrial inputs and raw materials due to diversion of limited economic resources to the production of other goods found to be commercially more profitable by producers and sellers, and also restriction of output to keep prices high.
(b) Creation of artificial scarcities by hoarding or holding up of stocks of commodities or controlling their regional or territorial distribution in a manner which would deliberately starve certain areas to keep prices high there.
(c) Deterioration in the quality of goods produced or production of substandard goods, adulterated goods or goods of such low quality as to be harmful to their consumers or users.
(d) Resort to unfair practices by manufacturers, traders or distributors, deliberately misleading consumers or users in order to promote sales.
(e) Causing unemployment of human resources and keeping installed capacity unutilized or underutilized.
(f) Deliberate restriction of the expansion of industrial capacity or creation of additional or new capacity in areas which may be vital for the economic well-being of the mass of consumers or for desired growth in vital sectors of the economy despite the existence of large, unsatisfied demand or unfulfilled need.
(g) Emergence of an inflationary spiral with wages and prices of wage goods chasing each other, aggravating inflationary pressures.
(h) Rapid erosion of the value of money due to steady, steep rise in the general price level.
(i) Steep fall in real incomes of the weaker or vulnerable sections of the community accentuating disparities in the distribution of real incomes, creating conditions for social and political unrest and economic instability.
(j) Emergence of a resource allocation and production pattern and a structure of relative prices which is not found to be consistent with the basic objective of economic growth with stability, considerations of equity, national priorities, or the pattern planned for or envisaged in the national plan.

The above list is not exhaustive, merely illustrative. There could be several other situations which would call for direct intervention in the market mechanism. From the viewpoint of government, the need has arisen as soon as, factually and on empirical evidence, such a distortion has become manifest, and there is reason to believe that the situation cannot be remedied by monetary and fiscal measures (which operate through the market mechanism) without direct control and management of prices and, if need be, production and distribution as well.

Having decided that the need for direct intervention in the market mechanism has arisen, the next question which arises is which markets need to be interfered with, or what prices need to be brought under some kind of price discipline, or what should be the criteria for the selection of commodities for price control. Here again, it is ultimately a matter of economic judgement as to which prices are causing the distortions, and whether they have assumed the proportions or created a situation where price control has become imperative. Broadly speaking, price control may be resorted to in order to correct the distortion in the relative price structure, as an anti-inflationary measure to hold the price line, to reduce the general price level, or to prevent it from rising steeply. Most often, price controls have both purposes in view. If the free play of market forces has resulted in or is likely to result in a relative price structure which might inhibit the growth of certain vital industries or sections of the economy, or alter the relative incomes of those engaged there, creating undesirable disparities in income distribution, it might be found necessary to control certain prices so as to create conditions for the desired growth of such industries or sectors or to prevent such disparities from emerging or getting accentuated, as the case may be. For instance, if the prices of goods produced by the small-scale sector or handicrafts are increasing relative to the prices of the same or similar goods produced in the large-scale manufacturing sector using modern machinery and technology, it may sometimes be considered necessary to support the small-scale or handicrafts sector by subsidizing their products to enable them to sell them at lower prices and effectively compete with the competitive products produced at lower cost in the large-scale sector. Such subsidization is in effect a kind of price control which helps to keep the prices of the goods produced in the subsidized sectors at competitive levels, and thereby to help the survival of the industrial units in such sectors. Similarly, if it is considered desirable to maintain a certain parity between the incomes of the agricultural sector and of those engaged in non-agricultural occupations, it might become necessary to artificially keep the prices of agricultural products at a sufficiently high level by fixing minimum or floor prices (also known as 'support prices', below which the agricultural prices may not be allowed to fall, and arranging to buy any quantity at those prices.

Very often, price control is resorted to in order to control the rise in the general price level; this can only be done by identifying movements in the commodities (which could be essential consumer goods or industrial inputs or raw materials) whose prices might primarily be responsible for the general rise, and controlling the prices of commodities so identified. The first criterion for selection of a commodity for price control in such a situation would be its importance in terms of its influence on the general price level, or the proportion of consumers' income spent on it, or its linkages with other prices. In the case of industrial units and raw materials, the relevant factor would be the importance of the final products for whose production they are required, and the extent to which changes in their prices could affect the total cost of production of those final products. Other criteria could be a relatively inelastic demand due to either the essential nature of the commodity for consumers or industrial users, or lack of substitutes, and an ascertainable demand (so that the total production and distribution could also be controlled, if need be). From the administrative point of view, one could possibly add homogeneity of the product, and the requirement of relatively smaller numbers of inputs for production so that their prices could also be regulated, if necessary. These criteria could be used for the initial selection of the commodities whose production, costs, prices and distribution need to be monitored with a view to deciding when the need for interference with the market mechanism has arisen because it has created distortions of the nature indicated above due to various imperfections in its functioning.

Since the basic justification or rationale for price control in the case of any particular commodity arises out of its scarcity, real or artificial, price control has to aim at removing the basic cause, namely the scarcity itself. This cannot possibly be done by controlling the price alone, and it might become necessary simultaneously to:

(a) regulate demand by rationing;
(b) regulate distribution so as to ensure that all areas and all sections of the population and sectors of the economy which need the price-controlled commodity get it in the required quantity, to the extent possible; and
(c) identify the causes of shortages or scarcity, which could be real (e.g. low productivity due to low or outdated technology, financial bottlenecks, lack of infrastructural facilities, scarcity of essential inputs, etc.) or artificial (restrictive practices by producers in a monopolistic or oligopolistic situation deliberately stopping the flow of resources into any industry, restricting output, keeping installed capacity underutilized, or controlling the distribution of the product in such a way as to starve certain areas), and devise a suitable package of measures consisting of direct control of prices, production and distribution as well as monetary, fiscal and other measures designed to remove those causes.

Price control is obviously not an end in itself but a means to achieving certain ends. In several situations those ends might not be achieved, or might be achieved only partially, unless price control is accompanied by direct management of both demand and supply, involving control of both the volume of production and distribution of the goods produced in terms of quantity as well as coverage of different areas and different sections of consumers or users. Moreover, as has also been argued earlier, price control might not succeed in achieving its objectives if it were resorted to as an isolated measure: it has to aim at remedying the total situation which necessitated it. In most cases, not only a broader perspective covering both production and distribution might become a practical necessity, but pricing policy might also have to be conceived or formulated and implemented as a necessary part of a comprehensive and integrated economic policy, getting the requisite support and sustenance from other economic measures designed to remove the basic causes which had created the situation necessitating price control. The basic objective which price control, supplemented and supported by other measures, seeks to achieve is the creation of a situation where the causes which necessitated it have been removed, so that its continuance is no longer necessary, it could be lifted and the free functioning of the market mechanism restored. Whether the package of measures (including price control) is tending to move the system in that direction and whether the desired stage (where price control could be lifted) has been reached is again a matter of economic judgement based on available data regarding the behaviour of the relevant economic variables immediately preceding and during the period of price control, which have to be continuously collected and analysed through an efficient and effective monitoring system.

As regards the question of whether price controls need necessarily extend to inputs, raw materials or substitutes, all prices being interrelated, the entire integrated price system has to be kept in view while regulating the price of any commodity, so as to prevent avoidable distortions and maintain a broad internal consistency in the structure of relative prices, which might in many cases necessitate simultaneous control of prices of inputs or intermediate products, and sometimes even substitutes.

Another important issue which the policy-makers have to decide in regard to pricing policy is what should be the nature, degree and stage of interference in the market mechanism in any given situation. Broadly speaking, the issue is to what extent and in what manner should market forces be allowed the freedom to determine the price. This freedom could be curtailed almost completely or restricted drastically by government, for instance by:

(a) fixing a ceiling price above which the price is not allowed to rise (which would invariably be below the equilibrium price which might have otherwise prevailed); or
(b) freezing the price determined by the free play of market forces as it obtained at a particular point of time (which would have otherwise risen to higher levels); or
(c) fixing a ceiling on profit or trade margins at the production or distribution stage and allowing free price formation subject to that ceiling; or
(d) fixing a 'minimum', 'floor' or 'support' price (e.g. in the case of agricultural produce such as food grains, sugar-cane or cotton)

below which the price is not allowed to fall (which would be above the equilibrium price which might have otherwise prevailed); or
(e) fixing 'retention prices' based on 'standard' costs or approved cost norms in the case of oligopolistic industries (having only a few units whose unit costs differ due to differences in technology and feedstocks) which every unit in the industry is allowed to retain irrespective of its actual unit cost, the units with lower unit costs paying the difference into a common pool and those with higher costs getting reimbursed from it to the extent that their costs are higher than the standard costs.

Instead of almost total restriction of the nature indicated above by 'fixing' or 'freezing' a price, government could partially restrict the freedom of price formation in two other ways. A 'price bracket' or a range of minimum and maximum price could be fixed within which the price could be allowed to be fixed freely. Alternatively, a system of 'dual pricing' could be resorted to under which a fixed proportion of the output of the industry is procured by the government at a fixed price for being supplied to certain categories of buyers or for certain purposes at a controlled price, the remainder being allowed to be sold at whatever price it could command in the open market.

Besides total or partial restriction on free price formation, there could be various other measures designed to influence the level of market prices or the volume of production and distribution. The basic idea underlying these measures is to allow a kind of 'controlled freedom', i.e. freedom to fix prices subject to certain conditions or obligations or within a given framework or parameters of action. Some of these measures adopted in the EEC and other countries are as follows:

1. Price framework (le cadre de prix)

This is a system prevalent in some of the EEC countries (e.g. France and Belgium) under which producers are required to work out the maximum prices of their products on the basis of a number of predetermined factors. Such prices are allowed to prevail with the prior approval of the authorities and subject to the detailed cost calculations being checked by them. In France, items like wallpaper, petrol, building works and pharmaceuticals have been brought under this system.

The price initially fixed on the basis of the price framework is allowed to be revised subsequently 'by the application of a formula containing predetermined parameters'.[1] The need for such revision arises particularly in industries where the execution of orders may involve a considerable time lapse, for example the mechanical and electrical industry, construction and public works. The initial price in such cases could be varied in the event of an increase in wages or prices of other inputs according to a prescribed formula, 'subject, however, to possible total or partial freezing of one of the parameters included in the revision formula'.[2]

2. Stability contracts (contrats de stabilité)

These are contracts voluntarily entered into between business enterprises and the price control authority which give them 'freedom to vary certain prices, provided that they undertake not to increase the overall price level of their production programme'.[3]

Stability contracts were introduced in France in March 1965 'with a view to relaxing the general price freeze instituted in 1963',[4] and converting it 'into a freezing of price levels'.[5] The idea is to permit variations in individual prices so long as the weighted average of the entire range of products produced by an enterprise is maintained in order that the 'price level of the whole of its production programme'[6] is stabilized. In the event of the failure of the enterprise to fulfil the obligations under this contract, it is deemed to be subject to the general price freeze. While these contracts permitted increases in certain input costs, e.g. 'raw-materials, electricity, transport and imports to be passed on in the form of higher prices, certain other cost increases, e.g. wage increases were not allowed to be passed on'.[7] This arrangement represented what has been described as 'the first attempt by the French Government to achieve the aim of the stability of the price levels without creating a manifest obstacle to growth'.[8]

3. Programme contracts (contrats de programme)

These contracts are another innovation made by the French Government in March 1966 and constitute a system which 'transcends price policy and comes within overall economic policy in the Fifth Economic and Social Development Plan'.[9] Like stability contracts, programme contracts also give an enterprise the conditional freedom to fix the prices of its products.

> Accession to a contract gives enterprises the freedom to increase their prices within the limits of the growth rates specified in the Fifth Plan. But the authorities retain the right to object to prices which they regard as too high. Although specially fixed for each branch of the economy, the conditions to be observed are inspired in each case by the targets of the Fifth Plan and relate to the volume of production, the amount of investments, wage levels, productivity increase and exports.[10]

Programme contracts are thus not only a form of price control, but 'an instrument of achieving the Plan',[11] and aim at achieving a 'stable price level without loss of growth'.[12]

There may be yet another set of measures designed to influence the level of prices through the market mechanism in order to keep it at the desired level, or to prevent undue price increases. Such measures could be positive in nature, requiring the enterprises concerned to act in a particular manner, as well as negative in character, prohibiting certain practices or requiring them to refrain from acting in a way considered to be undesirable. Some of these measures could be as follows:

1. Prescribing rules for costing

These rules may lay down the manner in which cost accounts are to be maintained, 'defining the costs or profit components which can or must be taken into account by each enterprise in determining its own prices',[13] or imposing 'a maximum or a minimum limit on prices',[14] or prohibiting 'sales below cost price'.[15]

2. Compulsory reporting of prices

This is another kind of 'controlled freedom', the enterprises being free to fix their prices but required to report the fixed prices or price changes to the competent authorities, who could object to the prices so reported within a specified period.

3. Compulsory display of retail prices

This rule operates for the information of the public (for example, garages in the United Kingdom must display the prices of a standard grade of petrol).

4. Prohibition of resale price maintenance

Manufacturers sometimes bind the resellers or those to whom they supply their products 'to maintain determined resale prices and to impose the same obligations on subsequent acquirers until sale to the final consumer'.[16] Laws have been enacted in the EEC countries prohibiting this practice as it deprives the resellers of the freedom to fix their prices by adjusting their trade margins and practically eliminates all possibility of competition among them.

5. Prohibition of discriminatory practices

Price discrimination consists in a seller asking or a buyer offering 'different prices for the same service'.[17] The Federal Republic of Germany, France and Luxemburg have enforced prohibitions which 'mainly affect price discrimination by the seller'.[18] In the FRG the law 'prohibits groups of enterprises and market dominating enterprises which impose prices from unfairly interfering with other enterprises or discriminating against them without justifiable reason. The ruling legal opinion is that price discrimination may constitute unfair interference'.[19] In France, the law prohibits 'the habitual practice of discriminatory price increases unjustified by corresponding increases in costs'.[20] This prohibition 'is further strengthened by the prohibition of refusal to sell'.[21] In Luxemburg, the law prohibits the offer, announcement, or grant, on the purchase of merchandise, of rebates to customers in their capacity as members of associations or societies',[22] and also 'price discrimination designed to circumvent the prohibition of resale price maintenance'.[23]

Another measure which may have a similar effect to the

prohibition of discriminatory practices is control of rebates. There are rules regulating the grant of rebates in the Federal Republic of Germany. These rules

> do not prohibit uniform changes in the gross price, but they do limit the possibilities of adaptation of particular market situations by granting rebates on a uniformly fixed gross price. If the sellers want to reduce their net prices to a larger extent, the limitation on the legitimate amount of rebates compels them to reduce their gross prices.[24]

6. Prohibition on overcharging

The Federal Republic of Germany 'prohibits overcharging in general terms'.[25] There are legal provisions for

> 'penalties in the case of goods and services of basic necessity, the wilful charging, promise, contracting, acceptance or grant of unfairly high remuneration as a result of:
> (i) restraint on competition;
> (ii) exploiting a dominant position;
> (iii) exploiting a state of shortage.
> In assessing the fairness (*Angemessenheit*) of a price, the main criterion is not the relationship between costs and price, but the comparison with a national price unaffected by the special market situations listed.[26]

There may be several other price control measures which could be devised, depending on the nature of the market situation which is sought to be controlled, the specific objective(s) of control and the ingenuity of the policy-makers. Certain things are, however, self-evident. Firstly there could in fact be no standard price control measure for dealing with any particular market situation. Even an apparently similar situation in two different economies might have some distinctively different or unique feature of its own, which may sometimes call for some subtle, but significant, variation in the details of the conception, formulation and implementation of ostensibly the same measure adopted by both of them. Secondly, in any economy, at any particular time, different situations may prevail in different markets or sectors of the economy, calling for different control measures. In one sector, the problem might be one of ensuring a reasonable rate of return to the producer on the investment made in the face of falling prices or the reasonable expectation of a fall in prices to unremunerative levels; in another the situation might demand the protection of the consumer against steeply rising prices of consumer goods; in yet another market, consumers might need protection against the activities of the unscrupulous traders exploiting their oligopolistic or monopolistic position by unduly inflating their trade margins. An economy, at any time, might, therefore, need not one but a package of suitably devised measures according to its own peculiar requirements. Thirdly, price control measures need to be so devised as to promote the stability of the general price level and be consistent with the programmes and policies of the national plan. Fourthly, the implementation and enforcement of price control measures involve costs. Besides administrative costs, there may be costs incurred by way of payment of subsidies if the controlled price is found to be unremunerative or insufficiently remunerative to the producers; or if, as in the case of the food grains sold through the public distribution system, the price at which it is decided to sell the essential commodity (the 'issue price') does not fully cover the costs of procurement, storage, transportation and handling. These costs have to be carefully considered and weighed against the benefits which are expected to accrue in deciding on the advisability or otherwise of a price control measure. Fifthly, because of the multiplicity of the variables and complicating factors involved in any situation, and also because of conflicting claims by various pressure groups of producers, traders, consumers, etc., as well as the variety of objectives to be achieved (some of which could be mutually inconsistent or even contradictory in the short run), the package of price control measures actually adopted in any economy at any time would ultimately depend on the economic, political and administrative judgement of the policy-makers who might not always be guided or governed solely by absolute principles, but by practical considerations of acceptability, feasibility and expediency.

The countries which have comprehensive systems of price controls, such as France, Belgium, the Federal Republic of Germany, Italy, Luxemburg, Netherlands, Austria and the United Kingdom, have all enacted a number of laws covering various aspects of pricing policy. In the EEC countries, while there are no enactments regulating 'the prices offered by buyers',[27] there are laws binding the sellers in regard to the 'three phases'[28] of price formation, namely 'first, ascertaining the necessary and possible level of price demands, secondly, determining prices and, thirdly, bringing them to the notice of customers'.[29] Thus, these enactments can broadly be grouped into three categories: these 'governing price formation',[30] those 'concerning the general limitation of price levels'[31] and those 'governing publicity'.[32] Enactments prohibiting resale price maintenance and discriminatory price practices and those concerning control of rebates as well as those relating to 'stability contracts' and 'programme contracts' come in the first category. The second category consists of laws which lay down principles for determining or assessing price levels, which may relate to a minimum price limit and/or a maximum price limit. Legal provisions prohibiting 'sales below cost price', prohibition of 'overcharging', or laying down rules of costing also come in this category. The third category comprises enactments regarding the compulsory display of retail prices, or compulsory reporting of prices to the authorities, who may have the right to object to the reported prices within a specified time limit.

All price controls need not necessarily have statutory bases or legal sanctions. Prices could also be regulated on the basis of an informal understanding or arrangement with the industry. For instance, many items are covered by such informal controls in India (such as certain varieties of paper, *vanaspati* (hydrogenated edible oil) and tractors). Formal legal controls might make enforcement easier. Statutory controls would, in any case, be unavoidable if price control were coupled with compulsory levy and procurement, as in the case of food grains, cotton, cement, etc. in India. Legislation might also become necessary to enforce prohibition of any practice by producers or traders (e.g. prohibition of price discrimination, overcharging or sale below cost).

Appropriate institutional set-up and administrative procedures need also to be evolved for proper formulation, implementation and monitoring of pricing policy. Every country using price controls has developed its own institutions and procedures and these appear to be similar in many ways. In France, there is a National Prices Committee, which is a consultative body headed by the Director-General of Internal Trade and Prices, and it consists of representatives of the government departments concerned and the 'organizations representing agriculture, industry and trade, small business, production workers' cooperatives, nationalized enterprises, trade unions, large families, consumer cooperatives and academic economists'.[33] Price control measures are introduced by order from the Minister of Economic Affairs and Finance or by Prefects, if so empowered by the Minister. The Minister is advised by the National Prices Committee (whose advice is, however, not binding), and the Prefect by the Departmental Prices Committee, which is chaired by the Prefect himself. In Belgium too, the Minister of Economic Affairs issues similar orders on the advice of a similarly constituted Prices Commission, whose 'Chairman has always been drawn from academic circles'.[34] The United Kingdom had, some time ago, a National Board for Prices and Incomes, which was a statutory authority set up under the Prices and Incomes Act. The Board consisted of a Chairman and twelve members, 'drawn from both major political parties, from both sides of industry and from independent professions such as the law and universities'.[35] The legal powers of the Board were 'confined to the conduct of investigations',[36] and it was the government which decided on the 'subjects of such investigations'.[37] 'Within the framework of references to the National Board for Prices and Incomes',[38] the government could 'demand statutory notification of proposed increases in prices, wages and salaries and cause increases to be postponed for periods up to twelve months',[39] and could also get 'existing prices reduced'[40] where the PIB so recommended.

For policy-makers, several significant questions arise in the process of conception, formulation and implementation of pricing policy. Firstly, whether conditions exist or a situation has arisen which call for interference in the market mechanism, what kind of price control measures need to be adopted? Secondly, what adjustments need to be made in other interrelated prices or the relative price structure to ensure a broad internal consistency in the integrated price structure, that no distortions are created in the process, and that the package of price control measures adopted is also consistent with the objectives of the national plan in a planned economy? Thirdly, what measures, other than price controls, need to be taken to support and reinforce price control measures and make them more effective? Fourthly, where the government decides to fix a maximum or minimum price directly, how should it be done. If the prices fixed are to be cost–based, how should costs be determined for the purpose of price setting and what rate of return should be allowed so as to arrive at a price which is both fair to the consumer and remunerative to the producer? Moreover, how should the price fixed initially be revised so that it adequately reflects changing input costs and does not cause avoidable distortions in the relative price structure, the consequent flow of resources and the volume and pattern of output because of unduly delayed or lagged adjustments between costs and prices? Fifthly, how can the price control authority know how price controls have actually been working, whether they have been achieving their objectives, and whether a stage has been reached when they are no longer necessary and could be lifted? To answer all these and similar relevant questions, a suitable institutional set-up needs to be evolved. Since proper answers to these questions can only be given by taking an overall and integrated view of the entire economy, we find that it is the Department of Economic Affairs of the Government which has been in charge of work relating to pricing policy, and the Minister of Economic Affairs gets the expert advice of a statutory body like the National Prices Committee in France, or the Price Commission in Belgium. The National Board of Prices and Incomes in the United Kingdom generally consisted of the representatives of the government departments concerned, and those representing agriculture, industry and trade as well as professional experts and academics. Besides these national institutions, the following kinds of institutions also appear to be necessary to enable policy-makers to get proper answers to the various questions posed above, for the proper functioning of price controls:

(a) Some kind of central research organization with requisite field formations for collection and analysis of data required to monitor the behaviour of agricultural and industrial costs, prices and production, and also the distribution and availability of industrial goods and of agricultural produce in different areas, and to different classes of society, with a view to identifying significant distortions which might have arisen in the process of the free functioning of the price mechanism to justify intervention in it. The same organization could also monitor the effects of price controls generally as well as the effects of specific price control measures, report on their actual functioning, and whether and to what extent the desired results were being achieved, and also whether the stage had been reached when a particular price control measure could be discontinued as being no longer required, to enable the government to take appropriate and timely action. This kind of organization should consist primarily of professionals with expert knowledge of industry, trade, commerce and agriculture, and also professional economists and statisticians.

(b) A pricing body which can collect necessary cost data and work out the costs of production of the commodities whose prices are to be fixed by the government, and also check and verify information regarding costs and prices furnished by individual firms required to report their fixed prices and subsequent price changes, together with supporting cost data. The same body could also examine the cost accounts of individual units, wherever necessary, to ensure that the costing rules, if any, are properly observed. As both industrial and agricultural prices are interrelated, and both have to be kept in view when considering the effect of any price control measure on the relative price structure, it seems advisable to have the same body dealing with the costing of both industrial products and agricultural produce such as food grains, cotton, sugar-cane, etc. This body may report on both the initial fixed prices as well as subsequent revisions which may become necessary owing to periodical changes in input prices. Such an institution can only function effectively if it has legal powers to demand the necessary cost data and other relevant information, and to inspect cost accounts/records and associated papers of individual firms. Like the research organization suggested above, this should also be an expert body consisting of people with

professional expertise in industry, trade and commerce as well as trained economists, cost accountants and statisticians.
(c) A statutory body of a quasi-judicial or judicial nature consisting of legal experts, professional economists, statisticians, cost accountants as well as those representing trade, commerce and industry to investigate any cases of alleged price discrimination, overcharging, hoarding, blackmarketeering or any other practice prohibited by law on a reference received from the Government or on a complaint from anyone or *suo moto* (of its own accord). This body could submit its reports to government which could pass the necessary orders in each case.

There are several institutions of more or less the nature indicated above in those countries where price controls are prevalent. For instance, in India we have a Bureau of Industrial Costs and Prices set up in January 1976 by a Government Resolution to advise the Government 'on the various issues pertaining to cost reduction and improvement of industrial efficiency and pricing problems in relation to industrial costs'.[41] 'In order to advise the Government on these issues, the Bureau undertake cost studies pertaining to industries referred to it . . .'[42] The Bureau may also take up cost studies of other industries *suo moto*, 'where it feels such investigation to be desirable, and advise the Government suitably after a study of the cost structure of the industries in question'.[43] The Government of India had also set up an Agricultural Prices Commission earlier, in January 1965, to advise the Government on the pricing policy of various food grains, pulses, oil seeds and cash crops to be indicated by the Government from time to time with a view to evolving a balanced and integrated price structure in the perspective of the overall needs of the economy and with due regard to the interests of producers and consumers'. There is also a Monopolistic and Restrictive Trade Practices Commission in India which is a statutory body consisting of a Chairman who is, has been, or is qualified to be, a Judge of the Supreme Court or of a High Court; and not less than two and not more than eight other members appointed by Central Government, who have to be persons with knowledge and experience of dealing with problems relating to economics, law, commerce, accountancy, industry, public affairs or administration. The Commission has power to enquire into any restrictive trade practice on receipt of a complaint, or a reference from Central Government or a state government, or an application made to it by the Director-General of Investigation and Registration, or upon its own knowledge or information. It can similarly enquire into any monopolistic trade practice upon reference made to it by Central Government or upon its own knowledge or information. For the purpose of such enquiries, the Commission has the same powers as are vested in a civil court, and any proceedings before it are deemed to be judicial proceedings.

As regards administrative procedures, both internal procedures governing the functioning of the institutions connected with pricing policy as well as procedures in the government departments concerned have to be such as to minimize the time taken at each stage of processing and decision-making. Time is of the essence in all operations relating to pricing policy, as dealys may aggravate the existing distortions or create new ones (which might not have been considered at the time of the formulation of the pricing policy), sometimes rendering the entire exercise virtually futile, or adversely affecting the efficiency and the effectiveness of the measures adopted. There may of course be no unique answer to the question as to what would be the most efficient and time-saving procedure in any concrete case, and appropriate procedures would have to be evolved over a period of time in the light of actual felt needs and practical experience.

Notes

1. M.A.G. van Meerhaeghe, *Price Theory and Price Policy*, London, Longmans Green, 1971, p. 70.
2. Ibid.
3. Westphal, op. cit., p. 35.
4. Ibid.
5. Ibid.
6. Ibid.
7. Ibid.
8. Ibid., p. 36.
9. Van Meerhaeghe, op. cit., pp. 70–1.
10. Westphal, op. cit., p. 13.
11. Ibid.

12. Ibid., pp. 13–14.
13. Ibid., p. 53.
14. Ibid., p. 53.
15. Ibid., p. 15.
16. Ibid., p. 15.
17. Ibid., p. 42.
18. Ibid.
19. Ibid., p. 48.
20. Ibid.
21. Ibid.
22. Ibid.
23. Ibid.
24. Ibid., p. 50.
25. Ibid., p. 67.
26. Ibid.
27. Ibid., p. 14.
28. Ibid.
29. Ibid.
30. Ibid.
31. Ibid.
32. Ibid.
33. Van Meerhaeghe, op. cit., p. 68.
34. Ibid.
35. Ibid.
36. Ibid.
37. Ibid.
38. Ibid.
39. Ibid.
40. Ibid.
41. Government of India, Ministry of Industrial Development, *Internal Trade and Company Affairs Gazette of India Extraordinary*, Pt. I, sect. I, 15 January 1970.
42. Ibid.
43. Ibid.

5 Some problems and issues relating to the determination of controlled prices

Government interference in the market mechanism may take the form of:

(a) setting a maximum or ceiling price beyond which the market price is not allowed to rise, or a minimum or floor price below which it is not allowed to fall; or

(b) setting a maximum and a minimum limit or a 'price bracket' within which individual units are given complete freedom to fix price; or

(c) determining a certain proportion of the output of each unit in the industry to be procured from it at a price fixed by the government, leaving the remainder to be sold in the open market at whatever price it can command (often called 'dual pricing'); or

(d) setting retention prices (which is generally practicable in an oligopolistic situation) — either a uniform price which each unit in an industry is allowed to retain irrespective of its actual unit cost (the difference between the unit cost and the retention price being contributed to or reimbursed from, as the case may be, a common equalization account), or a different retention price for each unit or a group of units according to its/their actual unit cost (which might vary from unit to unit depending on the age of the plant, technology, feedstock, etc); or

(e) setting a maximum rate of profit leaving the price to be fixed by each unit subject to the prescribed ceiling on the profit margin; or

(f) enabling uneconomic units (e.g. certain small-scale or handicraft units) or 'sick' units to survive by subsidizing them so that they are able to sell their products at competitive prices which might not even fully cover their unit costs; or

(g) enabling industrial units in certain industries to export their products or sell them at competitive prices in the international market by giving them direct subsidies or indirect subsidies by way of tax concessions, etc. to bridge the gap, if any, between their actual unit costs and the competitive international prices at which the products are exported, and leave them adequate margins of profit to provide incentive for greater exports to earn more foreign exchange.

Although cases (e) (f) and (g) are not, strictly speaking, cases of price setting, they have an important bearing on the price actually fixed (as in the case of (e) above) and the ability of the industry or of the individual units comprising it to face price competition in the domestic or international markets (as in the case of (f) and (g) above). These measures thus constitute significant interference in the market mechanism and are, in effect, price control measures affecting the setting or determination of prices of indigenously produced goods sold either within the country or exported. Moreover, measures such as (f) and (g) above involve government subsidy, which is an economically important aspect of pricing or price determination.

There are several other possible ways of fixing and determining prices, price ranges and maximum profit margins, directly or indirectly, by government action. There appear to be some obvious considerations and guiding factors in any such exercise. Firstly, the price, whether fixed directly by government or allowed to be fixed freely by individual units in industry within a price range or subject to a ceiling on the rate of profit, has to be cost-based. Secondly, the controlled price has to be generally fixed on a cost-plus basis, so that the individual units in the industry are, by and large, able to cover their costs and also earn a reasonable margin of profit over and above the costs incurred. Thirdly, any rational system of price setting must reward efficiency in some way so that there is always sufficient incentive to reduce costs and increase the productivity of the entire input mix used in the process of production and distribution of the goods produced. Fourthly, in a planned economy, the system of determination of controlled prices has to aim at evolving a structure of relative prices which will result in the allocation of scarce national resources in general accordance with the priorities and objectives of the national plan. Fifthly, practically speaking, controlled prices may not always be based solely on economic considerations; sometimes some non-economic compulsions, ideological considerations or considerations of political and administrative expediency may have also to be kept in view.

As all controlled prices have to be cost-based, the following questions arise in connection with the setting of and implementation of controlled prices:

(a) What costs need to be covered by the controlled price?
(b) How should costs be determined under different market conditions, and what measures are necessary to ensure that costs are properly determined?
(c) Should the units which have a lower capital cost because their plant and equipment are old be allowed to earn a larger margin of profit because the controlled price is fixed on the basis of some sort of average capital cost of the industry or the norm for capital cost adopted in the price setting exercise? Or should the higher profits of such units in excess of the rate allowed in working out the controlled price be sequestered in a separate fund or reserve in each such unit for that unit itself, or elsewhere, in the form of a common fund created and operated, statutorily or otherwise, to finance modernization/expansion of the individual units generating the fund, the reserve or any units in the industry?
(d) Is there a case for building in a certain contribution towards the development of the industry in the controlled price itself, to create a separate Development Fund for the price-controlled industry for financing research and development (R & D) for the industry as well as modernization and expansion of individual units? This would provide funds for the growth and development of the industry at least partly out of the surpluses generated by the industry itself, and to that extent would reduce dependence on government funds or finance from the public financial institutions (which might be deriving their finance for industrial projects, largely or even wholly, from the government budget)?
(e) Whether, in subsequent price revisions, after the initial setting of the controlled price, regard should be had for the fact that certain units in the industry have in the meantime enhanced their profit margin (beyond the average allowed in working out the

initial controlled price or that being achieved at the time of the setting of the initial controlled price) through cost reduction or greater efficiency of production, and the revised price fixed in a manner so as to allow these efficient units to retain a sizeable part of these higher earnings as a reward for their superior performance?

(f) Whether two separate controlled prices need to be fixed — one for existing units and the other for the new units set up after a certain specified date in order to at least fully cover the increases in costs which might have taken place in the meantime to provide incentive for the growth and development of the industry?

(g) What should the long-term policy of government be in regard to the substantial expansion of existing units and the setting up of new units in any industry? Should it allow existing units to grow in size and also set up new units nearby, concentrated in a few centres, or should it prevent big units from getting bigger and encourage new units, dispersed over different regions, particularly backward areas where no such units exist?

(h) How should transport costs be dealt with in any exercise for setting a controlled price? Should transport costs be artificially equalized for all units in the industry irrespective of the distance between the production sites and the consumption centres where the goods are to be transported for distribution and sale by operating some kind of a freight equalization account, or should sale prices be allowed to vary according to variations in transport costs which are due to differences in the distance between production units and distribution or sale points?

(i) How should controlled price be determined in the case of an industry with individual production units or groups of production units which have differing unit costs because of plant and equipment of different vintages and differences in technologies, feedstocks and scales of production? Should there be a uniform controlled price for all units in the industry or different retention prices for such different units or groups of units related to their unit costs?

(j) What are the categories of cases in which controlled prices might justifiably not cover costs fully? Or might there be a case for government interference in the market mechanism by way of subsidizing an industry or certain units in it to enable them to complete effectively in the market with larger or more efficient units by selling at a price which, if the element of subsidy is excluded, might not cover their unit costs fully or leave them an adequate margin of profit (the difference between the actual unit costs of such units plus reasonable margin of profit and the competitive market price being covered by the subsidy)? How should such subsidies be financed and how long shoud they be continued?

(k) How frequently and in what manner does the initially fixed controlled price need to be revised?

The question of whether the controlled price needs to be equated to the marginal or the average cost, and the problems relating to the determination of the rate of return which arise in any exercise for setting a controlled price, are not being dealt with here, since they require separate detailed consideration. In attempting to answer the questions posed above, frequent references have been made to price controls as they operate in India and to the Indian experience, with which the author is a little more familiar. The answers have been attempted bearing in mind the practical problems which might arise in any price setting exercise by an independent body required to submit a report regarding setting the controlled price of any particular commodity for the consideration of the government.

The term 'costs' may refer to either:

(a) 'historical costs', i.e. the costs which have already been incurred by an enterprise in producing a certain amount of a product; or
(b) 'projected costs', i.e. the costs which could reasonably be expected to be incurred in producing any product, taking into account the prices at which various inputs would be procured and all other costs; or
(c) 'standard' or 'normative' costs, i.e. costs worked out according to certain standards or norms regarding the quantities and values of the various inputs required for production.

It is obvious that while (a) are actual costs already incurred, (b) and (c) are hypothetical costs from which the actual costs may differ to the extent that the projections, standards, norms or assumptions on which they rest differ from the actual. Some of the practices followed and the difficulties encountered in fixing and implementing cost-based prices can be stated as follows:

(a) The cost on the basis of which the controlled price is determined might be some kind of an average cost of the industry which might not (and need not) correspond to the actual average cost of any particular firm, or group of firms in the industry. This average cost is generally determined mainly on the basis of the data relating to all or a sample of firms in the industry of the costs currently being incurred, or incurred over a period of time, which would therefore be 'historical costs' in a certain sense.

(b) Since the price is determined on the basis of the average cost of the individual firms or of the group of firms from whom the cost data relating to a particular point or period of time are collected, no cost functions showing the behaviour of costs at different levels of output with given or different technologies could possibly be constructed; and it cannot, therefore, be said how the costs would behave with variations in the quantities produced or changes in technology, and whether the average cost is still falling and has not yet reached its minimum level from which it would start rising.

(c) There may be elements of both 'projected costs' as well as 'normative costs' in the price worked out in any price setting exercise. In so far as the costs actually taken into account in working out the average cost are not the actual costs incurred but the costs expected to be incurred when the exercise is undertaken or at some future point in time (making allowances for factors like likely increases in prices or changes in technology which could occur in the meantime), they represent projected costs. All average cost calculations might also be based on certain assumed norms regarding the size, age and value of the plant, technology, feedstock, capacity, utilization and consumption of raw materials, energy and fuel per unit of output, overhead costs, etc., determined separately and suitably revised from time to time. These norms introduce a built-in incentive for efficiency, as individual units, which are or could operate at levels of efficiency in respect of any one or more of the factors

covered by these norms, and could earn a larger margin of profit at any given controlled price.
(d) The collection and analysis of the cost data of various firms for setting the controlled price might result in the identification of the relatively high-cost firms, and also the reasons for their high costs, such as old and outdated technology, small size of plant and low scale of production, low capacity utilization, high overheads, high inventory levels, low managerial or operational efficiency, etc. It might help further in identifying the units with relatively high debt/equity ratio due to greater reliance on initial borrowings and subsequent low generation of internal surpluses and consequent defaults/delays in the repayment of loans/interest instalments and the slower building up of reserves. Price fixing bodies could analyse the causes of high costs and high debt/equity ratios in such cases and suggest suitable remedial measures.

If controlled price has to be cost-based, necessary cost data have to be collected. Since the scope of the functions of any price-fixing body could be wider than merely recommending a cost-based price, it might have to collect data relating to several associated aspects such as the technology adopted, extent of utilization of licensed/installed capacity, overhead costs, transport costs, overt and covert subsidies, debt/equity ratio, etc. When collecting and analysing cost data, the distinction between fixed and variable costs might also need to be kept in view. It might in some cases be necessary to work out the average total cost and the average variable cost separately so that the price recommended is such that it covers at least the average variable cost of most of the firms in the industry, to enable them to survive in the short term and take necessary measures to reduce their costs so as to cover their average total cost at the controlled price fixed as quickly as possible. Maintenance of proper cost accounts and availability of reliable cost data covering all relevant aspects such as the ones indicated above is, therefore, essential for determination of the controlled price as well as being in the firm's own interest. It is so even in cases where the government refrains from fixing the price itself, but requires industrial units to do so themselves within the minimum and maximum limits prescribed, or subject to their observance of a ceiling on the rate of profit fixed, or their simply notifying the initial fixed price together with any subsequent changes, the government having the right to object within a specified period (as is done in the case of certain commodities in some of the EEC countries); as in all such cases, the observance of minimum and maximum limits, the profit ceiling, the reasonableness of the fixed price or of subsequent price changes, as the case may be, can only be checked, both by the firm concerned and by the government, from the cost accounts that are kept.

Countries using price control of any kind have generally prescribed costing rules statutorily. 'In Belgium, Germany, France and Luxembourg, there are rules relating prices to costs ... In Belgium, the Ministerial Order of 1 July 1967 governing the price of pharmaceutical specialities includes rules for costing'.[1] In Luxemburg, public contracts are awarded in certain cases on the basis of production costs 'calculated on the basis of direct labour and material costs with a reasonable addition for overheads and profits'.[2]

In India, legal provisions relating to the maintenance of cost accounts, the furnishing of cost data to the government and price fixing bodies seem to be somewhat involved and not adequately to serve their purpose. Firstly, there are provisions in the Companies Act, 1956 (Section 209 (1)(d), p. 129, introduced by an amendment made in 1965) which create a legal obligation on any company engaged in production, processing, manufacturing or mining activities to include in its books of account 'such particulars relating to utilization of material or labour or to other items of cost, as may be prescribed', if required to do so by Central Government. Another provision of this Act (Section 615) gives general power to Central Government to require such a company 'to produce such records or documents in its possession or under its control for inspection before such officer and at such time as may be specified by the Central Government', and also 'to furnish such further information as may be specified by the Central Government and within such time as may be fixed by it'. Secondly, there is a Government Resolution setting up the Bureau of Industrial Costs and Prices which says that

> the Bureau would have full powers under Section 19 of the Industrial (Development and Regulation) Act of 1951 to call for any data, records or papers pertaining to any industry listed in

Schedule I of the Industries Act, or to take such action as is allowable under the said section of the Industries Act.[3]

The wording of Section 19, however, makes it clear that it does not give any power to call for information. It only gives the power to enter and inspect any premises, to order the production of any documents and to examine persons. These powers can be exercised by any person authorized by Central Government. Thirdly, there are the Cost Audit Report Rules, 1968 (as amended from time to time)[4] framed by Central Government under the relevant provisions of the Companies Act, 1956, prescribing, *inter alia*, the form in which the cost audit report is to be submitted and the power of the cost auditor to obtain cost accounting records/statements/books for the purpose of audit. The Annexe to the prescribed form for Cost Audit Report (which forms a part of it) also indicates the various cost items, e.g. capital employed, depreciation on fixed capital, raw materials, power and fuel, wages and salaries, interest on borrowings, bonus to employees, taxes, etc. Fourthly, there is no uniformity in the cost accounting procedures and principles followed by different industries. There is, however, an exercise being carried out to standardize these by framing cost accounting rules by different industry groups under the relevant provisions of the Companies Act.[5]

The scattered, incomplete, inadequate and somewhat unrelated legal provisions outlined above need to be systematized into a body of coherent and comprehensive substantive and procedural law and rules with a view to ensuring that:

(a) all industrial units (irrespective of whether they are private or public companies, sole traders, co-operative societies, or have any other form of organization) are classified into specific groups for purposes of cost accounting; and

(b) all cost items are identified and standard rules and procedures regarding maintenance and furnishing of cost accounts, records and all related papers are prescribed for each such industry group so as to ensure that data relating to all costs, cost components or constituents, as well as significant related aspects such as fixed and variable costs, various overhead costs, transport costs, subsidies, debt/equity ratio, licensed/installed/utilized capacity, internal resource generation and its utilization, reserves and surpluses, capital/output ratio, capital/labour ratio, etc. are properly maintained, regularly audited, inspected by price fixing and other appropriate bodies and also furnished to such bodies within the specified period.

While the provisions in the Companies Act may continue, since they are part of the regulatory mechanism envisaged in that Act, there seems to be a strong case for suitably amending and amplifying the existing relevant provisions of the Industrial (Development and Regulation) Act and also framing the required rules under those provisions, wherever necessary, to ensure (a) and (b) above. This is imperative because, in the absence of necessary provisions under the relevant law, price fixing bodies might sometimes be severely handicapped, encountering numerous practical problems in obtaining the requisite data. This could sometimes vitiate the entire price setting exercise, rendering it farcical owing to inadequate coverage and unreliability of the data that they can collect, which forms the core of their exercise and the basis of their recommendations. Incidentally, availability of comprehensive and reliable cost data is also vital in checking the observance of costing or any other related rules regulating or influencing price formation by individual firms within the prescribed constraints. Further, it may be necessary for ascertaining the reasonableness of the rates offered by various parties in the tenders received for government contracts, and may help in selecting the appropriate parties for the award of government contracts.

Having somehow collected the required cost data on reasonable reliability, the question faced by a price fixing body is how should the average cost be assessed? The simplest cases are those of a monopoly or an oligopoly with a few units: in the case of the former the average cost of the single firm can be calculated, while in the latter the average costs of each of the oligopolistic units can be calculated and then a weighted average cost for the entire industry worked out to form the basis of the controlled price. The situation becomes increasingly difficult with the increase in the number of units which might be using different technologies and operating at widely varying levels of output and efficiency.

In India, the Bureau of Industrial Costs and Prices (BICP) and the various pricing committees set up by the Government have been following different methods in working out the average cost. For instance, in its report on vanaspati (which is a competitive industry with a large number of units), submitted in December 1980, the BICP worked out the weighted average cost of selected units in each geographical zone separately. In the case of white printing paper (which is the only kind of paper whose price is controlled), the price recommended by the BICP is based on the weighted average cost of the most efficient units accounting for two-thirds of the total production of the industry. In their report on cement pricing submitted in December 1981 by the committee set up by the Government, yet another approach was adopted. The average costs of the units of production were arranged in an ascending order, and the average cost of the unit at the cut-off point of two-thirds of the country's total production in 1980–81 was adopted as the basis for the recommended controlled price.

It appears that in an industry with only one unit, or with a large enough number to make it practicable to collect the cost data of all those units, price-fixing bodies can work out the average cost of each unit; and in the latter case also the weighted average of the average costs of all the units, to form the basis of their recommendation for a controlled price. In other cases, namely where the number of units is so large that it is impracticable to collect the cost data of all the units in the industry, the cost data of the relatively more efficient units which account for a major portion (say, two-thirds) of the output of the industry can be collected, and the units arranged in an ascending order of their average costs worked out separately for each unit on the basis of the data collected. Here, of the two available alternatives, i.e. the weighted average cost of all the relatively more efficient units accounting for two-thirds of the output of the industry, or the average cost of the unit at the cut-off point where two-thirds of the output is accounted for, the latter may be preferable since the price recommended on that basis would be higher than the one fixed according to the former alternative; and would, therefore, enable a larger number of units to cover their costs. But the real problem may be one of identifying the relatively more efficient firms which account for a major portion of the industry's output. Strictly speaking, this could only be done when the average costs and outputs of all the units in the industry are known. Moreover, even if this could be done, the number of units in a competitive industry accounting for two-thirds of the total output of the industry might be too large for the collection of cost data from all of them, or there might be too many cost variations among a large number of units spread over several geographical regions to ascertain the relatively more efficient of them which account for two-thirds of the industry's output. In such a situation the only practicable way might be to take some kind of a sample which was representative of the units of different levels of output and efficiency; and sometimes to take such separate samples from different regions and recommend a different controlled price for each region based on the cost data relating to it.

Assuming that an industrial unit or firm must, under any market conditions, at least cover its average cost (average variable cost in the short run and average total cost, which might include an element of reasonable profit, in the long run), the controlled price could be lower than the prevailing market price or the price which would otherwise have prevailed in a free market to the extent that the average cost is lower than such a price. Theoretically, under conditions of perfect competition, the long-run equilibrium of the firm would be at the point where the price (average revenue) is equal to the minimum average cost (where it is equal to marginal cost), and the difference between the average cost and price might arise due to market imperfections because the profit maximization (where marginal cost is equal to marginal revenue) under such conditions might be at a point where the price (average revenue) is higher than the average cost, the gap between the two widening with the increase in the degree of market imperfection. It follows that the extent to which the controlled price could be lower than the prevailing market price at the time of the imposition of the price control or the market price which would have otherwise prevailed would vary inversely with the degree of competitiveness of the industry. Whereas market prices in competitive industries would be nearer average costs and would, therefore, provide less scope for reduction through price control, market prices under conditions of monopoly or oligopoly could be substantially higher than average costs, providing much greater scope for the lowering of controlled prices.

In any exercise to set a controlled price, a certain level of capital cost (cost of fixed capital per unit of output) is to be assumed, and this could be either the industry's average or else the norm adopted for the industry. The actual capital cost of any particular unit in the industry might differ from this average or norm depending on several factors, such as technology, type of capital equipment, age of the plant, etc. Even if a uniform method of valuation of capital assets (e.g. depreciated value worked out by the straight-line method, the declining balance method, or the estimated replacement value at the current or some future price) is adopted, the old units using older (and, therefore, in most cases, cheaper) capital equipment might have a lower actual capital cost than the relatively newer ones which might have procured their capital equipment at a higher cost. A uniform controlled price would, in such a situation, yield an excess profit to the older units, owing to their actual capital cost being lower than the average or the norm adopted in the price setting exercise. The more capital intensive an industrial unit is, and the larger the proportion of relatively older capital assets to its total capital assets, the greater would be the aggregate excess profits earned by such a unit. The determination of controlled price, therefore, raises the question of how such excess profits from the old units should be regulated. This question is not germane to the price setting exercise as such, but arises as a related problem as a consequence of the setting of controlled prices.

Problems arising out of the age of the capital equipment in the old units need to be studied in the course of the collection and analysis of cost data in any exercise to set the controlled price. In fact, several old units need not necessarily make any excess profit because of the low cost of their capital equipment since they may be using an old and outdated technology which may be adding to both their maintenance and operational costs. It may also be necessary, in the case of such units, to set apart a larger amount as a reserve for the replacement of old capital equipment, if adequate reserve for the purpose has not already been built up; and there could possibly be cases where the reserve already built up, together with the possible additions to it during the remaining span of life of the capital equipment, might not be sufficient to replace the old capital equipment at the appropriate time, and the unit might be required to raise the necessary finance from some other sources as well. It cannot, therefore, be assumed that the problem of excess profits would necessarily arise in the case of all old units — in reality, there might be no problem in the majority of cases, and the excess profits earned by old units in a few cases might be found to be too small to call for any regulatory action. Where some old units with specific problems are identified in the course of the price setting exercise, price fixing bodies can suggest remedial measures. It does not appear that the problem of excess profits of old units could be of such magnitude as to call for any special regulatory measures, statutory or otherwise, to sequester them into a separate reserve within the unit or outside, to ensure that they are not diverted to inessential uses or frittered away in any other manner.

Another question sometimes raised in connection with setting a controlled price is whether an element of contribution towards the development of the price-controlled industry needs to be built into it to create a separate development fund. Such industries need funds for expansion and modernization of existing units as well as for setting up new units so that production increases to required levels, and the shortages which necessitated price controls are eliminated. The need to create such a fund has, in fact, been felt. In India, a Steel Development Fund was created in June 1978, and there have been suggestions for the creation of a Special Sugar Development Fund and a Cement Development Fund also. The need for funds for expansion and modernization of any industry may not be fully met either by the issue of shares or by public borrowing, long-term finance from public financial institutions, government subsidies, direct loans, or even all these put together (or any combination of them) in many cases, because of the magnitude of the need and the practical limits to these sources of finance. It is, therefore, imperative that a growing industry increasingly generates its own internal resources in order to progressively reduce its dependence on other sources of finance, particularly on the public financial institutions and government. However, the pooling of these resources into a common development fund may be necessary, because, while the larger and more efficient units in the industry may be generating more internal resources, the smaller and less efficient units may need more funds for modernization and expansion to bring them up to a reasonable level of efficiency and internal resource generation. The basic question which thus arises is, how should this fund be created? Should it be by:

(a) building an element of contribution into the controlled price itself (as was done in the case of the Steel Development Fund in India); or
(b) levying some kind of a cess (tax) based on the annual value of output, turnover or profits; or
(c) donations on a voluntary basis.

Raising the controlled price to include a contribution to the development fund might not always be advisable if this price has to be kept sufficiently low to make it affordable by the bulk of consumers or users. It may also be difficult to get a sufficient amount for the development fund on a continuous and regular basis through voluntary contributions. Levying a tax to raise the required funds by making necessary provision for it in the relevant law seems to be the only practicable alternative. In India, the Industrial (Development and Regulation) Act does contain such a provision (Section 9). The rate of tax levied under this provision, however, cannot exceed '13 paise per cent of the value of goods'. As the amount collected at this rate might not be adequate in all cases, this provision needs to be suitably amended to enable the government to raise a larger amount for the creation of a development fund to meet developmental needs and to finance the modernization and expansion plans of the individual production units in an industry. The advantage of creating a development fund in this manner is that the burden of the cess cannot be shifted in the form of higher prices, and according to the capacity of the individual units, they must contribute proportionately in terms of the value of their respective outputs (or turnovers or profits, which could also be alternative bases for the levy).

Any exercise to fix a controlled price has to be based on a study of the industry producing the particular commodity which covers all relevant aspects, such as the regional and overall demand and supply position, the estimated gaps between actual and projected production and requirements, the causes of shortages and the remedial measures necessary for their speediest possible removal so that the control can be lifted, being no longer needed. It is necessary to keep this perspective in view, as the price control might otherwise adversely affect the growth of the industry and tend to become self-perpetuating, which may not be desirable from the economic as well as the administrative or even political angle. Continuous and sustained growth of the price controlled industry, by way of both the expansion of existing units, the setting up of new units and also growth in productivity through technological improvement and the adoption of newer and better technologies, is essential for increasing production to a level where shortages are eliminated and price control rendered unnecessary. After the initial price determination, therefore, the situation needs to be kept under constant review; and in every subsequent revision of the controlled price the questions as to whether the industry has been achieving the desired rate of growth in production and productive efficiency, and what other measures are necessary for achieving it need to be carefully examined. In the course of the revision exercise, if it is found that certain units have enhanced their profit margins by achieving higher levels of efficiency and lowering their costs, thereby bringing down the average cost of the industry which would form the basis of the revised controlled price, the price needs to be revised such that the benefits of cost reduction or gains in efficiency are shared equitably between the industry and consumers by allowing a reduction in price which is proportionately smaller than the reduction in costs, the exact proportion being suitably determined taking into account the interests of both consumers and producers. Such a policy would preserve the motivation for greater productivity and efficiency and at the same time benefit consumers and be conducive to the healthy growth of the industry.

Price fixing bodies may sometimes recommend two prices, one for existing units and the other for new units set up after a specified date. This has been done, for instance, in the Report on Cement Industry (1981) in India. The price recommended for new units set up at green-field sites is said to be based on what the report calls 'long-term marginal cost', which is actually the projected average cost of a unit set up after a certain date, and is not the 'marginal cost' in the sense in which the term is generally used. The concept of marginal cost is applied to individual firms under conditions of static equilibrium, and cannot properly be applied to an entire industry consisting of several firms with widely varying cost structures owing to differences in plant size, technology, feedstock, levels of capacity utilization, scale of production, etc. and operating under rapidly changing or dynamic conditions.

Apart from the conceptual difficulty regarding 'long term marginal cost', another difficulty involved relates to the implementation of two prices — one for the existing and the other for the new units. Two such prices could probably only be implemented under conditions of 'dual pricing' where a given proportion of the industry's output is procured by the government at a procurement price fixed by it to be sold at a controlled price to certain categories of consumers or users or for specified purposes in rationed quantities, leaving the remainder to be sold in the open market at a price determined by the free play of market forces. In such a situation the government could pay a high procurement price to the new units and adjust the controlled price, whenever necessary, to cover the increases in the average procurement price caused by payment of a higher price for the quantities procured from the new units.

In the case of total price control, it might not be practicable to have two controlled prices — one for the existing and the other for the new units. There could possibly be two alternatives in such a situation. The controlled price could be a pooled average price based on the average costs of the existing and the new units. This price would be higher than it would have been had it been based on the average cost of the existing units alone, if the average costs of the new units were higher. Such a price might yield a higher profit to existing firms, but it might not fully cover the higher costs of the new units, which might have to be subsidized to make them meet their costs fully. Alternatively, the government might procure the entire output — the output of the existing units at the uniform price fixed for the industry, and of the new units at a higher price which covered their average costs — and arrange to sell it through its own outlets at a uniform controlled price which might be fixed so as to cover the entire cost of procurement, distribution, etc. A controlled price such as this would, however, be higher than it would have been had the new units also been allowed the same price as the existing ones (as payment of a higher price to new units would push up the average procurement price), and had all the units been allowed to sell directly to consumers/users at the controlled price (as that would have avoided incurring extra expenditure by the government on procurement, transportation, storage, distribution, etc.). It might also necessitate frequent revisions of the procurement as well as the controlled price owing to the setting up of new units. To eliminate these practical difficulties arising in a situation of total control, it might be advisable to consider some other ways of compensating the new units or covering their higher costs so as to provide the necessary incentive for the expansion of the industry by the addition of new units, such as liberal licensing and imports of machinery and technology, tax concessions, concessional finance, and better and cheaper infrastructural facilities (e.g. land, transport, fuel, power, water, etc.), rather than setting a higher price for the new units.

The practical difficulties involved in giving a price incentive for the substantial expansion of existing units or the setting up of new units in a price-controlled industry and the consequent reliance on non-price incentives of the kind indicated above, raises a related question as to what the nature and direction of growth of such industries and the degree of their regulation by government should be. This question too, though not germane or directly relevant to any exercise to determine the controlled price, is nevertheless important in this context, and no simple or categorical answer can be given to it. The answer to this question would depend not only on the immediate economic objectives sought, but also on the long-term perspective adopted, and several non-economic considerations might also have to be kept in view. Two possible alternative courses and their consequences could be as follows:

(a) The existing units could be allowed to expand and grow, and the existing large industrial houses allowed to set up new units wherever they find it profitable or convenient, without restriction. The chief advantage claimed for this approach is that it would greatly accelerate the rate of growth of output and efficiency and also of technological transformation. Owing to the absence of restrictions on plant size, technology and location, the combinations of the chosen three would generally maximize the combined advantages of all three factors, which might simultaneously increase output, improve its quality and lower costs rapidly. The process might leave fewer but more efficient firms, using the most modern technology and earning larger aggregate profits. Fewer and bigger firms earning larger profits could be perfectly consistent with greater output and greater availability of goods at lower prices. But this approach might well also result in greater concentration of economic power in the form of economic resources and productive assets in fewer hands, and a pattern might emerge where giant-sized industrial units got concentrated in a few areas with ancillaries growing up around them, while other economically backward or underdeveloped areas might continue to remain so and their potential remain unexploited. Moreover, since individual enterprises need not necessarily have a broader economic perspective covering the entire economy, the resultant growth may be haphazard, unbalanced and not always self-sustaining. The technology adopted, whether developed indigenously or imported, might also be unsuited to the factor endowment of the country (i.e. the relative availability of labour, land or capital) inasmuch as it might be making less use of the more abundant factor of production as compared to the use of the scarcer factor and creating less scope or fewer opportunities for the use or employment of the abundant factor of production. In most of the underdeveloped countries where labour is relatively abundant, such growth might aggravate the problem of unemployment.

(b) The expansion of existing units and the setting up of new units could be allowed, subject to their being consistent with certain broad objectives, such as, dispersal of industries to cover the economically backward areas and avoid concentration, congestion and pollution at a few urban or sub-urban centres only; balanced growth in keeping with the regional and total demand pattern which could be self-sustaining; generation of greater employment opportunities; more even distribution of economic power and incomes; adoption of technology suited to the factor endowment of the country which economizes in the use of the scarce factor and makes more liberal use of the relatively abundant factor as far as possible; and so on. This approach may sometimes result in slower and not so spectacular growth as the other one, but may be considered socially, politically and even economically more desirable.

The question of how transport costs should be treated in determining the cost of production of a price-controlled commodity for the purpose of price setting needs to be examined. There are two different kinds of transport costs which we have in mind, namely the cost of transport of raw materials and other inputs from their source to the factory/plant site, and the transport cost of the finished product from the factory/plant to the consumption centre. While the former are incurred in the process of production itself and have necessarily to be taken into account in determining the cost of production, the latter are incurred in the course of the sale of the finished product. If the price-fixing body has only to fix the ex-factory price, the latter does not enter into the calculations, but if they are required to fix the consumer price (f.o.r. [free-on-rail] destination), the latter has to be taken into account. There is no doubt that the cost of transport of the finished product has to be reckoned as cost. The question is whether the consumer price for different consumption centres should vary according to the distance from the production site, or should be made uniform by a system under which the production units near the consumption centres are made to subsidize those located in relatively distant places through the operation of a freight equalization account. In India, in the case of commodities like pig iron, steel, cement, nitrogenous fertilizers, etc., this system of freight equalization has been in operation. It is directly related to pricing and has an important bearing on the profitability of the production units in the indutries in which it is used. It has had several deleterious economic effects. Since the cost of transport of the finished product from the production sites to the consumption centres or sale points is equalized for all units irrespective of their locations, the entrepreneurs seek to locate the plant in places where they minimize other costs. This has resulted in sub-optimal locations, far away from consumption centre, which might have only minimized the commercial costs to individual producers and not the economic costs to the economy; and has rendered several units set up near the consumption centres prior to the introduction of this system virtually null. The economy has to bear higher transportation costs involving the use of larger quantities of scarce resources such as diesel, and heavier demands on limited rail and road traffic capacities. The system has also resulted in the clustering of production units near sources of raw materials, and has thus prevented their dispersal to various areas of consumption, thereby accentuating regional disparities in industrial growth.

In view of the distortions indicated above, the system of freight equalization needs to be gradually phased out. One way could possibly be to allow the existing units near consumption centres (whose average transport cost per unit of output is less than the average for the industry) to retain the advantage by not being required to pay the difference into the freight equalization pool. Other units (whose transport costs are higher than the industry's average) may be given a transport subsidy on a sliding scale, say at the rate of cent for cent for the first 250 kms. above the average lead or distance between the plant and the consumption centre, 60 per cent for the next 250 kms. and 40 per cent for distances above 500 kms. This subsidy need not come from the government budget, but from a development fund, the creation of which has been suggested earlier. There may be no such subsidy in the case of the new units, so that their location may be decided keeping in view the need to minimize all costs (including transport costs) of finished goods. The proposed arrangement would maintain the profitability of the existing units in remote areas; increase the profitability of existing units near consumption centres, leading to their expansion and modernization; lead to optimum location of the new plants (minimizing total costs, including the cost of transport) and reduction of avoidable pressure on rail and road transport, and avoid the drain on the limited budgetary resources of government.

Another practical way of gradual withdrawal of the existing freight equalization arrangement could be a reduction in the rate of transport subsidy every year (in the case of both old and new units alike), such that it was completely withdrawn within five years. The schedule of reduction could be as shown in Table 1.

In the case of cement in India, freight equalization is carried out by a system of freight pooling, introduced in 1956. Under this system, a pooled average freight charge is built into the f.o.r. destination price of cement. The difference between the pooled average freight charge and the freight charges actually incurred is paid into or received from the freight equalization pool, as the case may be. The gradual withdrawal of this scheme in accordance with the schedule suggested above would mean tapering off the contributions to and

Table 1 *Schedule of reduction in transport subsidy*

Financial year	Percentage of transport subsidy
1985–86	84
1986–87	68
1987–88	52
1988–89	36
1989–90	20
1990–91	Nil

disbursals from this pool over a period of five years, and the abolition of the pooling arrangement altogether for the purpose of freight equalization from the sixth year onwards.

Similarly, in the case of fertilizers in India, while the cost of transport from the factory site/ports to the warehouses for stocking is included in the retention price, the transportation cost from the warehouses to the Block headquarters is borne by Central Government. The Government has been bearing the burden of this transport subsidy in pursuance of its policy to promote the use of fertilizers, particularly in the interior areas. However, it should not be necessary to continue this subsidy for ever. If the available empirical evidence shows that the off-take of fertilizers has reached a sufficiently high level in a particular area and cultivators are convinced of the usefulness of fertilizers, a gradual reduction and eventual withdrawal of the subsidy could be considered in the case of such an area more or less in the manner indicated above. Similar arrangements could also be worked out in the case of steel, pig iron, etc.

The scheme suggested above should motivate those units with relatively higher transport costs of finished product from production site to consumption centre to adopt cost reduction measures to compensate for the reduction in the amount of transport subsidy every year and its eventual withdrawal in five years. Since the scheme would apply to new units as well, entrepreneurs will have to take into account the transport costs to be incurred in the year of setting up the unit and subsequent years while deciding the location of any new unit so as to minimize the total cost, including transport cost.

Another important question which arises is whether a uniform price should be fixed or different retention prices fixed for different units or groups of units in the industry based on their cost differentials. Different retention prices are feasible if the product of different units is uniform and the number of units in the industry is not very large (e.g. in the case of aluminium or fertilizers in India). It may be necessary to fix different retention prices in the case of units in an industry whose production costs are different due to differences in feedstock and technology, particularly in the case of industries whose products are in short supply (e.g. fertilizers in India), so that high-cost units also earn a certain minimum rate of profit and find it worthwhile to continue production. The system of different retention prices is accompanied by a pooling arrangement to maintain a uniform consumer price, which may, in effect, amount to low-cost units subsidizing high-cost ones, or to the government bearing the cost of subsidy. Such a system would reduce the profitability of low-cost units and reduce the surpluses available to them which could be used for modernization and expansion. It would also tend to perpetuate cost differentials among different units by assuring a minimum rate of return to high-cost units, thus providing them with no incentive to reduce costs. Therefore, even where fixing different retention prices is considered necessary, certain norms regarding costs or efficiency of production need to be adopted and adhered to, and the number of different retention prices kept to the minimum by grouping units on the basis of the age of plants, feedstocks, production processes, etc. Moreover, the efficiency norms need to be suitably revised or improved in each successive price setting round, so that the incentive for achieving higher levels of efficiency is sustained.

A uniform price is more conducive to efficiency since it leaves a larger margin of profit to more efficient or lower-cost units. In an industry in which different retention prices for different units are considered necessary, an alternative arrangement could, therefore, be as follows:

(a) fixing one standard price for all the units in the industry on the basis of standard costs worked out in accordance with norms regarding technology, feedstock, input–output co-efficients, capacity utilization, etc. adopted;

(b) allowing the units whose actual costs are lower than the standard or normative cost to retain the relative cost advantage; and
(c) directly subsidizing from the government's general budgetary resources those units whose costs are higher due to unavoidable differences in feedstock, technology, etc. to make up for the differences between actual cost and normative cost, the quantum of subsidy gradually tapering off over years.

The chief merits of this alternative arrangement would be:

(a) the financial burden of the subsidy would not be borne by the relatively more efficient units, and they would be able to retain the larger surpluses generated internally owing to their greater efficiency, to be ploughed back for their expansion and modernization; and
(b) as the rate of subsidy gradually tapered off, the relatively high-cost units would be urged to reduce their costs progressively so that they did not need any subsidy by the time it was completely withdrawn.

The main demerit of this arrangement would be that it could involve substantial outgoings from the government's budget, and that the taxpayer could ultimately be made to subsidize the high-cost units.

As a general rule, the controlled price has to cover costs (including a reasonable margin of profit) fully. But there could, however, be cases where setting a controlled price at a level where it covers costs fully militates against the basic objective of price control, namely providing protection to the vulnerable sections of the community against the rapidly rising prices of essential consumer goods, or to producers against similar increases in the price of essential industrial inputs. There could also be categories of producers who are not able to cover their costs fully at prevailing prices in the domestic or international markets, and who need protection to help them survive and sell their products. Such cases might call for either round of setting a controlled price at a level lower than the one at which costs are fully covered, or giving direct or indirect subsidies to certain categories of producers to enable them to sell at competitive prices, as the case may be. Some instances of cases necessitating government subsidy in various forms could be as follows:

(a) Cases where setting controlled price at a level where it covers costs fully might make it unaffordable by the category of consumers for whose protection the price is controlled. Controlled prices of food grains and other essential consumer goods such as edible oil, *maida* (fine wheat flour used for making bread, cakes, etc.), *suji* (semolina) or kerosene which are sold through fair-price shops in India come into this category. Sometimes, prices of such commodities which fully cover the costs of procurement, storage, transportation, distribution, etc. may be considered too high to be affordable by the poor, for whom the fair-price shops were primarily opened by the government; and the controlled prices may have to be fixed at lower levels, the difference between the prices so fixed and the prices which would have covered the costs fully reflecting the extent of a subsidy by government. Similarly, in cases where the government arranges to supply an essential input at a controlled price to some categories of producers to keep the costs of production of their products low (e.g. supply of yarn to weavers), such supplies may sometimes have to be made at subsidized rates.
(b) There could be industrial units in the small-scale or handicrafts sector or in rural areas whose products have to compete with the large-scale or mill-made products of units located in big urban industrial centres, whose production costs are lower due to better technology, economies of scale and other economies available to them on account of their locational advantage. Such units might not be able to survive without some direct or indirect subsidy from government to keep their costs sufficiently low to be able to compete in the market; and their survival might be considered necessary in the interest of balanced regional growth, development of local arts and crafts, opportunities for gainful employment available to the local population, etc.
(c) Direct or indirect subsidy may also be considered necessary in the case of certain products meant exclusively for the export market to enable exporting units to sell them there at competitive prices, and to earn valuable foreign exchange.
(d) In order to encourage the setting up of industries in the

backward areas, the government may sometimes give a 'capital investment subsidy' to the new units set up in such areas, besides the indirect subsidies by way of tax concessions, and availability of land, water, power, etc. at concessional rates. Such subsidies are also intended to have the same effect, namely to enable the newly set-up units in the initial phase of their existence, when their costs are generally high, to survive and effectively compete in the market.

The financial burden of these subsidies can be very high and is increasing every year, especially in the developing countries, as the figures in Table 2 reveal.

Table 2 *Growth of subsidies in India, 1950/51–1982/83 (Rs crores)*

Year	Fertilizer subs.	Food subs.	Subsidy on controlled cloth	Export subs.	Other subs.*	Total subs.	Total subs. as % of total tax revenue	Total subs. as % of total govt. exp.	Export subsidies as % of total value of exports
1950–51	—	32	—	—	—	32	5.1	3.5	—
1955–6	—	19	—	—	—	19	2.5	1.3	—
1960–61	—	19	—	—	7	26	1.9	1.0	—
1965–66	—	−56	—	—	103	47	1.6	0.9	—
1968–69	—	31	—	—	20	51	1.4	0.8	—
1973–74	—	251	—	66	44	361	4.9	3.0	2.6
1978–79	342	578	38	375	142	1,475	9.5	5.7	6.5
1979–80	603	601	60	361	196	1,821	10.3	6.2	5.6
1982–83	648	722	57	500	451	2,378	8.7	4.9	5.7

* Derived figures
Source: 'Economic and Functional Classification of the Central Government Budget and Economic Surveys', published by the Government of India and the data collected from the Ministry of Industry and Ministry of Finance, Government of India.

In India, the burden of subsidies has been growing, particularly since the year 1968–69; and it was as high as Rs 2378 crores in 1982–83, which constituted about 9 per cent of the total tax revenue and 5 per cent of total government expenditure. Export subsidies too have been increasing, and were of the order of Rs 500 crores in 1982–83, constituting about 6 per cent of the total value of exports in that year.

It has been suggested above that the fertilizer subsidy in India could gradually be tapered off over a period of time. The burden of food subsidy and the subsidy on controlled cloth also needs to be progressively reduced in the same way. Alternatively, if feasible and considered advisable on other considerations as well, part of the burden of the food subsidy could possibly be passed on to the producers or traders from whom the procurement is made by lowering the procurement price; and in the case of controlled cloth, to textile manufacturers by a gradual reduction in the rate of subsidy without allowing a corresponding increase in the price of the controlled cloth. Export subsidies could similarly be gradually tapered off by adopting a conscious policy of encouraging the upgrading of technology and the adoption of other cost reduction measures. The long-term strategy in all cases has to be to create conditions by a continuous process of technological improvement, cost reduction, greater managerial and operational efficiency, etc., where subsidy can be progressively reduced and ultimately dispensed with altogether.

After initial fixation, controlled prices have to be kept under constant review by an efficient system of monitoring so as to ensure that they move more or less in line with the movement in the cost of essential inputs, and there are no unduly long time lags to create distortions.

There is, therefore, a need to evolve a system which makes short-term adjustments in prices to changing costs of major raw materials and inputs automatic. The desirability of making frequent small changes in prices in response to short-term changes in costs of essential inputs (which the economic system can easily absorb), instead of large changes at long intervals, needs to be stressed. The price fixing body may determine the major raw materials and other inputs for each price-controlled industry, and evolve a suitable price adjustment formula, keeping in view factors like their proportion to total cost, the degree of their substitutability in the short-term, the price elasticity of demand for finished products, etc. and also the off-setting factors which might cause a reduction in costs. They can then closely monitor movements in their prices, and take action as soon as they have changed to the extent warranting a corresponding change in the prices of the price-controlled commodities concerned, according to the formula evolved by them. The entire process could be computerized. Producers could be asked to adjust their prices accordingly as soon as notification is given and inform the government immediately. These adjustments could be allowed every six months or so.

The price fixing bodies also need to take up a comprehensive review of costs and prices of price-controlled industries of their own accord periodically, say every three years or so. They could maintain a roster so that the review is initiated well in advance. They should have the power to require units to furnish the required cost data to them in the form of an annual return in a prescribed form to enable them to undertake such comprehensive reviews.

Once a product has been referred to a price fixing body, that body should have continuing concern for the product's initial price setting and subsequent short-run price adjustments as well as comprehensive reviews at specified intervals.

Notes

1. Westphal, op. cit., pp. 53–5.
2. Ibid., p. 61.
3. 'The Industries (Development and Regulation) Act, 1951' (as amended by Act No. 4 of 1984), Current Book House, New Delhi, 1984, p. 40.
4. 'The Cost Audit (Report) Rules 1968' (as amended up to 2 February 1971), Cost Accounting Record Rules under the Companies Act 1956 (brought up to 3 June 1977), Ministry of Law, Justice and Company Affairs, Government of India, New Delhi, pp. 771–780.
5. 'The Companies Act, 1956' (as amended up to 1 July, 1975), Ministry of Law, Justice and Company Affairs, the Controller of Publications, Delhi, 1976, pp. 334–5.

6 Marginal cost pricing versus average cost pricing

The question whether the controlled price needs to be equated to the marginal or the average cost is important, theoretically as well as from a practical angle; and has, therefore, engaged the attention of both the economic theorists and those concerned with the actual formulation and implementation of economic policies.

It is argued, particularly with reference to public utilities, public sector, or nationalized industries run by the government, that the controlled price should be fixed at a level where it is equal to marginal cost. The argument is based on the reasoning that such pricing will ensure that output is produced 'up to the point of its actual "worth" to the consumers',[1] and that if 'firms have been producing at less than capacity, an increase in output resulting from adoption of a marginal cost pricing policy will reduce the average cost of production'.[2] It is further claimed that marginal cost pricing is superior to any other system of pricing as 'it meets the marginal conditions for maximizing welfare and that for this reason it represents an optimum'.[3]

The case for marginal cost pricing rests essentially on the theory of perfect competition, and of 'welfare optimum' flowing from it, developed to a very high degree of refinement and mathematical precision by using the tools of marginal analysis. Under perfect competition where every producer has a perfectly elastic demand curve for his product at the prevailing market price in the sense that he can sell any quantity at that price (his share in the total output of the industry being so infinitesimally small that he has to take the ruling market price as given and unalterable by any action of his own), and the point at which he maximizes his profits (by equating his marginal revenue to his marginal cost) or his equilibrium position is necessarily at a point where price (average revenue) is also equal to marginal cost. This automatic equalization of price to marginal cost for all firms arises because of the perfectly elastic or horizontal demand (average revenue) curve for each individual firm under perfectly competitive conditions, which indicates equality of marginal revenue to average revenue at all levels of output. The price being given, competition forces every firm under such conditions to reduce costs in order to increase its profit margin until the point of minimum average cost (where marginal cost is equal to average cost) is reached. In the long run, every firm thus reaches an equilibrium where, simultaneously, its profits are maximized, costs minimized and a level of output attained which is the largest consistent with profit maximization. Such a position is obviously attained because of the following three factors:

(a) the individual firm's inability to change the ruling market price and its ability to sell any quantity at that price which gives a horizontal average revenue curve indicating equality of marginal revenue and average revenue at all levels of output;
(b) competition which impels every firm to go on reducing costs and producing more to earn larger and larger aggregate profit until the level of minimum average cost is reached; and
(c) operation of the law of diminishing returns or increasing costs after a certain point which gives a U-shaped average cost curve which could become tangent to a horizontal average revenue curve at its lowest point where the marginal cost is equal to average cost, as the marginal cost has just ceased falling and not yet started rising.

Obviously, if all the firms in a perfectly competitive situation reach their long-run equilibrium positions, the following five conditions would be simultaneously achieved:

(a) the price of everything would be equal to its marginal cost, i.e. everything would sell at a price which is equal to its 'worth' in terms of what it costs to produce it (which should include a minimum margin of profit per unit of output to provide the necessary incentive to produce it);
(b) every firm or producer would reach his optimum position where his aggregate profits are maximized;
(c) efficiency of production would be maximized as all firms would be producing at the minimum average cost achievable under given conditions;

(d) the output of each firm would be the largest consistent with the minimization of cost and the maximization of profit; and
(e) a position of 'welfare optimum' would be reached where all the 'marginal conditions' of it (into which we need not go here for our argument) are satisfied.

The entire scheme of things outlined above is upset in any real life situation where competition is far from perfect. The two crucial factors which materially change the situation are:

(a) the individual firm or producer's capacity to influence the market price and his ability to sell more by reducing his price which results in a downward sloping demand or average revenue curve for him (so that marginal revenue is less than average revenue throughout the slope of the curve); and
(b) decreasing costs or increasing returns over considerable ranges of output due to economies of large-scale production, indivisibilities, 'lumpiness' of investment in large-size plant and equipment, modern technology, etc. which, on the one hand, increase the output of an individual firm or unit to the extent where it forms a sizeable portion of the total output of the industry and is large enough to enable it to influence the market price by altering his own production plans and, on the other hand, also give it the ability to restrict its output to a point where its own profits are maximized.

Unlike perfect competition, where in the long run each individual producer's profit maximization point coincides with the efficiency maximization point (minimum average costs) and also the point of welfare maximization (where 'marginal conditions' are satisfied), the profit maximization point of a producer under imperfect competition may be at a level below the level of maximum efficiency (minimum average cost), and the output at that level may be smaller than it would have been under competitive conditions (by pushing production up to the point where the average cost is minimized). Because of the downward slope of the average revenue curve, the price (average revenue) is also higher than the marginal cost at the equilibrium position (where marginal revenue is equal to marginal cost) of any producer under conditions of imperfect competition. In other words, in this situation, the community is made to pay a higher price for any commodity than it is 'worth' in terms of the cost involved in producing it. The 'welfare optimum' would, therefore, not be achieved under conditions of imperfect competition without price control, i.e. unless the price is reduced by government intervention to the level at which it is equal to marginal cost. At this level not only would the price be lower, but the output would be larger. Thus, even leaving aside the sophistication of the satisfaction of 'marginal conditions', consumers will get a larger output at a lower price, and producers may also get a reasonable, though somewhat smaller, profit. But there could be two objections to setting the controlled price at the level of marginal cost under such conditions. It would not be an equilibrium price for the producer since it would be lower than the price at which the aggregate profit is maximized, and this price could only be enforced and the producers compelled to produce more at this price by coercion. This is perhaps not a serious objection since any controlled price may only be enforceable through some sort of coercion. But another somewhat serious objection is that the controlled price which is equated to marginal cost need not be the price which would achieve either the maximum efficiency (minimum average cost) or the maximum output consistent with minimum cost (both are achieved only at the long-run equilibrium price conditions of perfect competition, which is equal to both marginal cost as well as average cost). In fact, if the average cost curve is U-shaped, as it is generally assumed to be, it cannot be tangent to a downward sloping average revenue curve at its minimum point (where the marginal cost curve cuts it from below, marginal cost having just ceased falling and not yet started rising) and, therefore, any price (average revenue) which is equal to marginal cost can achieve neither maximum efficiency (minimum average cost) nor the largest output which could have been produced had it been pushed to the point where the average cost is minimized, under such conditions.

Marginal cost pricing is essentially based on the static equilibrium theory of price formation, and is largely irrelevant under dynamic conditions. In the real world where the cost functions are constantly changing because of changes in technology, and higher and higher levels of production and productivity are being achieved through factors such as greater capacity utilization, economies of scale, better inventory management, better labour/management relations, better management and marketing techniques, etc., the real problem from the viewpoint of economic policy is not that of maximizing so-called 'welfare' by dubious devices like equation of the prices of controlled commodities to their respective marginal costs. The real problem under such conditions is to identify the areas where cost functions are not changing or not changing rapidly enough, and to create favourable conditions and provide necessary incentives for changing the cost functions themselves through a package of policies, which might include measures like liberal licensing of additional industrial capacity wherever needed, quicker availability of finance at easier terms for worthwhile projects, research and development activities for development of suitable technology, import of technology wherever necessary and creating the necessary infrastructure so that greater and greater output is achieved at lower and lower cost. In this dynamic perspective, it may be more prudent and advisable to fix the controlled price at a level where it covers the average cost of a reasonably efficient producer in the industry, and also conforms to certain efficiency norms, so that, besides being low enough to be affordable by consumers, it is high enough to be remunerative for most of the units in the industry, and does not impair their will or capacity to make improvements and reduce their costs; and, simultaneously, to take measures to shift the average and marginal cost curves themselves so that the consumer gets more at the same price or has to pay less for the same quantity.

The concept of marginal cost (all 'marginal' concepts for that matter) has been developed in price theory to determine the equilibrium position of an individual firm under certain given conditions. It applies to individual firms and probably cannot be applied to an industry which might consist of a large number of firms producing under different conditions. Even if it were possible, theoretically, to conceive of the marginal cost of an industry (arrived at by some kind of summation of the marginal costs of individual units comprising it), operationally it would be a nearly impossible proposition since it would involve the construction of marginal cost functions of all the individual units and then summing them up to get the marginal cost function for the entire industry. Moreover, even assuming that some statistical and mathematical manipulation or jugglery could produce a marginal cost function for the entire industry, such a function would change with even the slightest change in the conditions governing even a single unit comprising that industry. Then the basic question would be, whether such a game is worth the candle? In a developing economy where cost functions are themselves getting rapidly changed, and the objective of economic policy is not to force the system to attain an equilibrium position and to remain at it, but to keep on pushing it to progressively higher and higher levels, there is little practical relevance of marginal cost in the context of the setting of controlled prices.

Yet another point which arises in respect of marginal cost pricing is what should be the level of output at which price should be equated to marginal cost. Under static conditions of long-run equilibrium in a perfectly competitive situation, there is a unique level of output at which price is equal to marginal cost and also to average cost and marginal revenue. There is also a unique level of equilibrium output under conditions of imperfect competition at the point where marginal revenue is equal to marginal cost, which is the profit maximization position. But once the equilibrium and profit maximization constraints are removed, there need not necessarily be a unique level of output at which the controlled price needs to be equated to marginal cost. If the industry's demand curve is given, then perhaps a unique level of output could be found where price could be equated to marginal cost. But if the demand function is not known, the price could be fixed at any point on the marginal cost curve; and which levels of output and marginal costs should be chosen for the determination of the controlled price in such situations is both a theoretical and a practical problem. If both the average and the marginal cost functions are known, one alternative could perhaps be to fix the controlled price at a level where the average cost is minimum and the average and marginal costs are equal to each other. However, if the price is so low at this level that most of the units with their existing levels of efficiency and output cannot cover their costs, setting the price at this level might create problems. The position might become much more complex in a dynamic situation where the cost and demand functions are changing or could be changed by government action. Assuming that the changing demand and supply functions over a period of time could be constructed, the question would be which of them should be taken as the basis for equalizing price to marginal cost in order to determine the controlled price. Moreover, these functions might themselves change while the price setting exercise was going on, necessitating a fresh exercise all over again, and so on.

Yet another complicating factor in marginal cost pricing is the refinement introduced by Professor A.C. Pigou's concepts of marginal social cost and marginal social benefit. If the distinction between marginal social costs and benefits and marginal private costs and benefits is valid, then the external economics which cause divergencies between marginal social benefits and marginal private benefits, and external diseconomies resulting from divergencies between marginal social costs and marginal private costs also need to be taken into account in the price setting exercise, which might create almost insuperable practical and operational difficulties, into which we need not go here.

Leaving aside the concepts of marginal social costs and marginal social benefits, even the adoption of the simple marginal cost pricing principle is beset with formidable practical difficulties. Marginal cost pricing would necessitate the construction of a cost function (or several cost functions based on different sets of assumptions under dynamic conditions), which would be a highly complicated engineering and accounting exercise.[4] Even the determination of the marginal cost at any given level of output without constructing the cost function would be a much more complicated exercise than the determination of simple average cost. What the engineers and accountants would be required to work out would be the costs incurred in terms of tangible physical inputs (both fixed and variable) as well as intangible inputs of skilled and unskilled labour, supervisory and managerial effort, and so on, in producing an incremental unit of output, and then to work out the value of all such costs in monetary terms. This would involve estimational and allocational problems of staggering magnitude, and the degree of error in any marginal cost so worked out could be very high. Similar exercises will have to be undertaken in respect of all the units whose costs are to be considered for price determination, and then a weighted average of marginal costs of all such units worked out and a controlled price fixed at that level. Alternatively, instead of working out the marginal cost on the basis of the data regarding the costs already incurred (historical costs), an exercise could be undertaken to determine what it would now cost to produce an incremental or extra unit of output in the case of each production unit and then to work out a weighted average of the marginal costs so discovered. But whether we work backwards on the basis of the costs already incurred, or forwards by projecting what an extra unit would cost, apart from the engineering and accounting problems of considerable magnitude, the marginal cost so worked out would only be hypothetical. In the case of a monopoly, where there is only one unit, or an oligopolistic situation where there are a few units, the marginal cost so worked out could perhaps have some meaning under static conditions, but in a competitive situation where there are numerous units of different vintages operating at varying levels of output and efficiency, and under dynamic conditions, the usefulness of the marginal cost so worked out for determining the controlled price could be questionable.

Unlike marginal cost, the practical difficulties involved in working out average cost are of relatively much lesser magnitude. Average cost could be worked out for any unit largely on the basis of the available cost data at any point in time or over a period of time without necessarily constructing on average cost function, and a weighted average cost could also be worked out on the basis of the average costs of the selected units, if necessary. The average cost so worked out would reflect the costs actually incurred in producing a unit of output, and would not be an entirely hypothetical figure based on the estimate and judgement of engineers and accountants regarding what it actually cost to produce the last increment of output at any level of total output, or what it would now cost to produce an incremental unit at any existing level of output. Moreover, average cost, in whatever manner worked out, is operationally a more significant concept, as all technological improvements and measures to increase productivity and reduce costs could be directed towards minimizing it. In fact, it is the marginal cost at the level of output where it is minimized and becomes equal to average cost that is a desirable objective to achieve; and it is the price fixed at that level which would achieve both maximum efficiency and the largest output at minimum cost. From the viewpoint of economic policy, therefore, average cost is a much more significant and useful concept, and is operationally much more simple and relatively free from estimational bias, for any exercise for setting the controlled price, or formulation of a set of policies designed to reduce costs, or promote efficiency, or increase productivity.

Average cost pricing is practically speaking a more desirable alternative for another reason: it obviates the need for subsidizing decreasing cost industries whose marginal cost is lower than average cost because the industries cannot meet their total costs, or for managing surpluses arising in the case of increasing cost industries, if the controlled price is fixed at a level where it is equal to marginal cost. Several alternative ways have been suggested to overcome the difficulties arising owing to decreasing or increasing cost industries in the case of marginal cost pricing, but we need not go into them here. While these problems may not be practically so important in the case of competitive industries with large numbers of units operating at varying levels of output and efficiency (as any method of price determination might result in some units incurring losses and some making larger profits than they might have made had there been no price control), they might create genuine problems in the case of state monopolies or public utilities like, for instance, electric supply undertakings, roads or railways in some countries. Setting the controlled price at a level where it covers the average cost (which could include a reasonable margin of profit), accompanied by suitable cost reduction measures on a continuing basis, and subsequent timely revision of the controlled price to keep it in line with changing costs, might be a better policy prescription in such cases.

Notes

1. H.H. Liebhafsky, *The Nature of Price Theory*, Homewood Ill., Dorsey Press, 1963, p. 405.
2. Ibid.
3. Nancy Ruggles, 'Recent Developments in the Theory of Marginal Cost Pricing', in *Public Enterprise*, R. Turvey (ed.), Harmondsworth, Penguin, 1968.

4. See Ralph Turvey, 'Practical Problems of Marginal Cost Pricing in Public Enterprise, England' and James R. Nelson, 'Practical Problems of Marginal Cost Pricing in Public Enterprises, United States', in *Prices: Issues in Theory, Practice and Public Policy* (ed. Almarin Phillips and Oliver E. Williamson, Philadelphia, University of Pennsylvania Press, 1967.

7 The problem of rate of return in relation to price-controlled industries

The controlled price needs to be fixed at a level where it not only covers the cost, both fixed and variable, fully, but also leaves an adequate margin of profit to preserve the incentive for greater production and productivity. The cost covered is generally some kind of an 'average cost' worked out for the entire industry on the basis of the cost data of a sample of individual units, and also certain assumed norms of consumption of various raw materials and other inputs, scale of production, overheads, etc. and of capacity utilization. A price which covers this 'average cost' may only accidentally or by chance happen to exactly cover the average cost of some particular units: it may in fact turn out to be higher or lower than the average costs of most of the individual units, depending on the degree of variation in their actual costs from the average worked out in the price setting exercise in the manner indicated above. This system of price setting provides a built-in incentive to reduce costs, as the more efficient units whose actual cost is lower than the average cost on which the controlled price is based, or which could by technological improvement or greater managerial and operational efficiency reduce their costs below the level of this average cost, could earn a larger profit in terms of the difference between their average cost and the controlled price. However, the controlled price has not only to cover the cost but also to provide a margin of profit over and above it, so that all reasonably efficient units make enough profit to induce them to stay in the industry and constantly endeavour to earn more and more aggregate profit by achieving higher and higher levels of productive efficiency. While this profit margin cannot be too large since it would defeat the very purpose of price control, namely the protection of the consumer or the user against unduly high and steeply rising prices, keeping it too low could also have deleterious economic effects, as it could slow down or stifle the growth of the industry or else result in diversion of resources away from it. Basically, it is a problem of reconciling the interests of both producers and consumers so that the controlled price is fixed at a level where it is high enough to be remunerative to the former and low enough to be affordable by the latter. Two basic questions arise: to what should this margin of profit over costs be related or what should be the base for allowing it, and what should be the rate at which it should be allowed in the determination of any controlled price?

One thing is obvious and needs to be plainly stated at the outset. Production involves investment in both fixed and 'variable' capital, in infrastructural facilities, plant and machinery, raw materials and other inputs, skilled and unskilled labour and supervisory and managerial personnel. The entrepreneur who undertakes production relates the profit earned by him (in the sense of the difference between the costs incurred in production and the revenue earned by the sale of the product) to the entire investment made by him in the production and marketing of the product, including the taxes paid at various stages. The controlled price has, therefore, ultimately to allow a reasonable rate of return on the entire capital invested or employed or the total costs incurred in production; and whatever base is adopted in working out the rate of return (whether capital employed, net worth, turnover, output or value added), it is always translatable, and is actually translated, into a rate of return on total investment made or costs incurred. The controlled price which is fixed on the basis of an average cost worked out for the industry, and a reasonable rate of profit over and above it, should provide sufficient incentive to achieve both higher production and greater productivity by reducing costs for the reasons stated in the preceding paragraph. Statements like the following are fallacious and misleading in this context:

> Prices which are made up of true costs calculated by post costing, and a profit margin, can hardly afford an incentive to cut costs. If the legal profit is fixed as an absolute figure, it is not affected by cost variations. If it is fixed as a percentage of unit costs, *increased costs become a means of maximising profits*.[1] [author's italics]

Firstly, any cost-based controlled price is determined by 'post-costing', but, as indicated earlier, any price so determined on the basis of an average cost of the industry has a built-in incentive to reduce costs. Secondly, the profit margin allowed in any controlled price cannot reasonably be an 'absolute figure', which is 'not affected by cost variations'. The profit margin has to be related to some base, capital employed, net worth or turnover, or any other base, and could not conceivably be an 'absolute figure'. Thirdly, there could possibly be no profit whose *quantum* remains unaffected by cost variations. If profit is, by definition, the difference between the costs incurred in the production and the revenue earned by the sale of a product, reduction in costs would, other things being equal, always increase profit and vice versa. Fourthly, 'increased costs' could never 'become a means of maximizing profits', so long as by profit we mean an excess of revenue earned over the costs incurred.

An entrepreneur, whether in a free economy or in a regime of controlled prices, is interested in maximizing his aggregate profits. In setting the controlled price, the rate of return needs to be so allowed as to provide adequate incentive for maximization of aggregate profits by expansion of output and cost reduction. The aggregate profits of the entrepreneur would basically depend on the following three factors:

(a) The base chosen for working out the rate of return. The alternative bases could be capital employed (fixed capital plus working capital), net worth (paid-up capital plus reserves), turnover (total sale proceeds of the goods sold), value of output and value added in the process of production. Of all these bases, net worth and value added may empirically be found to be the smallest, and turnover and value of output the largest bases. Capital employed should be larger than the net worth and the value added but smaller than the other bases. The larger the base chosen for working out the rate of return, the smaller could be the rate allowed to yield a given amount of aggregate profit on a given output.

(b) The rate of return allowed on the base will also determine the aggregate profit, as it could be larger even on a smaller base if the rate allowed in terms of percentage of the base is sufficiently high.

(c) The aggregate profit would ultimately depend on the level of output on which it was earned. The controlled price, or for that matter, any price is in terms of per unit of output; and the higher the output, the higher would be the aggregate profit earned. Given the base, the rate of return and the average cost, the aggregate profits would be a function of the growth of output.

In deciding both the base on which the rate of return is to be worked out as well as the rate itself in any exercise for setting the controlled price, a combination of the two is to be chosen which yields a price which is both adequately remunerative to the producer and sufficiently low for the consumer. While the choice would essentially be a matter of judgement based on several considerations, the implications of alternative approaches need to be analysed in order to make a proper choice.

In India, prior to 1975, capital employed (i.e. fixed capital plus working capital) was adopted as the base for working out the rate of return in the case of industries whose price was fixed by the government. Capital employed has since been abandoned as a base mainly on the grounds that it gives equal return on investors' own capital as well as on borrowed funds. In a situation where the rate of interest payable on borrowed funds is lower than the rate of return on capital allowed, the investor can increase the effective rate of return on his own capital as well as on the borrowed funds by increasing the proportion of borrowed funds in the total capital employed. Greater reliance on borrowed funds is further encouraged by the fact that the interest on borrowed funds is generally deductible from profits for taxation purposes. It is, therefore, argued that the rate of return should be worked out only on the net worth of a company, excluding borrowed funds altogether. The main grounds on which net worth has been adopted as a base in preference to capital employed are as follows:

(a) Equity capital needs to be encouraged, as it is a measure of the actual risk taken by an entrepreneur by investing his capital in a productive venture instead of keeping it in the form of riskless bank deposits.
(b) Net worth provides a base which makes the rate of return neutral

in regard to the contribution of borrowed funds to total capital, and, therefore, discourages borrowings and encourages the use of equity capital or own funds.

It is true that in the case of an enterprise in the corporate sector in which the shareholders have limited liability, the entrepreneur's risk is limited to the *quantum* of his share holding. Hence it may be desirable to encourage ventures in which the proportion of equity capital is higher than that of borrowed capital. The financial institutions, therefore, generally insist that the debt/equity ratios do not exceed certain maximum limits. However, the desirability of discouraging the use of borrowed capital *vis-à-vis* equity capital in all cases may be questionable. The primary consideration in regard to any project is its economic viability in terms of productivity, technology, marketability of the product, generation of internal surplus, etc. The mode of financing is a question of relatively secondary importance. A worthwhile project need not be discouraged simply because it involves a greater use of borrowed capital, nor a project which is not economically viable encouraged, if it can be financed by equity capital to a larger extent. The relative desirability of different projects is to be judged on the basis of several economic factors, and the pattern of financing may be only one of these factors.

It is not correct that net worth as a base is neutral to the contribution of borrowed capital to total investment, i.e. the effective rate on net worth remains the same irrespective of the debt/equity ratio or the proportion of borrowed funds to net worth. As debt/equity ratio differs from unit to unit in any industry, the price has to be fixed on the basis of an average debt/equity ratio of the entire industry. Any price fixed with reference to such an average ratio cannot be neutral to the contribution of borrowed capital; in fact, in a situation where the rate of interest on borrowed capital is lower than the rate of return allowed on net worth, the higher the ratio of borrowed capital to equity capital than the average adopted for price setting, the higher would be the rate of return on equity capital, and vice versa. Adoption of net worth worked out on the basis of an average debt/equity ratio calculated for each industry could thus result in the firms trying to increase the effective rate of return by raising the debt/equity ratio. The extent to which individual firms would actually be able to raise their debt/equity ratio would, however, depend on several factors, the most important of which is the lending policy of the term-lending institutions (which may not permit the ratio to rise beyond a specified maximum limit in any individual case) and the taxation policy of the government (which would affect the *quantum* of reserves which could be built up). Debt/equity ratio may, in fact, fall over time in the case of units making profits, owing to the repayment of debts and the building up of reserves. To the extent, therefore, that the rate of return, on whatever base calculated, generates internal surpluses and thereby creates the capacity to repay debts and build up reserves, it tends to reduce the debt/equity ratio. Debt/equity ratio itself is thus a function of the rate of return, in whatever manner determined.

In adoption of net worth as the base for working out the rate of return has also been criticized on the following grounds:

(a) A guaranteed rate of return on net worth has encouraged over-capitalization or an excessive increase in capital intensity in the sense of substitution of capital for labour, which is not warranted by the real cost of capital *vis-à-vis* labour in the Indian economy.

(b) Net worth as a base may discourage further investment in and expansion of certain industries by causing prices to be fixed at very low levels. This may be true of industries mainly involving assembly jobs in which the capital used may be minimal. This may also be true in the case of certain service industries (e.g. transport services, particularly coastal shipping) where the depreciated value of the capital is very low because it is worked out on the basis of the historical costs of the old capital equipment.

On grounds (a) and (b), it is suggested that turnover should be adopted as the base for working out the rate of return.

Some of the points made to counter the arguments contained in (a) and (b) above, which do not seem to be valid, are as follows:

(a) There would be no tendency to over-capitalize or increase capital so long as a uniform price was fixed for each industry based on the average cost of the industry. The tendency to over-capitalize would only arise if the cost-plus formula were used for each firm separately, irrespective of the industry average.

(b) The tendency to increase capital intensity would only arise if the level of capital investment taken into account for price setting were too high. If the price-fixing bodies used capital investment norms instead of actual capital costs, there would be no such tendency.
(c) Since 'net worth' is only a fraction of the total capital employed, the adoption of net worth as a base could not result in inefficient or excessive use of capital, as net worth could be increased without increasing the total capital employed by increasing the proportion of net worth in the total capital employed. The argument would have been valid had the rate of return been worked out on capital employed rather than net worth.

Capital intensiy (in the sense of the proportion in which capital is combined with other factors, particularly labour) depends on several factors, such as the nature of the product, the technological choices available and the relative prices of different factors of production, particularly capital (interest rate) and labour (wage rate). Certain industries may by nature be more capital intensive than others. There may, however, be a limited range of choice among available technologies at the initial stage when an investment decision is taken; and the initial choice may be made keeping in view the relative prices of different factors of production, the cost of acquiring the technology or know-how, productivity, etc. Having made the initial choice, the scope for changing capital intensity subsequently without changing the technology is rather limited. In any case, no causal relationship could possibly be established between working out the rate of return on 'net worth' or capital employed and the tendency to use more capital in relation to other factors of production. The adoption of capital employed or 'net worth' as the base may, under certain conditions, encourage the use of borrowed funds relative to equity, but that need not cause greater use of fixed capital or a more capital intensive technology.

There is no reason to believe that in cases where net worth has been adopted as a base, if a uniform price were fixed for an industry, there would be no tendency to increase capital intensity, whereas this tendency would arise if separate prices were fixed for each firm separately on a cost-plus basis. A uniform price would leave larger margins of profit to those firms whose costs of production are lower than the industry's average on the basis of which the uniform price may be fixed, and relatively smaller margins of profit to other units (and possibly even losses to some units). This price should, therefore, reward efficiency and penalize inefficiency. Separate prices on a cost-plus basis for different firms would in a way guarantee a certain rate of return to each unit and thus neither provide incentive to efficient units nor discourage inefficient ones. Such a system may, therefore, tend to perpetuate inefficiencies. Fixing uniform price or different prices for different units has no relationship at all with encouraging or discouraging capital intensity in the sense of providing incentive to use more or less fixed capital relative to labour or other factors. The point mentioned at (a) above is thus not valid.

Similarly, the level of capital investment taken into account for price setting has nothing to do with encouraging or discouraging capital intensity. If a high level of capital investment is assumed for price setting, the price so fixed may be higher than it would have been had a lower level been assumed. A high price should, other things being equal, leave larger profit margins with all firms, which should encourage the growth of that industry. Such a price may, however, adversely affect consumers or users of the product of that industry, and distort the relative price structure, which may have other adverse economic effects also. A high price fixed because of an excessive capital investment assumed could not possibly have the effect of encouraging the use of more fixed capital relative to other factors of production in that industry. Of course, if there is a wasteful use of capital in any industry because of which the level of capital intensity is very high, that level could be perpetuated if the actual capital costs were taken into account in price fixation. In such cases, the adoption of a norm regarding the use of fixed capital which is lower than the actual cost of fixed capital used in certain units in the industry would result in lower price setting, and a consequent lowering of profits for the units making an excessive use of capital. Such units may, therefore, try to reduce costs so as to increase their profit margins; and the reduction in cost could be brought about in several ways, not necessarily by reducing the use of fixed capital. The point at (b) above is also, therefore, not valid.

As regards the point mentioned at (c), it may be pointed out that the terms 'net worth' and 'capital employed' are not of the same genre. Whereas 'capital employed' refers to capital assets (fixed capital plus working capital), net worth is a method of financing the creation of those assets. There is, therefore, no question of 'net worth' being a fraction of 'capital employed'. Theoretically, a situation is conceivable in which the entire capital employed is created by use of own capital or net worth only. The statement that 'net worth' could be increased without increasing the total 'capital employed' could perhaps mean that more equity capital relative to borrowed capital could be used for the creation of the same quantity of capital assets, which has nothing to do with the efficiency of capital use. The adoption of 'net worth' or 'capital employed' as a base has no relationship with encouraging or discouraging the use of fixed capital relative to other factors of production or efficiency in the use of capital, which depends on other factors. Thus the point mentioned at (c) above has also no validity.

There is no validity in the contention that net worth as a base encourages excessive use of fixed capital. As discussed above, capital intensity depends on other factors, and there is no causal relationship between working out the rate of return on net worth and increase in capital intensity. As stated earlier, there is also no guaranteed rate of return if the price is fixed on the basis of an average cost worked out for the industry based on certain assumptions regarding technology, levels of capacity utilization, scale of output, etc., as those operating at higher than the assumed levels will actually get a higher rate of return, and vice versa.

There is also no validity in the argument that net worth as the base discourages investment in the lines of production where the use of fixed capital per unit of output is very low (e.g. industries primarily involving assembly jobs), or where the depreciated value of the old capital stock is very low (e.g. coastal shipping), as the price worked out in such cases (with net worth as the base for the rate of return) is very low. The incentive to invest is primarily a function of the return per unit of capital invested; and it cannot be argued that net worth as a base would necessarily result in setting a low rate of return per unit of capital invested in industries in which fixed capital per unit of output is low or the depreciated value of the capital stock is low because it is old. Net worth in the case of such industries could yield a low rate of return per unit of capital invested if the average net worth per unit of output worked out for the entire industry for the purpose of price setting were low, because of either a very high debt/equity ratio permitted by the financial institutions owing to the highly capital intensive nature of the industry and the size of the initial investment required (e.g. the shipping industry), or generally low profitability which does not allow any sizeable build-up of reserves; or a recessionary phase through which the industry might be passing, causing considerable erosion of net worth of most of the units comprising it. In such cases, instead of the average worked out, a suitable norm of net worth needs to be evolved and adopted which could yield a reasonable rate of return per unit of capital invested to any reasonably efficient unit in the industry. Similarly, if the controlled price is likely to get unduly depressed owing to most of the units in the industry having very old capital equipment, instead of taking the depreciated value of such equipment at its original cost of acquisition (which might have been very low), its estimated current replacement cost could be considered and a suitable norm adopted to avoid any possible distortion of costs on this account. Moreover, the rate of return on net worth (or on any base for that matter) could, in the case of any particular industry with such distinctive features, always be suitably adjusted to yield an adequate rate of return on the capital invested so that further investment in that industry was not discouraged.

Thus it can be seen that neither the arguments advanced against the adoption of net worth nor those urged to counter them are valid. Further, of the two arguments put forward in favour of net worth, namely that increase in net worth is desirable and needs to be encouraged, and that net worth as a base is neutral in regard to the contribution of borrowed capital and, therefore, discourages borrowing and encourages the use of equity capital or own funds, the first one is only partly valid and the second has no validity at all. Also there is no empirical evidence either to support the contention that the proportion of net worth has in fact been rising and the debt/equity ratio falling in the price-controlled industries in India since the adoption of net worth as a base in 1975.

Growth of net worth actually reflects profitability and is a function of efficiency of production resulting in the generation of surpluses which are ploughed back into the enterprise itself. But net worth, being an accounting concept as well, could be manipulated by the accounting procedures followed which might not be uniform in all industrial units. It would also depend on the policy followed by the enterprise regarding the creation of depreciation and other reserves and payment of dividends, and the taxation policy of the government. But even if it is assumed that adoption of net worth as a base for the rate of return would encourage increasing the proportion of net worth in the total financing of the setting-up of a new unit or the running and expansion of an existing unit, the question is how could this be a feasible proposition under all market conditions. The controlled price has initially to be fixed on the basis of some kind of an average net worth or norm adopted regarding net worth per unit or output, and the entrepreneurs could get the price fixed at a higher level by increasing the average net worth per unit of output when the initial price is subsequently revised or in the subsequent rounds of price setting. In a competitive situation, no individual unit could assume that if it increases its own net worth by, say, issuing more share capital or building up more reserves by paying less dividends or in any other way, other units would do the same, thereby pushing up the industry's average. It is only in the case of a monopoly or in an oligopolistic situation where one or two producers could, by their own effort or by acting in combination with other units, increase the industry's average net worth per unit of output, that they could possibly take advantage of it in the subsequent revision of the controlled price. In such market situations, net worth as a base could indirectly encourage efficiency, as greater efficiency means lower costs per unit of output, generating larger internal surpluses at any given controlled price which could be used for building up larger reserves, thereby also increasing the net worth. However, the extent to which the internal surpluses generated would be ploughed back into the unit itself and not invested in alternative projects elsewhere in the non-price-controlled sector would also depend on the relative levels of the rates of return allowed in the case of price-controlled industry and those prevalent elsewhere. While the certainty of the rate of return in the price-controlled industry might be a factor favourable to the ploughing back of the surpluses in the unit itself, the entrepreneurs could take some degree of risk and invest the surpluses generated in units in the price-controlled sector in alternative non-price-controlled industries promising a much higher, though fluctuating and somewhat uncertain, rate of return. The conclusion seems to be that unless the rate of return in the price-controlled industry (at whatever base worked out, as it is translatable into the rate per unit of capital invested) is sufficiently high, there could conceivably be a diversion of resources internally generated away from it causing an actual decline in net worth in the units comprising it.

The point that adoption of net worth as a base might cause an increase in capital intensity has also been made in other terms. 'It has been contended that in so far as the formula has an in-built tendency to raise the net worth, it has introduced a bias in favour of capital intensive technology'.[2] This line of reasoning has several snags. Firstly, the adoption of net worth as a base has no such in-built tendency. Whether it would actually result in an increase in net worth would depend on so many factors, such as the degree of competitiveness in the industry, the depreciation and dividend policy and the accounting procedures followed by individual units, the taxation policy of the government, and above all, the relative rates of return in alternative industries where the internally generated funds could be diverted. Secondly, net worth only reflects the extent to which the capital (both fixed and working) has been financed through equity and reserves intead of borrowings, and has nothing whatsoever to do with capital intensity, which means the proportion in which fixed capital is combined with other factors, particularly labour and the fixed capital/labour ratio. As suggested earlier, the fixed capital/labour ratio would primarily depend on the technological choices actually available, the relative costs of financing the creation of fixed capital assets (the long-term interest rate) and of meeting working capital requirements (interest rate on short-term borrowings), and the prevailing money wage rate. To encourage an input mix which uses more labour and less capital so that a given amount of fixed capital generates larger employment, and greater use is made of the relatively abundant factor (labour) and use of the scarcer factor (capital) is thus economized on, an entirely different set of policies needs to be adopted. Even this policy (which could include measures such as indigenous development of capital saving and labour absorbing technology through research and development efforts, making long-term finance for financing fixed capital dearer, making fixed capital costlier, insisting that the fixed capital/labour ratio does not exceed a particular limit at the time of clearance of an industrial project for licensing and financing, etc.) might not always succeed in making entrepreneurs adopt a labour-intensive technology. The entrepreneur is interested in maximizing the productivity of the entire input mix or minimizing the total cost, and not in maximizing the productivity or minimizing the cost in terms of any single factor of production. He is not interested in either labour-intensive or capital-intensive technology as such or in technology which makes more liberal use of the abundant factor and economizes in the use of the scarce factor, but in the most cost-effective technology irrespective of the proportions in which different factors of production are combined. It is quite possible that in spite of the government's following a set of policies designed to discourage a higher fixed capital/labour ratio or encourage a lowering of this ratio, entrepreneurs will still adopt a technology which uses more fixed capital relative to labour and does not 'economize' in the use of fixed capital, because they find that a more capital-intensive technology increases the productivity of the total input mix to an extent that it more than offsets the increase in cost due to fixed capital having been made costlier by measures taken by government. In such circumstances, there could hardly be a case for labour-intensive technology on economic grounds. In any case, the base for working out the rate of return in the setting of the controlled price has nothing to do with the technology adopted which depends on several other factors, and government might not always succeed in promoting labour-intensive technologies with a view to generating greater employment for the reason indicated above.

It has been argued that the incentive to use more labour relative to fixed capital could be provided by ensuring 'that an entrepreneur is able to get a higher rate of return by lowering capital intensity'.[3] It is further argued that, in the case of total price control, 'this is possible only if the profit margin is allowed to be de-linked with capital invested. A cost plus formula, which allows a reasonable minimum rate of return on own capital invested, but is de-linked with capital invested as a base, can be expected to be more favourable to the employment objective'.[4] This reasoning has several snags also. Firstly, the base on which the rate of return is calculated has nothing to do with the type of technology used, and cannot possibly be used to encourage the lowering of capital intensity by ensuring a higher rate of return on capital invested to entrepreneurs who use more labour relative to fixed capital. The effective rate of return, which an entrepreneur will in fact earn at any controlled price fixed by the government, will depend on the degree of efficiency of production achieved by him as reflected in his average total cost. More efficient units whose average total cost is lower than the average of the industry on which the controlled price is based would earn larger profits. An entrepreneur could earn a higher effective rate by 'lowering capital intensity' if by so doing he could reduce his costs. But a less capital-intensive technology need not necessarily be more cost effective, and there might be cases where higher productivity, lower costs and higher effective rate of return went with a capital-intensive rather than labour-intensive technology. Secondly, every pricing formula for determination of the controlled price has to be a cost-plus formula, if it allows a margin of profit over and above the costs. The question is how is the plus component of the controlled price to be determined, or more precisely, on what base should it be worked out, and at what rate. A pricing formula which allows a minimum rate of return on 'own capital invested' has to choose 'own capital' or equity capital as against the borrowed capital or total capital employed as a base. Such a base cannot be de-linked with capital invested, whch obviously means the total capital invested, including both the component financed by net worth (equity capital and reserves built up out of internal surpluses) as well as that financed by borrowings; as the rate of return worked out on the base of 'own capital' would, in practice, be translated into a return on total capital invested in this sense, in which the entrepreneur is ultimately interested.

It could be argued that, for certain reasons, 'net worth' is a better base than capital employed. Notwithstanding the fact that individual units by their own action may not always succeed in raising the average net worth of the industry to take advantage of it in the successive rounds of revision of the controlled price, adoption of net worth as a base could provide an incentive for greater use of equity capital and generation and ploughing back of internal surpluses in the unit itself, thereby reducing its dependence on the banks and financial institutions for meeting its short-term and long-term financial requirements. As suggested earlier, net worth is a function of productivity or efficiency of production, and its growth reflects how efficiently an industrial unit is being run. It should, therefore, encourage the adoption of measures designed to increase productivity and reduce costs which generate larger internal surpluses and might increase the net worth of the enterprise. Capital employed, on the other hand, does not provide any incentive to reduce reliance on borrowed capital. Although capital employed also has a link with productivity in the sense that a reduction in capital employed (fixed capital plus working capital) per unit of output reflects greater productive efficiency and lower costs, yielding a larger profit at any given controlled price, the base as such does not provide any incentive for cost reduction or increasing productivity in the manner in which net worth does. One disadvantage from which net worth as a base suffers is that it may not be easily determinable in the case of multi-product firms where allocation of net worth to each unit may be difficult because of practical accounting problems. Net worth could possibly also be manipulated by accounting procedures. The fact that net worth could be considerably eroded in the case of firms incurring losses (e.g. in the case of several public sector units in India) and could even become negative, might also create practical difficulties in adopting net worth as a base.

If price control is generally resorted to in a situation of shortage or inadequacy of supply, pushing up the price of an essential commodity beyond reasonable limits, and if the ultimate objective is to remedy such a situation by creating conditions where the shortage is eliminated by both supply and demand management, designed to increase production on the one hand and restrict and regulate demand by rationing and a public distribution system on the other, a base for working out the rate of return in the determination of a controlled price which more directly encourages higher production and efficiency of production should be preferable to either capital employed or net worth. Three such alternative bases could be considered in this regard, namely turnover (value of the output sold), value of output and value added in the process of production. Both turnover and value of production would be much larger bases than value added, and the rate of return to be allowed would have to be relatively lower in case either turnover or the value of the output were adopted as a base as compared to value added to yield the same aggregate return. Turnover has certain disadvantages. Since it is the value of the output sold, it can be larger or smaller than current production, depending on whether sales have actually been equal to current physical production, or have been less, adding to the inventory of finished goods, or greater than it, reducing the inventory which might have been built up in earlier years. Moreover, since turnover is the value of output sold, it has two elements — the cost element and the tax element. The turnover (in terms of value of the output sold) of items on which the tax rate or excise duty is very high may get unduly inflated relative to other items on which the tax rate is much lower. In some cases highly capital-intensive industries with a very large capital base may not have a sizeable turnover in the initial stages of their existence, whereas some smaller units with a much smaller capital base may have a much quicker and larger turnover.

The same position might also hold good in the case of value of output and value added. Although 'value added' may also have these two elements, it may be preferable since it would be a smaller base more directly related to productivity. Moreover, if value added at the production stage is taken into consideration, the tax element can be eliminated. But whether turnover or value of output or value added is adopted as a base, it has necessarily to be related to the capital invested and the rate of return on that base determined in a manner such as to allow a certain minimum rate of return on capital invested. In any system of rational price setting, the rate of return cannot possibly be divorced from capital invested. The price-fixing body will have to work out turnover, value of output or value added per unit of capital invested (fixed capital plus working capital) and fix the rate of return on whichever of these bases is adopted in such a way as to allow a certain minimum rate of return on the capital invested. The adoption of either of these three bases would directly encourage production and promote efficiency of production, as the units which achieve a higher rate of turnover, production or value added per unit of capital invested (whether by adopting a labour-intensive or a capital-intensive technology) than the rate assumed in the price setting exercise will get a larger margin of profit. Operationally also, either of these bases would be easily ascertainable, much less susceptible to manipulation by accounting procedures, and should pose no practical problem in the case of multi-product firms or firms incurring losses.

Having determined the base, the price-fixing body has to recommend the rate of return to be allowed on that base. It has been suggested above that whatever the base chosen, the rate on it has to be worked out in order to allow a certain minimum rate of return on the entire capital invested, whether financed by own funds or borrowings. This means that the minimum rate of return on the capital invested should be determined first, and then it should be translated into a rate of return with reference to the base chosen. For instance, if turnover is adopted as the base, and it is decided to give a minimum rate of return of 10 per cent on the entire capital invested, an average capital invested turnover ratio will also have to be worked out, and the rate of return on turnover fixed in such a way that it yields a 10 per cent return on the capital invested. Instead of working out the capital invested turnover ratio on the basis of the available data, a normative ratio could also be adopted. Such a formula should encourage a lowering of the capital invested turnover ratio by using the capital more efficiently, since individual units with a capital invested turnover ratio which is lower than the average or the norm adopted in the price setting exercise would earn a higher effective rate of return.

Empirical evidence relating to India shows that of the three bases, namely capital employed, net worth and turnover, net worth is generally the smallest and turnover the largest base. Table 3 based on Reserve Bank of India data brings this out clearly. In the year 1977–78, for instance, in the case of Central Government companies, net worth (453,971) was less than half of capital employed (966,024) and turnover was even more (1,090,865). But turnover was less than the value of output (1,110,709).

The rate will have to be higher if a smaller base is chosen and vice versa. In India, where price-fixing bodies now use net worth as the base, the rate of return allowed by those bodies has varied from industry to industry. In the case of *vanaspati*, newsprint and

Table 3 *Size of alternative bases for the rate of return* (Rs in lakhs)

	Central Government companies				Private sector companies			
Year	Capital employed	Net worth	Turnover	Value of output	Capital employed	Net worth	Turnover	Value of output
1976	782,418	308,505	770,166	794,883	783,104	391,685	1,294,908	1,321,060
1977	914,278	424,911	988,448	1,000,825	820,899	408,252	1,458,111	1,460,712
1978	966,024	453,971	1,090,865	1,110,709	879,491	434,292	1,594,853	1,605,766

agricultural tractors, for instance, the rate of return on net worth allowed has been 10, 12 and 9 per cent respectively.

It can be argued that the rate of return should have a fixed component and a variable component. The fixed component should be the minimum rate of return allowed to every industry, and the variable component should depend on several factors such as priority, need for internal resource generation, prospects for growth, etc. Alternatively, the price-controlled industries could be classified into different categories on the basis of priority, stage of development, generation of internal surpluses, etc., and a different rate based on such factors fixed for each category.

There is generally a rate of profit in each industry or trade which is considered to be 'normal' for it. The concept of 'normal' profit could be traced back to Alfred Marshall, who also refers to it as 'customary or fair rate of profit on the turnover'.[5] The 'normal' rate may change with changes in factors like technology, demand conditions and 'methods of trade',[6] and may differ from industry to industry depending on factors like the size of the initial investment required, the degree of risk involved, technology, 'traditions of the trade',[7] etc. If the 'producers charge a price which gives much less than this rate of profit on the turnover, they can hardly prosper; and if they charge much more they are in danger of losing their custom, since others can afford to undersell them'.[8] It is usually the rate which is just sufficient to induce an entrepreneur to remain in an industry and not shift to alternative industries. In some cases this rate may be ascertainable with a reasonable degree of accuracy, while in others a judgement may have to be made. Wherever it can be ascertained or a fair judgement regarding it made, it should be advisable to keep the rate of return in a price-controlled industry as near it as possible. But the priority industries, or the industries which need to expand at a higher rate need to be allowed a suitably higher rate.

It is often contended that any kind of price control is inimical to industrial growth, that price-controlled industries tend to stagnate, and that their rate of growth is, in any case, much slower than the growth rate of non-price-controlled industries. Although there is perhaps no empirical evidence to support this contention, it highlights the need for closely monitoring the rate of growth of the price-controlled industries *vis-à-vis* non-price-controlled ones, to ascertain whether there is any such observed tendency and to what extent it is due to a lower rate of return allowed in such industries, with a view to suitably revising the rate of return, whenever and wherever considered necessary, to ensure the desired rate of growth.

Notes

1. Westphal, op. cit.
2. 'Some Issues in Pricing Policy', paper presented by Dr C.H. Hanumantha Rao, Member, Economic Administration Reforms Commission (now Member, Planning Commission) at the symposium 'Price and Distribution Controls in the Indian Economy', 22–24 February 1982, at the Indian Statistical Institute, New Delhi, p. 8.
3. Ibid., p. 11.
4. Ibid.
5. Alfred Marshall, *Principles of Economics*, 9th (Variorum) ed, **I**, London, Macmillan, 1961, p. 617.
6. Ibid.
7. Ibid.
8. Ibid.

8 Dual pricing

Price control can be total or partial. Total price control implies direct fixation of the price of the entire quantity of a commodity, accompanied by the necessary regulation of production and distribution arrangements. Where the government only fixes a maximum or a minimum price, or a 'price bracket', issues some guidelines, prescribes rules for costing or price fixation, or resorts to any other regulatory system not involving total supersession of the market mechanism in determining the market price, the control cannot be said to be total. Any system of control which leaves some scope for the free play of market forces, or some freedom of action to the individual enterprises regarding determination of prices of their products within the framework of government regulation, could be called partial control. 'Dual pricing' is a kind of partial control where the government directly fixes the price of part of the production of a commodity and arranges its distribution. Such price control is partial, because although it may affect the entire quantity of the controlled commodity, direct interference in the market mechanism is not complete since it is only restricted to the quantity whose price is fixed and whose distribution is directly regulated by the government, allowing freedom of action to the market forces in regard to the remaining quantity. The essence of dual pricing in this sense is the existence of two prices — not two market prices, but one controlled price or set of prices relating to the portion of the total output whose price is fixed by the government, and a free market price or a set of market prices for the remaining quantity. The salient features of this system of dual pricing are:

(a) the determination of a certain proportion of the output of a commodity to be procured by the government, or the 'levy rate';
(b) the setting of the price at which the procurement is to be made, or the 'procurement' or levy price';

(c) arranging distribution of the quantity procured to specified categories of consumers or users, or for specified purposes, at a price often referred to as the 'issue price', which may cover the costs of procurement, transport, storage, distribution, etc.; and
(d) leaving the remaining quantity to be sold in the open market at the market price determined by the free play of market forces.

The government may not in all cases actually procure any quantity, but simply require the enterprises concerned to produce and also arrange to sell a certain proportion of the total production of a commodity to specified categories of consumers or users, or for specified purposes, at the price fixed by the government, in specified or rationed quantities. Thus, there need not be actual procurement and distribution by the government in all cases of dual pricing. Moreover, while in the case of more or less homogeneous commodities like sugar or cement, dual pricing may relate to the product itself, in the case of variegated commodities which have a range of products (e.g. paper, steel or cloth), dual pricing may take the form of regulating the price and distribution of one of the products in the range, leaving the other products free. In India, for instance, whereas both sugar and cement have been under dual pricing, only certain varieties of cloth and paper have been under this system of pricing.

Dual pricing in the sense indicated above raises a number of theoretical and practical issues, such as the following:

(a) Under what conditions does total price control need to be resorted to and when would dual pricing serve the purpose, and, therefore, appear to be a better alternative?
(b) What are the snags or difficulties involved in a system of total price control, and how and to what extent does dual pricing remove them or when is it free from them?
(c) What are the main issues in formulating and implementing a system of dual pricing and how are they to be resolved?
(d) What practical measures need to be taken to ensure the successful implementation of dual pricing?

Whether price control has to be total or partial would depend essentially on whether, under any given conditions, the desired objectives cannot be achieved unless the price of the entire quantity produced or available is fixed by the government, and administered and enforced by a public distribution system run by the government, and other regulatory measures taken by it; or they could be achieved by restricting government action to only a proportion of the total output and allowing the free play of market forces in regard to the remainder. There may be situations characterized by acute scarcity of a commodity caused by limited availability and highly inelastic supply in the short run, coupled with a similar demand owing to its being an essential item of mass consumption, or an essential industrial input, and there being no substitutes available at affordable or reasonable prices. In an underdeveloped country like India, where agriculture is mostly rain-fed, failure of the monsoon can create widespread drought conditions; and sometimes uneven distribution of rain or insect infestation creates similar conditions in large parts of the country, causing shortage of food grains. Similarly, in times of war, the entire production and productive capacities of the country may have to be geared to sustain the war effort, involving the large-scale mobilization of resources, and scarcities of essential commodities for civilian use. Such situations could conceivably leave no alternative to total price control, involving control of production and distribution as well. It could, however, be argued that in a situation where

(a) there is an article of mass consumption or a widely-used industrial input in short supply, which is consumed or used by a sizeable proportion of consumers or users, who could afford to pay a higher price without any serious detriment to them or to the economy;
(b) there are identifiable groups of consumers and users who need protection against rising prices and the quantity needed to meet their requirements is ascertainable with a fair degree of accuracy; and
(c) the market forces could reasonably be expected to expand production and remove the shortages, provided they are allowed sufficient scope for free play, and adequate incentives are provided or avoidable disincentives are removed; and
(d) there is no extreme situation or crisis calling for drastic and desperate measures;

dual pricing would be a better alternative, both theoretically as well as from a practical viewpoint. But whether any actual situation calls for total or partial control is essentially a matter of judgement on the part of policy-makers, which has to be based on both economic and non-economic considerations; and there could possibly be no hard and fast rule or any rigid guidelines or prescription to be followed. While essential consumer goods, which are articles of mass consumption and generally enter the consumer price index, strategic industrial inputs, essential life-saving drugs, or articles being produced under monopolistic or oligopolistic conditions causing unwarranted restriction of output to keep their prices at an unduly high level (and the resulting idle capacity), or deterioration in the quality of the product, may need to be brought under some kind of price discipline, there could perhaps be no clear, categorical and unique answer to the question as to whether the control should be total or partial in any particular situation.

There may be several snags or difficulties in a system of total price control. Firstly, administratively, it may be an expensive and difficult proposition, as its enforcement generally necessitates extensive distribution arrangements and other regulatory measures. Almost the entire government machinery has sometimes to be geared up to implement the scheme, involving great government expense. Secondly, since the controlled price has to be less than the equilibrium or market-clearing price, the resultant excess demand gives rise to a black market on the one hand and hoarding and stocks going underground on the other, thereby artificially accentuating the scarcity, helping unscrupulous traders to sustain a black market and keeping exorbitantly high prices there, swelling their profits without the corresponding legitimate increase in tax revenue for the government. Thirdly, the system may result in the appropriation of economic surpluses (in the form of black market profits) by the relatively unproductive classes of traders and middlemen, instead of their accruing to the industry, thereby swelling the parallel economy of black money at the cost of the industry. The black money generated generally flows into inessential or low priority enterprises like real estate, luxury hotels, etc., rather than augmenting the resources available for the growth of the industries producing essential consumer goods or industrial inputs, pushing up their prices and accelerating the inflationary rise in the general price level. Fourthly, total price control implemented through a public distribution system, which makes the price controlled commodity available at a uniform price to all sections of consumers or users, also gives the benefit of the low price to the richer sections of the community, who could afford to pay a higher price, and thus militates against the concept of equity. Fifthly, since the controlled price has to be kept at a level where it is within the means of the bulk of consumers (for the protection of whose real incomes the price is controlled), without in the process making it unremunerative to the producers and impairing their incentive for greater production, it may have to be heavily subsidized. The burden of this subsidy falls on the public exchequer and ultimately on the taxpayer. A regime of total controls might, therefore, also be one of high taxation and could give rise to a vicious circle, where taxes have to be increased to sustain a system of subsidized prices, which increase the prices of the commodities subjected to higher rates of taxation or newly brought under the tax net, necessitating further controls and the extension of the area of price control, which in turn might make still more taxation necessary.

Dual pricing may have fewer of the drawbacks of total price control. It could be easier and less expensive to administer. Since a part of the output is allowed to be sold in the open market, the pressure on the distribution system is reduced. Total price control almost invariably degenerates into a vicious kind of dual pricing, owing to the inevitable emergence of a black market: two prices prevail — one controlled and the other in the black market, and the quantity intended for sale at the controlled price tends to surreptitiously flow into the black market, defeating the purpose of the control itself. Dual price, in effect, amounts to some sort of legitimization of the existence of two prices, or making *de facto* dual pricing *de jure* by recognizing a reality and making the best possible use of it. Allowing a certain portion of output to be sold in the open market at whatever price it can command eliminates to a certain extent the cause of the emergence of the black market, namely excess demand not being allowed to exert an upward pressure on price. The excess demand at the controlled price, at which the part of the output is sold under the system of dual pricing, finds an outlet in the open market where the proportion of the output not procured or meant for sale at the controlled price is available. The industry could get a much higher price for the proportion of output left with it for sale in the open market, and could, partly or wholly, make good the loss, if any, sustained by being obliged to part with a portion of the production at the price fixed by the government. The surpluses or resources so generated internally may remain with the industry to be ploughed back into the industry itself for expansion and modernization rather than being appropriated by traders and middlemen who thrive in the black market. If the internal resources position of the industrial units improves in such a situation, their reliance on public borrowings should get correspondingly reduced, and their reserves built up, lowering their debt/equity ratio and leaving greater resources with the public financial institutions to finance new projects in the priority sectors. Under dual pricing, the benefit of price control can be restricted to the 'deserving' sections of the community in need of protection against high prices; and as the requirements of the vital public sector units or of priority sectors could also be met out of the portion of the output sold at the controlled price, costs and prices in these sectors could be kept under check and prevented from exerting an upward pressure on the general level of prices. The system could, in a way, achieve a balance between demand and supply, and the excess demand at the controlled price would find an outlet in the open market where the free market price should be the market-clearing price; and it could be a better balance than the tenuous balance brought about by the illegal, surreptitious and antisocial activities and distortions caused by the black market under a system of total price control. Moreover, dual pricing may cause comparatively much less of a drain on the limited budgetary resources of the government by way of subsidies than total price control, and to a large extent obviate the need for high taxation, and leave larger financial resources with the government for developmental expenditure. The financial burden of subsidies could, in fact, be substantially passed on to the industry itself by a suitable adjustment of the procurement price and procurement rate, so that the industry is largely able to make up the loss on the controlled quantity (which it is obliged to sell at a lower price) by the profits earned on the free sale quantity. Since the industry can only make up the loss by sale at higher prices in the open market (where the excess demand at the controlled price would spill over, and the demand of those not covered by the sale at controlled price would find an outlet), the burden would ultimately be shifted to those buying in the open market at higher prices, who would mostly be the more affluent. The controlled price may thus be largely subsidized by the richer sections of the community, who could afford to do so, and would, to that extent, be an instrument of social justice or redistribution of income as well.

The main issues relating to the formulation and implementation of any policy of dual pricing are as follows:

1. Identification of the commodities to be brought under a system of dual pricing

Practically speaking, any article of mass consumption or essential input in scarce supply whose price needs to be controlled to protect the interests of certain classes of consumers, to avoid undue cost escalation or fall in production in certain vital industries, as the case may be, can be brought under dual pricing. If the commodity has already been brought under total price control, the growth of the industry during the period of total control needs to be analysed with a view to deciding whether there is a case for partial decontrol and introduction of a system of dual pricing which might be more conducive to the growth of the industry. This has, in fact, been done in India in the case of three vital commodities, namely steel, sugar and cement.

Steel, which had been under total statutory price control in India for a long time, was brought under a system of dual pricing in the light of the recommendations of a committee set up by the government of India under the chairmanship of Dr K.M. Raj. The committee gave its report in October 1963. In March 1964, all categories of iron and steel other than pig iron, billets and flat products were decontrolled; and in 1973 a system of dual pricing was introduced under which only the supply of certain categories of steel required mostly by the government departments and public sector enterprises was to be made at controlled prices, allowing freedom of pricing in respect of the remaining non-priority categories of steel. There has been no control over the price or the distribution of steel produced by the mini-steel plants, price regulation being confined to the steel produced by the 'integrated steel plants' only. However, even in the case of non-priority categories of steel produced by the integrated steel plants, government has been exercising some control as the Joint Plant Committee (JPC) and Steel Authority of India Limited (SAIL) were required to fix the prices of non-controlled items, mostly with prior government approval, or after informal consultation with the principal user ministries. This informal government control has also been abolished and price control completely withdrawn with effect from 1 March 1981, and prices are now fixed without obtaining government approval.

Sugar had been under various forms and varying degrees of control in India since long before 1947 (when the country achieved independence). In August 1967 partial decontrol was announced, and in the 1967–68 sugar season, sugar factories were required to supply 60 per cent of their output to the government at the 'levy' price, the balance being allowed to be sold in the free market. The main objectives of this system were to provide an incentive to the sugar industry to maximize sugar production, and to meet the requirements of consumers at a reasonable price.[1] In August 1978 there was complete decontrol, followed by the reintroduction of dual pricing in December 1979. The levy ratio has, however, been varying, and was 65 per cent for the year 1981–82.

Cement has been under total price control for a long time in India. Based on the recommendations of the Report of the Committee on the Development of the Cement Industry, the Government of India announced a policy of partial decontrol or dual pricing on 27 February 1982 under which the existing cement units are required to give 66.6 per cent of their production as levy at the controlled price, units which started production after 1 January 1982 being required to pay only 50 per cent as levy. Food grains, cotton textiles, aluminium and paper are also under some kind of dual pricing in India.

2. Determination of the procurement or the levy rate

In order to determine the procurement, the levy rate or the proportion of the output to be procured or required to be sold at the controlled price, it is necessary to:

(a) identify the categories of consumers or users and also the priority sectors or public sector units needing protection, and work out their existing minimum requirement and the likely growth in it over the next few years; and
(b) ascertain the existing total production and make projections for the next few years to work out the rate at which the procurement needs to be made to meet the minimum requirement.

The procurement or the levy rate may have to be revised and re-fixed, based on a fresh assessment made at suitable intervals, and it has to be kept at the minimum necessary to meet minimum requirements. With the growth in production, the levy rate could gradually and progressively be brought down, enlarging the area of price determination by the free play of market forces. The levy rate should vary inversely with estimated production and directly with estimated minimum requirements of the categories of consumers or users identified for supply at the controlled price.

At the open market price for the free sale quantity would normally be higher than the procurement or the levy price, a lower levy rate would yield larger surpluses or profits. The levy rate, therefore, need not be uniform, and varying rates could be fixed for different regions, or for the new units set up after a specified date, or for old units whose costs of production are significantly lower owing to their old, low-cost capital equipment. A lower levy rate for the regions where the growth of the price-controlled industry has been sluggish, creating regional imbalance, could increase its relative profitability in those regions attracting larger investments, accelerating its growth there, and thereby reducing regional disparity. A lower levy rate for the new units, or for increases in production achieved by substantial expansion of capacities after a specified date, should encourage the growth of the industry by maintaining the level of profitability of such new units, or of the existing units which expand substantially, in spite of cost increases which may have taken place in the meantime, in setting up new units or expanding existing ones. (That is why, in India, in the case of cement, units which started production after 1 January 1982 are required to pay a lower rate of levy.) Similarly, if some larger units could be identified whose capital costs were much lower than the industry's average because of their old, low-cost capital equipment (even after making adequate allowance for its replacement), a part of their excess profits arising from this situation could be mopped up by fixing a higher rate of levy for them.

An example of how the levy rate could be varied to encourage the setting-up of new units is provided by the scheme of incentives approved by the Government of India in October 1980 for the sugar industry, under which the new sugar units in the low recovery areas (where the average sugar recovery is less than 9 per cent) were allowed to sell their entire production in free sale for the first seven years, and the percentage was to be reduced to 75 in the eighth year. For the medium recovery areas (where recovery is between 9 and 10 per cent) also, entire production in the first four years was allowed to be sold in free sale, the percentages being reduced to 65 in the fifth year and 35 thereafter. In the high recovery areas (where recovery was more than 10 per cent), the free sale quota was 90 per cent in the first, 80 per cent in the second, 70 per cent in the third, 60 per cent in the fourth and 55 per cent in the fifth year, and 35 per cent thereafter. The scheme envisaged higher free sale quotas for expansion of the existing capacities on the same lines in the low, medium and high recovery areas.[2]

In India, a case could perhaps be made out for differential levy rates for different regions in the case of cement, on the basis of regional disparities in the demand and production of cement. The Southern and Western Zones have been surplus zones while there have been deficits in the Northern and Eastern Zones. The position in 1977 was found to be as shown in Table 4. The figures suggest that the levy rate could be lower for the Northern and Eastern Zones to promote greater growth of the industry in those regions, so that they also become more or less self-sufficient in course of time and a better regional balance can emerge.

Table 4 *Capacity utilization and demand for cement in different zones in India*

	Capacity ('000 tonnes)	Capacity utilization (%)	Production as % of demand
Northern Zone	3,818	82	47.61
Eastern Zone	3,889	80	74.85
Western Zone	6,150	98	105.78
Southern Zone	7,682	90	116.99

3. Determination of the procurement or 'levy price'

Dual pricing seeks to achieve the twin objectives of growth and equity by allowing the market mechanism as far as possible to function freely and generate incentives for growth, and at the same time to meet both the minimum requirements of essential consumer goods for the vulnerable sections of the community at a price which they can afford, and also essential industrial inputs of priority sectors of the economy at a price which does not unduly distort their cost structures. An integrated view, therefore, needs to be taken of the entire scheme, including the levy rate and the final price at which the controlled commodity is to be made available to those for whose protection it is implemented. While, as a general rule, any price (levy price being no exception) has to cover the cost fully and also allow a reasonable margin of profit, the levy price under the dual pricing scheme need not in all cases be a remunerative price in this sense. The normal expectation under dual pricing is that where the levy price does not entirely cover costs, the loss incurred owing to the obligation to sell a certain proportion of the output at that price would be more or less made up by the profits made on the sale of the free sale quantity. In other words, the average price for the entire quantity of output (taking into account both the levy price and the open market price), would not be less than what the market price would have been had there been no price control. Although it may not be possible to verify whether this actually happens in practice, the broad conclusion is that the controlled price under dual pricing could be lower than it would be under total price control, since the producers could be given a lower price for the levy quantity so long as the free sale quantity was large enough to permit them to sell it at a higher price in the open market and make good the loss. It follows that, other things being equal, the lower the levy rate, the lower the levy price could be, and vice versa. As indicated earlier, by suitably adjusting the levy rate and the levy price, the need to subsidize the final price or the 'issue price' at which the levy quantity is sold could be largely eliminated. The 'levy price' could be fixed in such a way that levy quantity could be made available to the vulnerable sections of the community or the priority sectors at a price arrived at by adding the costs of procurement, transport, storage, handling, distribution, etc. to it without adding any element of government subsidy. In practice, it may not be possible to do this with any great degree of precision, and the estimates, which have essentially to be based largely on judgement, could go wrong; but conceptually, there could be a combination of 'levy rate' and 'levy price' which could avoid subsidization of the final issue price by the government, and a fair approximation to it could perhaps be made in any real-life situation.

The practical problems arising in the process of implementation of any scheme of dual pricing could be those relating to the collection of the levy, the building up of buffer stocks, ensuring timely releases from it, preventing leakages and monitoring the effects of the system on the economy, particularly on the growth of the industry.

In the case of industrial products like steel, sugar, cement, paper and cloth, collection of levy or procurement need not take the form of physically taking possession of the levy quantities and arranging their transport or storage at another place. The entire quantity of output generally remains with the production units, and is released by them for free sale, or sale at the controlled price, according to the instructions of the government. In the case of primary produce like food grains, dual pricing may take the form of procurement of a certain quantity and arranging its sale through fair price shops in the urban areas (and sometimes also in rural areas where scarcities may have been created by crop failure due to drought, insect infestation, or any other reason, in a developing country like India). The levy is generally imposed on traders (who may also be engaged in processing, as in the case of rice mills) and collected from them through a government agency, involving transportation and storage. The food grains collected in this way form a 'buffer stock' from which releases are made from time to time to run the public distribution system. The purchases made by government at the minimum agricultural prices announced by it (under 'support price operations'), as well as imports of food grains, are also used to build up this 'buffer stock'. Subsidies may sometimes become inevitable in the case of food grains since only part of the procurement may be made at minimum support prices, and because of the high cost of imported food grains and the various costs involved in the creation and operation of 'buffer stock'.

Table 5 gives an idea of the growth of procurement and public distribution of food grains in India over the period 1956 to 1983.

Table 5 *Production, availability, procurement and public distribution of food grains in India, 1956–1983 (quantities in million tonnes)*

Averages for 3 years ending	Net production	Net availability (including imports)	Procurement	Public distribution	Procurement as % of net production	Public distribution as % of net availability
1956	61.97	63.29	0.53	1.96	0.9	3.1
1961	69.44	73.02	1.21	4.69	1.7	6.4
1966	70.70	78.72	3.16	10.95	4.5	13.9
1969	76.79	82.10	5.88	10.93	7.7	13.3
1974	89.50	94.05	7.25	10.90	8.1	11.6
1979	107.76	107.94	11.62	11.19	10.8	10.4
1983	114.11	114.87	14.64	14.67	12.8	12.8

Source: Economic Surveys of the relevant years published by the Ministry of Finance, Government of India

From a little more than half a million tonnes in 1956, the procurement increased to more than fourteen-and-a-half million tonnes in 1983, the quantities distributed through the public distribution system increasing more or less in line with increases in procurement, both reaching almost the same level in 1983. Procurement rose from less than one per cent of net production to about 13 per cent, and public distribution from a little over 3 per cent of the total available to the same level (i.e. 13 per cent) over this period. In 1982–83, the amount spent by the government on food subsidies accounted for nearly one-third of the total amount spent on subsidies.

Besides running the public distribution system, buffer stocks can also be used to keep open market prices in check by timely releases. Even where separate buffer stocks have not been physically built up, timely releases are necessary for the success of dual pricing — both for the proper running of the public distribution system as well as for the exercising of a salutary effect on the open market price of the controlled commodity.

Another problem in administering a system of dual pricing is that of leakages. In the case of a competitive industry, the demand for whose product is fairly elastic, the open market price may not be very high (since, given the free sale quantity, the open market price under dual pricing is largely a function of the competitiveness of the industry and the elasticity of demand); but under monopolistic or oligopolistic conditions, the open market price may tend to be very high, particularly in the case of products whose demand is relatively inelastic because they are essential items, and acceptable substitutes are not available. Under these conditions, if the difference between the 'issue price' fixed by the government for the sale of the levy quantity and the open market price becomes too great, it may cause large-scale leakages, defeating the purpose of dual pricing itself. Those purchasing at the controlled price may themselves sell their ration to others at a much higher price (though lower than the open market price). This tendency, although undesirable, could still serve the purpose of increasing the relative income of the poor. What is more undesirable, however, is the tendency on the part of dealers to divert sizeable quantities intended for public distribution for sale at much higher open market prices. The risk of such a leakage could be very high in the case of dual pricing, as the same commodity could legally be sold at a higher price in the open market, and the stocks meant for sale at the controlled price may not be distinguishable from the free sale stocks in many cases. This tendency could be checked by strict enforcement and efficient distribution arrangements, and by ensuring that the same dealers are not allowed to sell the controlled commodity, both at the controlled price and on the open market. Leakages could perhaps be minimized if the controlled commodities were sold by government-run shops exclusively selling the controlled commodities. But this might, in practice, be a difficult and expensive proposition (necessitating raising the controlled price itself or increasing the government subsidy). Moreover, the level of bureaucratic efficiency and integrity at lower levels being what it is, there could possibly be considerable leakages in this arrangement also. Part of the excess profits being earned owing to the open market price being very high could be mopped up by levy on or increase in the rate of excise duty, as the case may be (particularly if the controlled commodity has a relatively elastic demand so that the incidence of excise duty cannot be entirely shifted by further raising the price).

In India, in the case of sugar, which has been under dual pricing, the available empirical evidence indicates that there has generally been a wide gap between the price of free sale sugar in the open market and the controlled price. The figures in Table 6 bring out this position clearly. The price of free sugar has generally been more than double that of levy sugar, which might have caused considerable leakages. However, empirical evidence of such leakages may not be available.

Table 6 *Variations in the wholesale price of levy sugar (all-India average) and free sugar (Muzaffarnager B-30), 1974–1981 (Rs per quintal)*

Last week of March	Levy sugar	Free sale sugar	Percentage difference
1974	199.57	421.00	+111.0
1975	199.57	455.00	+128.0
1976	192.72	453.00	+135.1
1977	193.32	428.00	+121.4
1978	208.69	380.00	+82.1
1979*	—	275.00	—
1980	258.04	555.00	+115.1
1981	321.40	752.00	+134.0

* Decontrolled in August 1978; control reimposed in December 1979.
Source: Office of the Economic Adviser to the Government of India, Ministry of Industry.

The need for timely releases, and for keeping a watch on open market prices, for taking timely remedial measures to check the leakages as well as the need for monitoring the effects of control on the growth of the controlled and other related industries, highlight the importance of an efficient monitoring system for the effective implementations of dual pricing. Collection and analysis of market intelligence and data regarding the behaviour of prices, costs, output and investment, with a view to giving timely signals for remedial action, are essential for the efficient administration of any scheme of dual pricing.

There seems to be some empirical evidence to support the view that dual pricing has been somewhat successful in achieving its basic objectives of equity and growth in the case of commodities where it could be combined with support price operations for primary producers or those providing the raw material or input. In India, sugar and food grains are just such commodities, both of which have been under some kind of dual pricing, and there have been support price operations in the case of both sugar-cane and food grains.

The Report of the Committee on Controls and Subsidies submitted to the Government of India in May 1979 has given the following factual findings regarding sugar on the basis of an analysis of the empirical evidence available:

(a) The policy of decontrolling sugar has been adopted in the past during three different periods, namely 1952–53 to 1957–58, 1961–62 and 1962–63 (up to mid-April 1963), and 1970–71 and 1971–72 (25 May 1971 to 21 December 1971). The decontrol on these three occasions was, however, partial since '(a) the price of cane had not been decontrolled, and (b) control over monthly releases of sugar had not been given up'.[3] 'After every period of decontrol there has been a decline in the area under sugar-cane, and a much steeper decline in the production of sugar.'[4]

(b) Another significant finding of this committee is that under [the] partial control system adopted since August 1967, sugar production had increased from 22.48 lakh tonnes in 1967–68 to 46.62 lakh tonnes in 1969–70. The partial decontrol was announced too late to affect the area under cane in 1967–68. But the policy made it possible for the factories to pay higher prices for cane during the 1967–68 season.[5]

The committee has explained the nexus between control over sugar prices and the growth of cane output, as well as sugar production, as follows:

> In the past, decontrol of [the] price of sugar has been accompanied by a fall in the price of sugar, and with a fall in the price of sugar there has also occurred a fall in the price of gur, which in any case consumes the bulk of sugar cane output. With a lower realization in the price of cane, there was a decline in the area (and output) of cane, and there has been, historically, a more than proportionate decline in sugar output, causing a pressure on sugar prices, which has brought back the control on the price (and distribution) of sugar. While, therefore, the minimum price of cane has given an incentive to the growing of more cane, as long as control has lasted, this has induced greater sugar production. However, this has also, periodically, led to over-production of sugar in relation to off-take, and a build-up of sugar stocks. With [a] comfortable stock position there has been a clamour for decontrol.[6]

In India, control of food grain prices and their public distribution, introduced during World War II, has continued since then in some form or other. The control of food grain prices has been accompanied by a compulsory procurement/levy of various types on the one hand, and other control measures such as movement control ('to cordon off surplus and heavily deficit areas, the former in order to help procurement and the latter in order to enforce regulated distribution and to avoid the large purchasing power in these areas sucking in a disproportionate quantity of food supply'),[7] the licensing of food grain dealers, and separate controls on 'flour milling and rice hulling',[8] on the other hand. Several measures designed to increase agricultural yields have been taken simultaneously, coupled with support price operations to prevent agricultural prices from falling to unremunerative levels and provide incentive for greater agricultural production. The Government of India set up an Agricultural Prices Commission in 1965 as an expert body to evolve a balanced and integrated agricultural price policy which would be fair to both producers and consumers, and would achieve an optimum land use and production pattern. It is precisely because the pricing policy in respect of food grains has been pursued

Table 7 *Total production, total cropped area and average annual yield of cereals in India, 1955–56 to 1982–83*

Year average ending	Total production of cereals (million tonnes)	Total area under cereals (million hectares)	Average annual yield of cereals (kgs. per hectare)
1955–56	57.35	86.88	660
1960–61	66.06	91.16	724
1965–66	69.97	93.29	749
1968–69	77.48	97.04	797
1973–74	91.95	100.64	913
1978–79	111.32	103.58	1,074
1979–80	111.76	104.11	1,073
1982–83	119.18	103.48	1,152

Source: (1) Directorate of Economics and Statistics, Government of India, 'Area and Production of Principal Crops in India, 1980–81'; (2) Ministry of Finance, Government of India, 'Economic Survey' of relevant years.

as part of an integrated economic policy in regard to agriculture; and a package consisting of measures which support and reinforce each other, and are designed to remove the basic cause of control, i.e., scarcity of food grains owing to low agricultural production, that price control in this sector has, in fact, resulted in a sustained growth in agricultural production and area under cultivation, and higher agricultural yields. The figures in Table 7 clearly bring out this position. Total production of cereals, total cropped area under cereals and their annual yield per hectare have been consistently rising (except a very small decline in the area under cereals in 1982–83) over the last thirty years (1955–56 to 1982–83). Total production more than doubled and productivity also nearly doubled over this period. As brought out earlier in Table 5 above, the quantity of food grains procured and distributed through the public distribution system also increased several times over this period.

Notes

1. See Report of the Committee on Controls and Subsidies published by the Ministry of Finance, Government of India, New Delhi, May 1979, pp. 158–61.

2. See 'Government Creates Sugar Scarcity Again', *Commerce*, 9 January 1982, Bombay, pp.55–7.
3. Report of the Committee on Controls and Subsidies, Ministry of Finance, Government of India, May 1979, p.160.
4. Ibid.
5. Ibid.
6. Ibid.
7. Ibid.
8. Ibid.

9 Some aspects of price controls and pricing policy in India

Price controls in India, many of which originated during World War II, have been existence for a long time, their nature, content, coverage and manner of enforcement and implementation changing significantly in the post-independence era, particularly since the inception of planning in 1951. Some broad features which have emerged, the shortcomings and weaknesses of the system which they reveal, and their policy implications, are briefly indicated in this chapter. An attempt has also been made to present a comparative picture of the growth of some selected controlled and non-controlled industries in terms of production, capacity creation, capacity utilization, profitability, etc., on the basis of whatever scanty empirical data could be obtained from various sources.

Price control in India, in the sense of the items covered, is quite comprehensive. It covers a wide range of essential commodities such as food grains, edible oils and *vanaspati*, sugar, textiles, drugs, etc., which are items of mass consumption, as well as essential industrial inputs and intermediate products like fertilizers, pesticides, steel, cement, paper, newsprint, aluminium and jute. The coverage, though fairly wide, is not wider than that we find in the EEC countries such as the Federal Republic of Germany, France, Italy, Luxemburg and the Netherlands, particularly in the FRG and France. Lists of items under various forms of controls in these EEC countries in a recent 'Research Report'[1] show that price controls extend to a very large number of items in these countries. Although no such exhaustive list is available regarding the coverage of price controls in India, it could safely be stated that price controls in India are not wider in coverage than in most of the EEC countries.

Price controls in India have generally emanated from some enactment, the provisions of which are legally enforceable through courts of law. Price controls on items like food grains, sugar, cotton, textiles, vegetable oil products, drugs, paper and newsprint have been statutory. Some of these controls were initially imposed by orders issued under the Defence of India Rules (DIR), but they are now enforced under various control orders or notifications issued under the Essential Commodities Act, 1955. Most of these control orders are issued by the Central Government, but some (e.g. in the case of food grains) are also issued by state governments; and their enforcement is overseen by the ministries/departments of the Central or state government concerned. There are innumerable notifications containing these orders and subsequent amendments thereto, which in some cases have rendered the controls too complex and difficult to administer effectively. A committee appointed by the government in February 1978 to evaluate and review, *inter alia*, the system of controls on prices, production and distribution in India has, in its Report submitted in May 1979, compiled a long ministry/department 'List of Commodities/Services under Statutory Control as on 31-3-1979', and also of control orders issued by various state governments under the Essential Commodities Act 1955, which runs into several papers.[2] The committee has found that 'a plethora of control orders, notifications and amendments thereto'[3] and 'the absence of any comprehensive up-dated version of the control system . . .'[4] has, on the one hand, made the existing control system 'so complex that even the executive authorities responsible for implementing the controls are unaware at senior levels of the exact control system which they have to implement',[5] and, on the other hand, given 'occasion for harrassment and graft'.[6] The committee has mentioned textiles as a typical example of the complexity of the control law. There are

> nine Control Orders — all issued or validated under the Essential Commodities Act of 1955 — on various aspects of the textile industry . . . there have been more than a hundred notifications issued . . . and it becomes necessary, for anybody who wants to know the full control law, to go back chronologically, and wade through diverse notifications issued from time to time, to fathom the control system.[7]

The committee has, therefore suggested a comprehensive review of all extant economic legislation by the ministries concerned, with a view to removing all redundant enactments or orders from the statute book, simplifying all extant control orders, abolishing the multiplicity of control orders on the same items by consolidating them into one comprehensive control order, and introducing a system of annual updating of all such orders and placing them before Parliament for its information.

In most cases, statutory controls in India are not confined to prices alone, but extend to the control of movement, production and distribution as well, in order to achieve their objectives properly and fully. Controls on food grains and textiles illustrate the manner in which controls have covered these aspects in India.

In the case of food grains there are price controls since the government has been fixing the support/procurement prices of food grains and also the retail prices at which they are sold through the fair price shops. There has also been statutory rationing in certain areas, thus controlling both the price and the distribution of food grains. State governments have also been imposing restrictions on the inter-state and sometimes the inter-district movement of wheat, rice, maize and other food grains, to prevent their movement from surplus areas to deficit areas in an unregulated manner, with a view to securing a more equitable regional distribution and preventing traders and middlemen from profiteering at the cost of the consumers. There is a system of licensing food grain dealers enforced by state governments, requiring them to maintain certain registers showing the position of their purchases, sales, stocks, etc., to prevent hoarding and black marketeering. State governments have also been controlling flour milling and rice hulling. Since buffer stocks of wheat and other food grains have to be maintained by the Food Corporation of India (FCI) (which is the government agency for procurement, buffer stocking and release of food grains for the public distribution system), the supply of wheat to the flour mills is regulated, and there is a system which allots wheat to the flour mills from the FCI stocks. Rice hulling is similarly regulated, to achieve various objectives, such as 'to check the proliferation of rice mills in order to develop the hand pounding industry',[8] and to modernize existing rice mills, to reduce breakage of rice and to increase the output of rice from paddy'.[9]

As regards cotton textiles, the area of control is broadly indicated by the names of various Control Orders issued since 1948. The committee referred to above has listed the following nine orders in its report:

1. Cotton Textiles (Control) Order, 1948.
2. Cotton Textiles (Control of Movement) Order, 1948.
3. Cotton Control Order, 1955.
4. Cotton Textiles (Production by Handloom) Control Order, 1956.
5. Textiles (Production by Powerlooms) Control Order, 1956.
6. Art Silk Textiles (Production and Distribution) Control Order, 1962.
7. Textile Machinery (Production and Distribution) Control Order, 1962.
8. Woollen Textiles (Production and Distribution) Control Order, 1962.
9. Textiles (Production by Knitting, Embroidery, Lace Making and Printing Machines) Control Order, 1963.[10]

The basic objective of pricing policy in regard to the cotton textile industry has been

> to regulate [the] weaving capacity of the mill sector with a view to encouraging the growth of production in the decentralized sector. Apart from this physical control on the number of looms, the same objective is also sought to be achieved through regulating the modernization of equipment and technological improvements in the industry. Purchase/sale/installation and dispersal of plant and machinery by the mills are also regulated to ensure that the mill capacity is controlled and does not expand at the cost of the decentralized sector.[11]

In fact, price control as such is only restricted to a section of mill output, namely the 'varieties defined as controlled cloth required for mass consumption'.[12] There has been a scheme for controlled cloth production in operation under which the mills are required to produce certain minimum quantities of the controlled varieties of cloth and to sell them at the controlled price. Most of the regulations, however, to which the industry has been subjected are designed to regulate the growth of the industry to achieve the broad objective stated above. Besides these regulations, the government has also been helping the industry to grow and develop in various ways, such as providing soft loans for modernization and rehabilitation, arranging increased supply of cotton yarn to the decentralized sector, fiscal concessions, etc.

The instances of price control given above are also broadly suggestive of the following characteristics of the various systems of price controls in India:

(a) Although price control in the case of some commodities may have originated as a result of wartime shortages or the immediate need to restrict civilian consumption and mobilize resources for military purposes, the form, content and manner of controls has been changing since then. And these changes have not only permeated to production, distribution and almost all their stages and levels, but they have also evolved into a comprehensive economic policy in respect of the price-controlled commodity covering nearly all aspects relevant to their growth, such as the pattern of output, size and location of production units, supply of essential inputs, technology, research and development, expansion of existing capacities and creation of new capacities, provision of finance for expansion and modernization, trade and marketing, etc. Generally, there has emerged a package of economic measures (by and large, mutually consistent and supporting and reinforcing each other) designed to regulate the entire industry in a manner such as to achieve the desired rate and pattern of growth of the industry, and also the distribution of the income considered to be socially just and equitable, providing necessary protection to those classes of consumers and producers who need it for the maintenance of their real incomes, or their levels of production, as the case may be, at certain minimum levels.

(b) Because of its very conception and coverage, various schemes of incentives (in the form of soft loans, fiscal concessions, supply of inputs at concessional rates, direct cash subsidies) as well as disincentives (in the sense of statutory regulation of the expansion of existing capacities and the creation of new capacities, taxes, levies, procurement, quotas, etc.), in a wider sense, form part of the pricing policy of India. The policy also involves subsidized sales to certain categories of consumers or producers, the burden of subsidy falling mostly on the state exchequer. This burden has been increasing steadily over the years; and, as pointed out earlier, in 1982–83 total government expenditure on subsidies was nearly two-and-a-half thousand crores rupees (which was nearly 5 per cent of total government expenditure and 9 per cent of total tax revenue), of which more than half was accounted for by food and fertilizer subsidies. This highlights the need for a conscious policy of gradual reduction of subsidies with a view to phasing them out completely or reducing them to the barest minimum by increasing production and productivity to a level where enough is produced at sufficiently low cost that subsidies, and possibly controls themselves (including price control), could be abolished or at least minimized.

(c) Price controls and pricing policy are significantly affected by the federal character of Indian polity and by varying degrees of state autonomy in many spheres covered by the Constitution of India. In the case of food grains, for instance, different states comprising the Indian Union generally have different types and degrees of control, and also the effectiveness of their implementation is not the same in all states. Since each state sometimes has its own individual interest to protect, co-ordination at the national level may be far from perfect in many cases, and the extent of achievement of the objectives of any particular price control measure may also not be uniform in all parts of the country. There are also informal controls in India, and even in the case of commodities under statutory control there are aspects of informal control. Tractors have, for instance, been under the informal price control implicit in the Surveillance Scheme applicable to certain models, which are considered to be 'price leaders' in their respective horsepower ranges. The producers of the controlled models have to submit the necessary cost data within two weeks of any price increase to the Cost Accounts Branch of the Ministry of Finance, which examines whether the proposed price increases are within the norms of 90 per cent capacity utilization, 16 per cent return on capital employed or 9 per cent return on net worth. In the case of fertilizers, which are under statutory control — mainly two orders issued under the Essential Commodities Act (The Fertilizer (Control) Order of 1957 and the Fertilizer (Movement Control) Order 1957 — the latter rescinded in 1967 but reimposed in 1973), the arrangement regarding 'price pooling' in determining 'retention prices' (to which we will refer a little later) has been informal. Similarly, in the case of *vanaspati*, although the industrial capacity and input mix are formally controlled, and there is statutory quality control too (under the Vegetable Oil Products Control Order, 1947, the Vegetable Oil Products (Standards of Quality) Order, 1975, and the Industrial (Development and Regulation) Act), the industry has also been under informal price control since 1976 in as much as manufacturers have to consult the government before effecting any change in prices. The government exercises informal control on prices on the basis of the advice in this regard received from expert bodies such as the Tariff Commission or the Bureau of Industrial Costs and Prices (BICP). The BICP has been recommending a fair ex-factory selling price on the basis of a study of the cost structure, and has also evolved a pricing formula based on factors like the proportion of imported oils supplied to the manufacturers by the State Trading Corporation and the price of such oils, the price of indigenous oils, conversion costs (including transportation costs), excise duty and inter-state sales tax, and a 12 per cent post-tax return on net worth. Manufacturers are required to use 80 per cent imported oils, 15 per cent cotton seed and other minor oils, and 5 per cent sesame oil (to prevent adulteration of *ghee* (clarified butter) with *vanaspati*).

In India there are various forms of price control, such as total price control, 'dual pricing', procurement/levy prices and 'support prices'. The price control systems also involve certain operational arrangements, like setting 'retention prices', 'pooling' of prices in the case of controlled products whose input mix consists of partly indigenous and partly imported inputs, or where the demand for the controlled commodity is met partly by domestic production and partly by imports. There has also been a system of freight equalization in vogue (which has already been briefly discussed in an earlier chapter). Moreover, the prices of both inputs and intermediate products, as well as final products, have been controlled in certain cases, involving at the same time setting retention prices, 'price pooling' and control of input mix.

Three major nitrogenous fertilizers, namely urea, ammonium sulphate (AS) and calcium ammonium nitrate (CAN), are under total price control in India under the Fertilizer (Control) Order, 1957 and the Fertilizer (Movement Control) Order, 1973, issued under the Essential Commodities Act. Retail prices of the entire quantity of urea, AS and CAN have been statutorily fixed since 1957. The retail prices of complex phosphatic fertilizers have similarly been statutorily controlled, since March 1979. The scheme is administered by the Fertilizer Industry Co-ordination Committee (FICC). Operationally, the scheme involves both setting retention prices and price pooling, for the following two reasons:

(a) Feedstocks and the technology adopted by different units producing nitrogenous fertilizers are different. In the case of nitrogenous fertilizers there are five different feedstocks, namely naphtha, natural gas, fuel oil, coal (or lignite), coke, oven gas and electricity, with 70 per cent (as on 1 January 1979) of capacity based naphtha. The feedstock affects both the capital and the operational costs, the cost of plants based on naphtha or natural gas being much lower than the cost of fuel oil or coal-based plants.

(b) In the case of phosphatic fertilizes also, cost variations arise from differences in the prices of indigenous and imported rock phosphate and sulphur, or metallurgical smelter gases and gypsum, particularly because import costs have been fluctuating.[13]

The cost differentials among different production units arising from the factors mentioned above have necessitated the setting of 'retention' prices, i.e. the prices which production units are allowed to retain irrespective of their costs being higher or lower than the industry's average. The system permits each production unit, which satisfies certain norms, to cover their costs fully and also get a margin of profit over and above it. As with the system of retention prices introduced in November 1977 on the basis of the recommendations of the Fertilizer Prices Committee set up by the government, the manufacturers of nitrogenous fertilizers are allowed a post-tax return of 12 per cent on net worth, subject to a capacity utilization of 80 per cent and the stipulated norms of consumption of raw materials, etc.[14] The fact that substantial quantities of fertilizers are imported has also necessitated an informal price pooling arrangement and setting a 'pooled' average price for the final users.

The pricing of fertilizers may thus involve several stages or steps. In the case of urea in 1978–79, for instance, a weighted average cost of production was first worked out on the basis of cost studies (which included return on capital). Then an assumed average ex-factory cost of production was worked out based on the norms adopted. The difference between these two costs was subsidized from a FPEC (Fertilizer Pool Equalization Charge) account maintained by the Department of Petroleum and Fertilizers. The final retail price was fixed by adding excise duty, notional freight, dealer's margin and a Fertilizer Pool Equalization Charge used to pay the higher-cost factories the difference between their cost and the 'pooled' price.[15] The FPEC Account was actually introduced in 1974, to be operated on a no-profit-no loss basis after the oil price hike of 1973 which caused a steep rise in the price of imported fertilizers, 'whereby the manufacturers were required to pay Rs 610 per tonne of Urea into the acount of FPEC, this amount being used to subsidize the high cost of imported fertilizers'.[16]

A system of retention prices and price pooling had also been in operation in the case of aluminium, (which had been under dual pricing), owing to differences in manufacturing costs of different units caused by differences in power rates, depreciation and interest cost, etc. While the retention price for each producer was worked out separately in respect of the 'levy metal', it was sold to the cables and conductors manufacturers at a 'pooled price'. The system was operated through the Aluminium Regulation Account on a no-profit-no-loss-basis. The manufacturers whose retention prices were lower than the pooled price (Indian Aluminium Company and Hindustan Aluminium Corporation) were required to credit the difference to this account, while those whose retention prices were higher than the pooled price (Madras Aluminium Company and Bharat Aluminium Company) were paid the difference between their cash costs and the pooled prices, from this account.

The major commodities which have been under a system of dual pricing in India are food grains, sugar, cement, steel and aluminium. The manner in which the system has been operating in the case of steel, sugar and cement has been briefly indicated in Chapter 8. In the case of aluminium, a system of dual pricing was introduced on the basis of the recommendations contained in the Report of the Bureau of Industrial Costs and Prices on aluminium pricing submitted in May 1975, under which 'the primary aluminium producers were required to supply 50 per cent of their output in the form of EC grade aluminium at "cash cost", i.e. without covering their depreciation or return on capital. This quantum was designated as "levy" metal and its price was controlled'.[17] The producers were left free to sell the balance at the market price. In the case of food grains also, there has been dual pricing as a certain portion of output is procured and stored to be sold through the fair price shops, while the remaining quantities are sold in the open market at prices determined by the free play of market forces.

Major oil-seeds, cotton and sugar-cane are examples of the prices of basic raw materials being controlled by the government. But in the case of these commodities, government has been announcing certain minimum or support prices, primarily to prevent them from falling to unremunerative levels, and the market prices have generally been higher. This has been clearly brought out in the statistical data presented in the Report of the Committee on Controls and Subsidies. In the case of groundnuts, for instance, the support prices announced on the basis of the recommendations of the Agricultural Prices Commission has been much lower than the average market price in Bombay. In the years 1976–77, 1977–78 and 1978–79, whereas the support prices of groundnuts (Bold Kernel) per quintal announced were Rs 140.00, Rs 160.00 and Rs 175.00 respectively, the corresponding average market prices in Bombay were Rs 350.00, Rs 340.00 and Rs 360.00.[18] The Committee, therefore, found 'evidence that in most parts of the country, and also specifically in Gujarat — the traditional source of the groundnut crop — the newly irrigated areas are being switched over from groundnut to sugar-cane.'[19] In the case of sugar-cane, the committee found that the statutory 'minimum prices for cane — as per the State advised prices for sugar factories — used to be considerably higher than the statutory prices notified by the Central Government',[20] and many states had been subsidizing the difference (between 'state advised' and statutory prices). The same situation had obtained in the case of cotton. The committee has reported that the minimum support prices announced by Central Government for a certain variety of cotton (Punjab-American 320F) in the years 1975–76, 1976–77 and 1977–78 was Rs 210, Rs 220 and Rs 255 per quintal, the lowest market prices in the corresponding years in Bombay being Rs 262, Rs 410 and Rs 271.[21] Since the government only makes purchases under the Support Price Scheme in the event of prices tending to fall below the minimum announced by it, it is obvious that there was no occasion to interfere with the market mechanism in these years in the case of these commodities whenever the ruling market prices happened to be higher than the support prices.

The position has, however, been different in the case of food grains. In 1979–80, whereas cereals (rice, wheat and others) accounted for 60.7 per cent of the total gross area sown in the country, the area under sugar-cane, cotton and oil-seeds (including groundnut) was only 1.7 per cent, 4.7 per cent and 9.1 per cent respectively. The vast majority of nearly 77 per cent of the population residing in rural areas thus earn their livelihood by food grain production alone. Most of the farmers producing food grains in India are subsistence farmers with very low capacity for holding stocks of grains, owing to both lack of storage facilities and their immediate cash needs, to be able to take advantage of a rise in market prices. They have to sell their entire produce, after keeping the minimum required for their own consumption and for seed, in the village itself, to often unscrupulous traders or middlemen, or else take it to the nearest market-place or *mandi*. The rush of arrivals in the market immediately after harvest, therefore, has the effect of unduly depressing agricultural prices, particularly prices of food grains, necessitating support price operations. Moreover, the government also needs to build up buffer stocks of food grains to make them available to the weaker sections of the community in the urban areas at reasonable prices through the public distribution system. Buffer stocks are built up by purchases made by the government in the course of support price operations, as well as by compulsory levy and 'procurement' of the levy quantity at the 'procurement' or levy price fixed by it. Support price operations for primary producers and compulsory levy and procurement from traders thus acquire special significance in the case of food grains in the context of Indian agriculture; and they serve to maintain the profitability of agriculture at a minimum level on the one hand, and to enable the government to stabilize food grain prices in the urban areas. Government has in fact been procuring large quantities of food grains, and, as indicated earlier, the quantity procured has been steadily increasing over the last few years, and amounted to 14.64 million tonnes in the triennium ending 1983, which was about 13 per cent of the net production of food grains in that year.

Another important aspect of pricing policy in India is the system of freight equalization, already briefly examined in an earlier chapter. As stated there, the scheme has been in operation in the case of pig iron, steel, cement, petroleum products and nitrogenous fertilizers. Freight equalization schemes generally cover rail freights, but in the case of areas not covered by rail transport, or where road transport is costly, the scheme is specially extended to cover transport by road as well. The schemes are operated by setting up self-financing freight equalization accounts. The weighted average expenditure on freight or the 'pooled freight' worked out on an all-India basis is included in the average cost for working out the f.o.r. (free-on-rail) 'destination' price, the units actually spending less than this average or pooled freight pay the difference into the equalization account, and those actually incurring more than it get the difference reimbursed to them from this account.

In the case of cement, it has been found that the system of freight pooling has had some deleterious economic effects. It has resulted in sub-optimal locations of cement plants, built with a disregard to the cost of transport, and has seriously affected the viability of many units set up prior to 1956 (when freight pooling was introduced) near consumption centres to take advantage of lower freight (which could then offset the higher cost of limestone, etc. of such units, owing to their being located far from the source of raw materials), rendering them virtually 'sick' units. The Committee on Controls and Subsidies has observed that 'this system has acted as a major disincentive to the setting up of the cement manufacturing capacity in the North and the East which are heavily deficit in cement, and has led to the concentration of cement production in the South, endowed with relatively superior quality limestone'.[22] The Committee has further noted that 'the average lead for the movement of cement by rail has increased from 456 kilometres in 1970-71 to 743 kilometres in 1975-76'.[23] Another committee set up by the government to go into the matter has noted that between 1960-1961 and 1973-1974 the average lead distance increased by nearly 70 per cent (from 377 kilometres to 635 kilometres) in the case of cement and by 46 per cent in the case of iron and steel (from 697 kilometres to 1017 kilometres), as compared to only 22 per cent on an average for all rail goods traffic. The committee also concluded that freight equalization policy had had the effect of increasing real transport costs to the economy, and also of encouraging the siting of production units where they might not otherwise have been set up.

Besides the measures discussed above, which are part of the process of price setting, or are incidental to it, in a broader and more general sense, price controls and pricing policy cover certain other measures which constitute significant interference with the free functioning of the market mechanism or determination of prices and the direction of the flow of economic resources in the free market. This interference is considered necessary to prevent the distortions, correct the imbalances, or remove the inequities which might arise if certain practices followed by producers or traders were not regulated in the public interest. As indicated in Chapter 4, there is such a statutory regulation in several EEC countries too, for example the prohibition of 'resale price maintenance', 'discriminatory practices' or 'overcharging'. There are similar provisions in the Monopolistic and Restrictive Trade Practices Act, 1969 of India. The main objective of these legal provisions is the prevention of trade practices which:

(a) prevent, restrict or distort competition in the production, supply or distribution of any goods and services; or
(b) limit or 'obstruct the flow of capital or resources into the stream of production';[24] or
(c) limit technical development; or

(d) cause unreasonable increases in the cost of production or sale or resale prices; or
(e) maintain prices at an unreasonably high level 'by limiting, reducing or otherwise controlling the production, supply or distribution'[25] of any goods or services; or
(f) cause deterioration in quality of any goods or services; or
(g) make any false or misleading representation regarding any goods or services causing loss or injury to their consumers.

The law defines trade practices as 'any practice relating to the carrying on of any trade',[26] which includes 'anything done by any person which controls or affects the price charged by, or the method of trading of, any trader or any class of traders'.[27] The trade practices (which have a direct or an indirect bearing on the prices which prevail in the market) sought to be regulated have been classified as 'monopolistic trade practices', 'restrictive trade practices' and 'unfair trade practices' in the MRTP Act. Both conceptually and operationally, there is not much difference between the monopolistic and the restrictive trade practices, the elements common to both being restricting competition, maintaining prices at an unreasonably high level by restricting output, and limiting or obstructing the flow of resources to any industry, thereby stunting its growth. 'Unfair trade practice' is, on the other hand, a consumer-orientated concept designed to protect the legitimate interests of consumers against misrepresentation and fraud by producers or sellers, causing 'loss or injury to the consumers'.[28] The law gives a comprehensive list of these unfair trade practices, which includes practices like false representation regarding the 'standard, quality grades, composition, style or model'[29] of any goods/services, and false or misleading 'warranty or guarantee',[30] or 'promise to replace, maintain or repair an article'.[31] While the provisions relating to monopolistic and restrictive trade practices had been incorporated in the original law itself enacted in 1969, the provisions relating to unfair trade practices were added to it by the Amendment Act of 1984. The salient features of the scheme (including the institutional framework for its implementation) envisaged in the Act are briefly as follows:

(a) The MRTP commission (which is a quasi-judicial body, generally headed by a serving or retired high court judge and vested with the powers of a civil court) has the power to enquire into a restrictive or unfair trade practice on receipt of a complaint from any trade or consumer association with a membership of not less than twenty-five persons, or from twenty-five or more consumers, a reference from the Central or a state government, an application from the Director-General of Investigation and Registration, or on its own information. The commission can similarly enquire into a monopolistic trade practice on a reference made to it by Central Government or a state government, or on its own knowledge or information. In the case of a complaint received from a consumer association or consumers, the commission may institute a preliminary investigation by the Director-General before issue of process requiring attendance of the person complained against. The Director-General can also institute such a preliminary investigation based upon his own knowledge or information, or on a complaint made to him, to satisfy himself as to whether or not an application should be made by him to the Commission for Enquiry.

(b) During the enquiry, the commission has the power to grant a temporary injunction restraining an undertaking or a person from carrying on any monopolistic, restrictive or unfair trade practice until the conclusion of such enquiry or until further orders, if it is proved 'by an affidavit, or otherwise'[32] that such a practice 'is likely to affect prejudicially the public interest or the interest of any trader, class of traders or traders generally or of any consumer or consumers generally'.[33] The commission is further empowered to award 'compensation for the loss or damage caused'[34] by any such practice on an application made to it by the Central Government or a state government or any person or undertaking, after necessary enquiry into the allegations made therein.

(c) For the purposes of the law, every monopolistic practice is deemed to be prejudicial to public interest except in certain specified cases, such as, a practice 'expressly authorized by any enactment for the time being in force',[35] or, in respect of which the Central Government, being satisfied that it is necessary to meet the requirements of the defence of India or any part thereof, or for the security of the state, or to ensure the maintenance of supply of goods and services essential to the community, or to give effect to the terms of any agreement to which the Central Government is a party, permits it by a written order. Similarly, a restrictive trade practice is deemed to be prejudicial to the public interest, except in certain specified cases, where the commission is satisfied, for instance, 'that the restriction is reasonably necessary having regard to the character of the goods to which it applies to protect the public against injury (whether to persons or to premises) in connection with the consumption, installation or use of those goods',[36] or its removal would deny the public 'specific and substantial benefits or advantages';[37] or would have an adverse effect on the employment situation in an area; or cause a substantial reduction 'in the volume of earnings of the export';[38] or was considered necessary for defence, security or maintenance of essential supplies for the community.

(d) If the commission finds, on enquiry, that a monopolistic trade practice 'operates or is likely to operate against the public interest',[40] 'it shall make a report to the Central Government as to its findings thereon'[41] and it may pass appropriate orders on it prohibiting the continuance of such practice and also such other orders as it may think fit to 'remedy or prevent any mischief which results or may result'[42] from the continuance of such practice. These orders may include an order regulating 'production, storage, supply, distribution or control of any goods';[43] or prohibiting any 'commercial policy which prevents or lessens'[44] competition; or 'fixing standards for the goods used or produced';[45] or 'regulating the profits'.[46] In the case of a restrictive trade practice, if the commission finds it, on enquiry, to be prejudicial to the public interest, it may itself, by an order, direct that it shall be discontinued or shall not be repeated, and any agreement relating to it shall be void or shall stand modified in the manner specified in the order. Alternatively, the commission may, if the party to any restrictive trade practice so applies, permit it to take such steps as may be specified in its behalf by the commission as may be necessary to ensure that the practice in question is no longer prejudicial to the public interest. The commission also has the power to pass similar orders in the case of an unfair trade practice if, after enquiry, it is of the opinion that the practice is prejudicial to public interest, or to the interest of any consumer or consumers generally. Any person contravening any such order of the commission in respect of an unfair trade practice shall be punishable with imprisonment for a term which may extend to three years, or with a fine, which may extend to ten thousand rupees, or with both. The contravention of any order of Central Government in regard to any monopolistic trade practice or of the commission relating to any restrictive trade practice is similarly punishable with imprisonment for a term which shall not be less than six months, but not more than two years, in the case of the first offence; and not less than two years but not more than five in the case of any second or subsequent offence in relation to the goods and services in respect of which the first offence was committed; and in either case, where the contravention is a continuing one, also with a fine which may extend to five hundred rupees for every day, after the first, during which such contravention continues. The court has, however, been given the discretion to impose a sentence of imprisonment less than the minimum term indicated above in the case of contraventions of orders regarding monopolistic and restrictive trade practices, if it is satisfied that the circumstances of any case so require.

Like the EEC countries, there is a legal prohibition of resale price maintenance in India. The relevant provisions are contained in the MRTP Act itself. 'Re-sale price' has been defined as 'any price notified to the dealer or otherwise published by or on behalf of the supplier ... as the price or the minimum price which is to be charged'.[47] The law provides that any term or condition of a contract or an agreement 'between a person and a wholesaler or retailer ... shall be void in so far as it purports to establish or provide for the establishment of minimum prices to be charged on the resale of goods in India';[48] and prohibits notification to dealers or otherwise publication of any price in relation to any goods which is 'stated or calculated to be understood as the minimum price which may be charged on resale of the goods in India'.[49] The law further prohibits the witholding of the supply of any goods by any supplier to a wholesaler or retailer on the grounds that he had sold or is likely to sell them in India, at a price below re-sale price; or had or is likely to supply them to a third party who had or is likely to do so. The commission may, however, on a reference made to it by the Director-General of Investigation and Registration 'or any other person interested, by order, direct that goods of any class specified in the order shall be exempt'[50] from the operation of these provisions, if it 'is satisfied that in default of a system of maintained minimum resale prices applicable to those goods',[51] the quality of goods available for sale or the varieties of goods so available would be substantially reduced, or their retail prices would be increased, or any necessary services provided in connection with or after the sale of goods in retail, would cease to be so provided or would be substantially reduced 'to the detriment of the public as such consumers or users'.[52] Any contravention of the provisions relating to re-sale price maintenance shall be punishable with imprisonment for a term which may extend to three months, or with a fine which may extend to five thousand rupees, or with both.

The existing institutional framework for the formulation, implementation, enforcement and monitoring of price control measures and pricing policies has been briefly indicated in Chapter 4. Of the three independent institutions set up by the government, namely the Bureau of Industrial Costs and Prices (BICP), the Agricultural Prices Commission (APC) and the Monopolies and Restrictive Trade Practices Commission (MRTPC), the first two are expert bodies which advise the government regarding the determination of controlled prices of industrial goods and agricultural commodities, and the third is a statutory body of a quasi-judicial character created for the purposes of *inter alia* enforcement of the legal provisions relating to the monopolistic, restrictive and unfair trade practices and prohibition of re-sale price maintenance. Some significant features of the entire institutional arrangement appear to be as follows:

(a) There is no single broad-based institution or body of a national or all-India character like the National Prices Committee in France, the Prices Commission in Belgium or the erstwhile Prices and Incomes Board in the United Kingdom. Neither the BICP nor the APC can be said to be national bodies representing all regions or states, or all interests and groups. There are several professional bodies and organizations which represent industry and trade, which project their viewpoints in various forums and in various ways, but there is no body or institution set up by the government which gives due representation to them or to divergent political views in order to consider major policy questions relating to price controls and pricing policy and to advise the government, generally, or on specific issues referred to it by the government.

(b) The exercise of setting controlled price is undertaken not only by the BICP in the case of industrial goods, and by the APC for agricultural commodities, but also by several formal and informal committees and groups set up within the government ministries and departments concerned, and by several other *ad hoc* committees. This has been the case with fertilizers, steel, coal, cement, etc. In the cae of fertilizers of fertilizers, it is the Fertilizer Industry Coordination Committee (FICC), and in the case of steel, the Inter-Ministerial Study Groups set up from time to time, the Steel Authority of India (SAIL) and the Joint Plant Committee (JPC), which have been responsible for setting controlled prices. For coal and cement the government has also set up similar committees. This multiplicity of price-fixing bodies, combined with a certain *ad hoc*ism, has several disadvantages. Firstly, each price-fixing body may tend to take an isolated view, restricted to the commodity whose price setting exercise is undertaken by it or its inputs and substitutes, and not a comprehensive view of the entire integrated price structure; and it may not consider the effect of a pricing policy relating to that commodity on the relative price structure and thereby on the resource allocation and the income distribution, as well as on the growth of the related industries and of the economy as a whole. Secondly, in certain cases where the same body has not been in continuous charge of price setting for any commodity, there may be lagged or considerably delayed adjustments of controlled prices to changing costs, causing avoidable distortions. Thirdly, this arrangement may not be conducive to evolving a relative price structure consistent with the objectives and priorities of the national plan, and the pattern of resource allocation and growth envisaged therein.

(c) There does not appear to be any regular system for monitoring the effects of any price control measure on the growth of the controlled industry, or of other related industries, or for ascertaining whether it is achieving the desired objectives, or creating certain distortions or problems, so that necessary signals could be given for timely remedial action. There also does not appear to be any one central organization for collection and analysis of data relating to the behaviour of agricultural and industrial costs, prices and production, and the distribution and availability of industrial goods and agricultural commodities with a view to identifying distortions caused by the free functioning of the market mechanism or, possibly, by any price control measure itself or the manner of its implementation, calling for interference with the market mechanism, or reconsideration of that price control measure, as the case may be. While individual ministries may be carrying out some kind of monitoring, there does not seem to be any institutional set-up with the necessary field formations and technical and professional personnel for regular, systematic, centralized and properly co-ordinated monitoring of all price control measures. This monitoring could reveal the effects and impact on the economy of each of these measures individually, of all of them collectively or of a combination of them, and indicate the direction or the manner in which pricing policy and its implementation or enforcement generally, as well as in respect of individual commodities, needs to be reorientated, reformulated, reinforced with other measures, or modified to ensure that the desired objectives are achieved without any avoidable distortions.

The Committee on Controls and Subsidies has also observed that

> the lack of adequate data hampers not only policy formulation but also the devising of an effective control machinery, or the subsidization of needy sectors. For a monitoring system to be able to evaluate the effectiveness of the control measure, there must be a machinery which will disseminate information on the functioning of the control system through the timely supply of all relevant data. The requisite data must not only flow automatically, and without delay, but there must also be a system or a machinery which would classify and convert these data into information essential for the evaluation and continuing appraisal of the

working of the control. The monitoring system must, therefore, provide for the collation and analysis of the data being collected. The analysis should highlight aberrations, distortions and departures from anticipated or intended results so that corrective steps can be taken in time.[53]

The committee has made several suggestions for the effective implementation and monitoring of price controls, such as the setting up of a monitoring unit in the Planning Commission to co-ordinate the monitoring system, the monitoring of controls by State Planning Boards at state level, 'developing a vibrant consumer movement ... encouraged and funded by Government',[54] and 'organizing citizen's councils in each area to oversee the functioning of the fair price shops',[55] which deserve serious consideration.

The absence of an efficient monitoring organization and the non-availability of adequate data required for a proper analysis and appraisal of the operation of price controls and the implementation of pricing policy in India has been a great handicap to both policy-makers and academic researchers alike. It is often contended, generally without any supporting empirical evidence, that price controls have kept the prices of controlled commodities unduly and artificially depressed, thereby reducing the profitability of the industries producing them and adversely affecting their growth. It would be worthwhile examining to what extent the scanty statistical data available from various sources substantiates this contention.

Table 8 shows the comparative movement of wholesale prices of certain price-controlled and non price-controlled items over the period 1971–72 to 1983–84, the Average Annual Growth Rate (AAGR) of prices of cement and aluminium (both of which are controlled commodities), being higher than the AAGR of 'All commodities' (controlled as well as non-controlled) over the thirteen-year period 1971–72 to 1983–84. Similarly, the prices of paper and paper products have also moved almost completely in line with the movement of the general price level over this period. The corresponding Annual Compound Growth Rates (ACGR) indicate almost the same position. The AAGR and ACGR of drugs and

Table 8 *Changes in wholesale prices (1970–71 = 100) of some controlled and non-controlled items over the period 1971–72 to 1983–84*

	Average annual growth rate (AAGR)	Average compound growth rate (1983–84 over 1971–72) (ACGR)
Controlled items		
Drugs and medicines	4.9	4.8
Vanaspati	6.2	7.5
Paper and paper products	9.9	9.4
Cement	12.2	11.7
Aluminium	11.5	10.5
Non-controlled items		
Cotton textiles	7.4	7.2
Machinery and machine tools	8.3	8.3
Electrical machinery	7.3	7.0
Jute hemp and mesta textiles	8.7	7.2
All commodities	10.1	9.2

Source: Ministry of Industry, Government of India

medicines and *vanaspati* have not been as high as the AAGR and ACGR of 'All commodities' over this period, but this has been the case with all four non-controlled commodities shown in Table 8. It cannot be said on the basis of these figures that the controlled prices have been kept artificially very low. It appears that, in many cases, controlled prices have been allowed to increase nearly as much or even more than the general price level; while in some other cases the prices of non-controlled goods have moved more rapidly, controlled prices do not seem generally to have been kept at unduly low levels.

That the movement in the prices of controlled items have generally not been significantly slower than in other prices is illustrated by changes in sugar prices, both when sugar was under total price control as well as during recent years when the control was partly lifted and dual pricing was introduced with effect from 28 February 1982. Table 9 is based on the available data.

As the figures in Table 9 reveal, changes in the controlled price of cement kept pace with movements in all prices of 'All commodities'

Table 9 *Percentage changes in the index number of wholesale prices (1970-71 = 100) of cement, non-food articles, raw materials, manufactures, etc. over the periods 2-8-74 to 3-5-81 and 28-2-82 to 19-5-84*

	Percentage change during the period of total price control – 3-5-81 over 2-8-74	Percentage change during the period of dual pricing – 19-5-84 over 28-2-82
Cement	51.83	56.62
Non-food articles	34.59	31.44
Minerals	174.39	−9.35
Raw materials	66.12	n.a.
Fuel, power, light and lubricants	105.28	16.27
Manufactures	61.22	17.19
All commodities	54.80	18.97

Source: Ministry of Industry, Government of India

during the period 2 August 1974 to 3 May 1981 (the former increasing by 51.83 per cent and the latter by 54.80 per cent); and the cement price also changed more or less in sympathy with the prices of manufactures and raw materials. During the brief period immediately after partial decontrol (28 February 1982 to 19 May 1984), the price of levy cement in fact increased much faster than other prices. However, cement prices sometimes changed at intervals of nearly a year, necessitating somewhat bigger jumps.

Data regarding growth in capacity, production and capacity utilization for the years 1970–71 and 1975–76 to 1983–84 relating to some price-controlled and non price-controlled industries are contained in Table 10, which shows how annual capacity growth in the controlled industries has been roughly between 5 and 14 per cent, the highest rates of growth being achieved by nitrogenous fertilizers (14.0 per cent), phosphatic fertilizers (11.0 per cent), agricultural tractors (9.6 per cent) and paper and paper board (8.1 per cent). The capacity growth of other controlled industries has been broadly between 5 and 6 per cent. Growth in production has been lower than growth in capacity, except in the case of phosphatic fertilizers and sugar whose production recorded a higher growth rate

Table 10 *Growth in capacity, production and capacity utilization in some controlled and non-controlled industries over the period 1970–71 to 1982–83*

	Annual compound growth rates, 1982–83 over 1970–71		Percentage capacity utilization	
	Capacity	Production	1970–71	1982–83
Price-controlled industries				
Cement	5.9	4.1	84.1	68.2
Aluminium	5.6	1.9	99.5	64.8
Agricultural tractors	9.6	n.a.	n.a.	69.2
Sugar	5.2	6.8	101.1	121.1
Vanaspati	4.7	3.9	68.3	62.6
Paper and paper board	8.1	4.0	98.3	61.7
Nitrogenous fertilizers	14.0	12.5	78.1	66.6
Phosphatic fertilizers	11.0	12.9	56.5	69.1
Non-price-controlled industries				
Jute manufacturing	n.a.	2.0	n.a.	n.a.
Cotton spinning	n.a.	0.6	74.9	n.a.
Electric fans	8.8	7.5	94.5	82.0
Dry cells	10.2	n.a.	n.a.	74.1
Railway wagons	−0.5	2.8	37.1	55.0
Electric motors	8.7	4.7	105.9	67.1
Commercial vehicles	4.6	6.3	68.7	83.5
Passenger cars	0.9	−0.6	98.5	82.3

n.a. — Not available
Source: Plan documents, Director General Technical Development and Annual Reports of Ministries, Government of India.

than the capacity growth. Nitrogenous and phosphatic fertilizers recorded annual growth rates of 12.5 and 12.9 per cent respectively, the latter exceeding the capacity growth rate. The other controlled items recorded production growth rates ranging roughly between 4 and 7 per cent (except aluminium where annual rate of growth in production was only 1.9 per cent as against the capacity growth rate of 5.6 per cent, causing considerable decline in capacity utilization as well). The non-controlled industries generally do not seem to have done better over this period in respect of growth in capacity and production — their annual capacity growth rate varying roughly between 5 and 10 per cent (except passenger cars which achieved the capacity growth rate of about 1 per cent and railway wagons whose capacity seems to have remained stagnant or to have slightly declined). Production in the non-price-controlled industries recorded an annual growth rate of 2 to 7.5 per cent (except cotton spinning where it was a little over 0.5 per cent, and passenger cars which recorded a negative growth rate of the same size).

A comparison between changes in percentage capacity utilization in the controlled and non-controlled industries during this period does not indicate any significant differences. Wherever growth in production has been higher than growth in capacity, the capacity utilization has understandably increased. In the controlled sector this has been the case with sugar and phosphatic fertilizers; and in the non-controlled sector in railway wagons and commercial vehicles. Capacity has been growing faster than production in the case of all the controlled items shown in Table 10, except sugar and phosphatic fertilizers, and the capacity utilization has accordingly declined in all cases except in the case of these two commodities where it has recorded increases over this period. Broadly speaking, the industries in the controlled sector present the same picture. The figures in Table 9, however, do not in any way bring out the fact that the growth in capacity, output or capacity utilization in the controlled industries has generally been slower than in the non-controlled industries, and that price controls have had a deleterious effect on the growth of the controlled industries.

The data available in the Reserve Bank of India (RBI) studies of the finances of selected medium and large government and private sector companies, each with a paid-up capital of Rs 5 lakhs or more (published in the RBI Bulletins), give some indication of the changing levels of profitability and internal resource generation in some of the price-controlled and non-price-controlled industries. Table 11, based on these data, indicates the position in this regard. Profits after tax as percentage of net worth were generally higher or at comparable levels in the three controlled industries, and they were consistently negative over several years in the case of non-price-controlled industries such as cotton textiles and jute textiles.

A similar situation seems to emerge in regard to internal resources from the data contained in these studies. Table 12, based on these data, brings out this position. In these industries, internal resources

Table 11 *Profits after tax as percentage of net worth in selected controlled and non-controlled industries, 1973–74 to 1977–78*

	1973–74	1974–75	1975–76	1976–77	1977–78
Price-controlled industries					
Cement	negative	negative	12.0	2.8	8.8
Medicines and pharmaceutical formulations	15.7	12.8	12.0	14.6	16.5
Sugar	11.3	9.6	negative	9.0	negative
Non-price-controlled industries					
Cotton textiles	24.7	12.3	negative	negative	negative
Jute textiles	negative	12.0	negative	negative	negative
Engineering	10.8	12.1	8.5	10.3	10.1

Source: Reserve Bank of India Bulletins, Department of Economic Analysis and Policy, Reserve Bank of India, Bombay

Table 12 *Internal resources as percentage of total resources in selected controlled and non-controlled industries, 1973–74 to 1977–78*

	1973–74	1974–75	1975–76	1976–77	1977–78
Price-controlled industries					
Cement	negative	19.2	65.6	48.5	75.2
Medicines and pharmaceutical formulations	69.0	45.8	89.7	63.7	61.0
Sugar	21.2	28.9	1.9	negative	4.4
Non-price-controlled industries					
Cotton textiles	75.3	37.1	negative	negative	14.0
Jute textiles	negative	58.3	negative	negative	negative
Engineering	44.4	34.8	45.3	45.1	48.7

Source: RBI Bulletins

Table 13 Outstanding loans as percentage of invested capital in selected price-controlled and non-price-controlled industries, 1973–74 to 1977–78

	1973–74	1974–75	1975–76	1976–77	1977–78
Price-controlled industries					
Manufacture of hydrogenated oils, *vanaspati, ghee,* etc.	50.72	43.91	48.11	50.01	34.83
Drugs and medicines	33.86	39.36	38.07	44.04	41.09
Manufacture of cement, lime and plaster	43.55	50.40	34.55	41.69	30.07
Non-price-controlled industries					
Manufacture of jute, hemp and *mesta* textiles*	48.46	44.94	48.89	50.35	62.58
Manufacture of cotton textiles	54.72	50.82	59.73	63.87	65.28
Manufacture of machines, machine tools and parts, except electrical machinery	51.92	55.15	48.49	45.22	46.21

* A fibre similar to jute, *Hibiscus sabdarisa.*
Source: Annual Survey of Industries, Central Statistics Organization, Ministry of Planning, Government of India

(which are primarily a function of the efficiency and profitability of an enterprise) as a percentage of total resources were comparatively higher in the price-controlled sector than in the non-price-controlled sector.

The position indicated by an analysis of the RBI data finds some confirmation from the data relating to the outstanding loans in some price-controlled and non price-controlled industries in the data published by the Central Statistical Organization, as presented in Table 13. Comparable, and in some cases even higher, profitability and resource generation in some of the price-controlled industries seems to have resulted in their somewhat lower and declining dependence on loans or borrowings relative to some non-price-controlled industries, as reflected in the figures regarding outstanding loans as percentage of invested capital in Table 13. Although these figures do not establish any trend or marked tendency, they indicate that this percentage was much lower in 1977–78 than in 1973–74 in the case of some controlled commodities like hydrogenated oils, *vanaspati*, *ghee*, etc. and also in the manufacture of cement, lime and plaster — the figures for the former being 50.72 and 34.83 and for the latter 43.55 and 30.07, respectively, in these two years. In the case of drugs and medicines — another price-controlled commodity — the percentage in 1977–78 (41.09) recorded an increase over 1973–74 (33.86). Of the three non-price-controlled industries concerned, those at (1) and (2) show increases in 1977–78 (62.58 and 65.28 respectively) over the year 1973–74 (48.46 and 54.72, respectively); and only (3) shows a small fall (46.21 in 1977–78 as compared to 51.92 in 1973–74). It could possibly be stated on the basis of this empirical evidence that some of the price-controlled industries, starting with a marginally lower dependence on borrowings, had over these years further reduced such dependence, whereas the position has been reversed in the case of some non-price-controlled industries. This may have been the result of a slightly higher rate of profitability and internal resource generation in these price-controlled industries which enabled them to repay outstanding loans to some extent and also to reduce further borrowings a little.

Debt/equity ratio is another indicator of the reliance on borrowings relative to equity capital, and changes in it over time may, in some cases, reflect the profitability of an enterprise. Table 14, based on the RBI data, shows the changes in debt/equity ratio in some of the price-controlled and non-price-controlled industries. The industries to which the figures in Table 14 relate are not exactly the same as those in Table 13. But the figures in this table also indicate that debt/equity ratio in cotton textiles and jute textiles was rising in the years 1975–76, 1976–77 and 1977–78, indicating increasing dependence on borrowings in these non-price-controlled industries over these years. Debt/equity ratio had also been rising slightly in the case of engineering industries over the years 1974–75 to 1977–78, whereas chemicals had shown no change over the three years 1975–76 to 1977–78. In the case of price-controlled industries, while fertilizers had shown a definite decline in the debt/equity ratio over the three years 1975–76 to 1977–78, the other controlled

Table 14 *Changes in debt/equity ratios in selected price-controlled and non-price-controlled industries over the period 1972–73 to 1977–78*

	1972–73	1973–74	1974–75	1975–76	1976–77	1977–78
Price-controlled industries						
Cement	0.40	0.39	0.58	0.52	0.49	0.53
Paper and paper products	0.39	0.42	0.38	0.39	0.43	0.47
Fertilizers	n.a.	n.a.	n.a.	0.58	0.46	0.35
Sugar	0.20	0.21	0.35	0.46	0.44	0.47
Non-price-controlled industries						
Cotton textiles	0.61	0.51	0.53	0.62	0.74	0.89
Jute textiles	0.21	0.23	0.19	0.22	0.33	0.81
Engineering	0.34	0.32	0.39	0.42	0.45	0.48
Chemicals	0.48	0.37	0.35	0.37	0.37	0.37

n.a. — Not available
Source: RBI Bulletins

industries recorded no significant changes over these years — the ratio remained in the neighbourhood of 0.50 in the case of cement, recorded marginal increases in the case of paper and paper products and showed very small changes in the case of sugar. On the whole, it could be said that these data also bring out a picture which is not materially different from the one revealed in Table 13. That the reliance on borrowings had been somewhat greater and increasing over the years in the case of some non-controlled industries, relative to some controlled industries, is broadly indicated by the data presented in Table 14 also.

Although the scanty data presented in the statistical tables above do suggest that those who decry any kind of control may not be on solid ground, empirically or otherwise, the limitations of these data have also to be indicated. Firstly, the coverage of these data may be rather limited, and it relates to only some of the commodities in the controlled and the non-controlled sectors and to only a few years. Any generalization concerning the entire controlled and non-controlled sectors on the basis of these data would have only limited validity. Secondly, in the price-controlled industries, there is a sizeable public sector in some of the items to which the data relate (for instance fertilizers, aluminium and drugs and medicines), in which growth could have been autonomous as a result of planned investment, and not due to the incentives or disincentives generated by controls. The conclusions would have had greater validity had they been based on comparable data relating only to private price-controlled and private non-price-controlled industries.

To sum up, some broad suggestions which could be made on the basis of the above analysis are, briefly, as follows:

(a) There is an urgent need to simplify the system of statutory price controls in India by a comprehensive review of the relevant laws, the rules made and innumerable orders and notifications issued thereunder, by both Central and state governments, with a view to withdrawing or cancelling those which are no longer necessary, retaining only the barest minimum, and consolidating, classifying and codifying them, so that they are easily ascertainable by policy-makers as well as those who have to implement them.

(b) The building up of an efficient monitoring system (which includes a co-ordinated system of collection and analysis of all relevant data and giving necessary indications based on it) is an essential prerequisite for both the formulation of a proper pricing policy as well as ensuring its effective implementation. This system needs to be built up as soon as possible.

(c) The multiplicity of price-fixing bodies needs to be dispensed with. A single central or broad-based institution consisting not only of professionals and experts, but also those representing the interests of agriculture, industry, trade and commerce at the regional and national levels could perhaps take a more integrated view of the entire structure of relative prices and price controls in advising the government on specific matters or issues referred to it.

(d) As recommended by the Committee on Controls and Subsidies, there is also an urgent need for building up a powerful consumer movement and creating voluntary organizations at the grass-roots level to ensure the proper functioning of the public distribution system.

(e) The entire system of price controls needs to be productivity and efficiency orientated, so that production is increased and costs lowered, benefiting both consumers and producers, eventually creating a situation where scarcities are removed, a sufficient lowering of price is also made possible by cost reductions, and controls can be lifted and not become self-perpetuating.

(f) There is also a need to adopt a conscious policy of minimizing the burden of subsidies on the public exchequer by measures such as their gradual phasing out over time, suitably adjusting the procurement price and the issue price in the case of commodities like food grains which are procured and sold through the public distribution system, providing incentives for greater efficiency (so that, with reductions in costs, the rate of subsidy could be reduced) and resorting to dual pricing, wherever considered feasible and practically advisable.

(g) Some more liberal and innovative forms of price control, for example 'stability contracts', 'programme contracts' and 'price framework' tried in the EEC countries (which have been discussed in an earlier chapter) could also be tried in India, in suitable cases, since they may not only provide greater freedom to market forces but be much easier and much less expensive to administer. These measures may also be of greater help in stabilizing the general price level, and evolving a relative price structure and a pattern of resource allocation, which are more consistent with the programmes and priorities of the national plan. For a list of products or groups of products covered by 'stability contracts' and also a list of main 'programme contracts' in France, see the Appendix.

(h) There is practically no significant difference between a 'monopolistic trade practice' and a 'restrictive trade practice' as defined in the MRTP Act at present. Both conceptually and operationally, the two merge into one. Both concepts cover similar practices which can only be resorted to under conditions of imperfect competition where an individual producer or a group can, by their own action, influence the market price; and both may involve restriction of output or determination of price which may be disproportionately high relative to cost. Both restrictive and monopolistic practices are, therefore, essentially monopolistic in nature and we need have only one concept of a monopolistic practice (not 'trade practice' which might make it unnecessarily restrictive in scope), defined as any practice adopted by an individual producer or trader or a number of them to control the production, supply or distribution of any commodity in a manner so as to unduly restrict its output, deteriorate its quality or initially fix or subsequently increase its price disproportionately to its cost of production or increase therein, as the case may be, to the detriment of consumers or users affected by it, or the economy. This concept would obviate the need to have two different procedures (one for monopolistic and the other for restrictive trade practices), and would make the law simpler, logically more rigorous and operationally easier to implement effectively.

(i) The provisions relating to unfair trade practices introduced recently in the MRTP Act are very wide in their scope, covering virtually every conceivable misrepresentation 'for the purpose of promoting the sale, use or supply of any goods or for the provision of any services'[56] causing loss or injury to their consumers or users in any way. Besides monopolistic and restrictive trade practices, the MRTPC has also been empowered to enquire into unfair trade practices. In a vast country like India there could be a large number of cases of such practices in all parts of the country, which the MRTPC alone might find difficult to cope with. There is, therefore, a need to decentralize the administration of these provisions and create adequate institutional set-up and enforcement machinery at the state levels (even if it requires further amending the existing law or enacting a separate law dealing exclusively with unfair trade practices), if these provisions are to be effectively implemented in order to have the desired effect.

Notes

1. See Westphal, op. cit.
2. Report of the Committee on Controls and Subsidies, May 1979, Ministry of Finance, Government of India, —Annexes pp.30–9 and 57–81.
3. Ibid., 'Summary of Findings and Recommendations', p.i.
4. Ibid., p.ii.

5. Ibid.
6. Ibid.
7. Report of the Committee on Controls and Subsidies, Ministry of Finance, Government of India, May 1979, p.193.
8. Ibid., p.136.
9. Ibid., p.137.
10. Ibid., p.181.
11. Ibid.
12. Ibid., p.182.
13. See Report of the Committee on Controls and Subsidies, Ministry of Finance, Government of India, May 1979, p.218.
14. Ibid., p.219.
15. See Report of the Committee on Controls and Subsidies, Ministry of Finance, Government of India, pp.219–20.
16. Ibid., p.219.
17. Ibid., p.145.
18. Ibid., p.145.
19. Ibid., p.146.
20. Ibid., p.163.
21. Ibid., p.177.
22. Ibid., p.286.
23. Ibid.
24. MRTP Supplement — 'A Manual', Directorate of Research, Institute of Company Secretaries, New Delhi, Section 2.(0) (i) of the MRTP Act, 1969 (as amended by the Amendment Act, 1984, September 1984, Appendix I) pp.ix–xi.
25. Ibid., Section 2(i)(i).
26. Ibid., Section 2(U).
27. Ibid.
28. Ibid., Section 36A, pp.li–liii.
29. Ibid., Section 36A(2) (i).
30. Ibid., Section 36A(2) (viii).
31. Ibid.
32. Ibid., Section 12A, pp.xix–xxi.
33. Ibid.
34. Ibid., Section 12B.
35. Ibid., Section 32, p.xxxxvii.
36. Ibid., Section 38, lvi–lviii.
37. Ibid.
38. Ibid.
39. Ibid.
40. Ibid., Section 31, xxxxiv–xxxxvi.
41. Ibid.
42. Ibid.
43. Ibid.
44. Ibid.

45. Ibid.
46. Ibid.
47. Ibid., Section 40, Explanation 1, pp.lvii–lxi.
48. Ibid., Section 39(1).
49. Ibid., Section 39(2).
50. Ibid., Section 41.
51. Ibid.
52. Ibid.
53. Report of the Committee on Controls and Subsidies, Ministry of Finance, Government of India, May 1969, p.373.
54. Ibid., 'Summary of Findings and Recommendations', p.li.
55. Ibid.
56. The MRTP Act 1969 (as amended by the Amendment Act of 1985), Section 36A.

10 Growth, performance and pricing of public enterprises in India

In the case of a private enterprise, growth is directly related to performance, and both depend, to a large extent, on the prices of inputs as well as on the finished products which determine the costs incurred and the profits obtained by it, and therefore its profitability. While growth is indicated by increases in size, output, scale of operations, coverage of the market, etc., good performance is reflected in increases in productivity, lowering of costs and the earning of profits or the generation of surpluses which provide the funds or investible resources for further growth; and both growth and performance are functions of prices, which have to be taken as given under perfectly competitive conditions, or influenced in various ways and in varying degrees, depending on the nature and degree of imperfection of competition, so as to yield maximum profit under any given conditions. These interrelationships among growth, performance and prices essentially arise because the driving force or the chief motive behind the activities of a private entrepreneur, or private enterprises generally, is the desire to earn maximum possible profits. In the case of enterprises in the public sector, which are owned or controlled by the government, these interrelationships generally do not hold good because the profit motive is replaced by the desire to achieve certain other objectives which need not necessarily be consistent with maximization of profits of any individual enterprise; and also because the vision and perspective of public enterprises may be much wider and longer. This may create a rather curious situation where public sector enterprises might be growing despite incurring losses or earning such small profit as would have made hardly any growth possible in a private enterprise; and yet it may be necessary to have such enterprises and to keep them growing or even multiplying. Growth may become autonomous or independent of performance or profitability, and performance considered a relatively less relevant factor under certain conditions; and pricing may sometimes be consciously carried out in a manner which does not enable the enterprise to earn profits and generate internal surpluses which could be used for its own growth.

In the underdeveloped countries, the growth of public investment and the public sector may be autonomous, particularly in the initial stages of economic growth. These countries are generally in 'the vicious circle of poverty', which Ragner Nurkse describes as 'a circular constellation of forces tending to act and react on one another in such a way as to keep a poor country in a state of poverty',[1] which 'exists on both sides of the problem of capital formation in the poverty-ridden areas of the world'[2]

> On the supply side, there is small capacity to save, resulting from the low level of income. The low real income is a reflection of low productivity, which in its turn is due largely to lack of capital. The lack of capital is a result of the small capacity to save, and so the circle is complete.[3]

Similarly,

> on the demand side, the inducement to invest may be low because of the small buying power of the people, which again is due to low productivity. The low level of productivity, however, is a result of the small amount of capital used in production, which in its turn may be caused at least partly by the small inducement to invest.[4]

The crucial factor in this vicious circle is investment, which can break the circle on both the supply as well as the demand side. Economic growth is basically a function of investment, which generates incomes and therefore both the capacity to save and the incentive for further investment. But the climate or the conditions in an underdeveloped country may not be congenial to investment. Lack of infrastructural facilities such as transport and communications, and critical inputs such as steel, power, irrigation, fertilizers etc., as well as a limited market, due to generally very low income levels, constitute major obstacles to investment and growth.

Creation of the required infrastructure requires large and costly investments in projects such as the construction of roads, bridges, and irrigation dams, hydro and thermal power generating stations, steel and fertilizer plants, etc. — all of which have long gestation periods, and which, being unrelated to existing consumer demand, do not yield immediate financial gains. Private entrepreneurs may have neither the required resources nor the incentive to invest in such ventures; and unless these investments are made and the required infrastructure created, the marginal productivity of capital may be low, discouraging private investment. Autonomous public investment in such a situation creates the proper economic environment or investment climate for the growth of private investment by removing the obstacles indicated above and also by expanding the market by means of the incomes generated in the process. Rapid growth of investment in the public sector and in the share of the public sector in the national income and capital formation is thus inherent in any process of planned development of this kind in an underdeveloped country.

The problems created in the course of this development, though not directly related to price controls or pricing policy in the sense in which the term is generally used, do indicate the direction in which some thinking needs to be done in regard to the pricing of the products of public enterprises by the enterprises themselves (where such enterprises are run by independent corporations), or by the government (in the case of departmental enterprises) in market situations where they have the power to determine or significantly influence the market prices of their products.

In India coverage of public sector enterprises is very wide. They cover the basic or 'core' industries like steel, minerals and metals, coal, and petroleum and other vital industries such as fertilizers, pharmaceuticals, heavy engineering, medium and light engineering, transportation equipment, textiles and agro-based products. The public sector also contains enterprises rendering services like trading, marketing, construction, transport and technical consultancy. Tourism and financial services are also provided by public sector enterprises. Public enterprises in India provide infrastructural facilities, intermediate products and critical inputs as well as consumer goods (e.g. bread, leather goods, footwear, paper and

Table 15 *Growth of investment in the public and private sectors over different plan periods* (in Rs crores)

	Private sector	Public sector	Total
1951–56	1,800	1,560	3,360
1956–61	3,100	3,731	6,831
1961–66	4,100	6,300	10,400
1969–74	8,980	13,655	22,635
1974–79	27,048	36,703	63,751
1980–85	74,710	84,000	158,710

Source: Department of Economic Affairs, Ministry of Finance, Government of India

textiles). The coverage is so wide that these enterprises include all kinds of market situations too — competitive, monopolistic and oligopolistic.

Investment in the public sector has been growing steadily and now constitutes more than half of the total planned investment in the economy over different plan periods. Table 15 brings out this position. Over the plan period 1980–85, planned investment in the public sector would be of the order of Rs 84,000 crores, which is larger than the investment envisaged in the private sector (Rs 74,710 crores).

Table 16 shows annual compound growth rates (ACGR) over different plan periods, and it can be seen that the ACGR of the public sector, both in terms of GDP as well as GDCF, has been significantly higher than in the private sector (except for plan period 1965–66 to 1968–69 when the public sector recorded a negative growth rate). GDS has also grown faster in the public sector over the plan periods 1960–61 to 1965–66, 1973–74 to 1978–79 and 1978–79 to 1982–83. That the public sector has been expanding at a much faster rate is confirmed by the data relating to the growth of the net domestic product (NDP) and net domestic capital formation (NDCF) also, as shown in Table 17.

Because of a higher growth rate, the share of the public sector in the GDP, GDS and GDCF has been increasing over different plan periods. Figures in Table 18 show that the public sector's share in the

Table 16 *Annual compound growth rates of gross domestic product, gross domestic savings and gross domestic capital formation in public and private sectors over different plan periods (at current prices)*

	Gross domestic product at factor cost			Gross domestic savings			Gross domestic capital formation		
	Public sector	Private sector	Total	Public sector	Private sector	Total	Public sector	Private sector	Total
1965–66/1960–61	14.0	8.8	9.4	13.7	12.7	12.9	13.9	9.4	11.5
1968–69/1965–66	13.0	11.3	11.5	2.0	8.8	7.4	-0.6	10.4	5.2
1973–74/1968–69	13.2	11.8	12.0	16.1	20.1	19.4	17.5	17.1	17.3
1978–79/1973–74	17.0	8.7	10.1	21.5	15.0	16.1	14.9	15.2	15.1
1982–83/1978–79	18.7	12.3	13.6	11.7	10.9	11.1	19.8	11.6	15.2

Source: 'National Accounts Statistics', Central Statistical Organization, Government of India

GDP as well as GDCF has been growing steadily over different plan periods; and the public sector accounted for about one-quarter of the GDP and half of the GDCF in 1982–83. This position is more or less confirmed if we look at the figures of NDP and NDCF over the period 1970–71 to 1981–82 in Table 19.

Table 17 *Percentage growth rates of net domestic product and net domestic capital formation over the period 1970/71 to 1981–82 (at current prices)*

	Net domestic product			Net domestic capital formation		
	Public sector	Private sector	Total	Public sector	Private sector	Total
Average annual growth rate	16.87	11.53	12.33	19.71	15.73	16.91
Annual compound growth rate (1981–82 over 1970–71)	16.21	11.30	12.16	18.41	14.15	16.28

Source: 'National Accounts Statistics', Central Statistical Organization, Government of India

Table 18 *Growth of share of public sector in gross domestic product, gross domestic savings and gross domestic capital formation over different plan periods (at current prices)*

	Percentage share of the public sector		
	Gross domestic product at factor cost	Gross domestic savings	Gross domestic capital formation
1960–61	10.9	20.6	44.7
1965–66	13.4	21.3	49.7
1968–69	14.0	18.3	42.0
1973–74	14.8	15.9	42.4
1978–79(P)	20.0	19.8	42.1
1979–80(P)	21.1	20.0	45.1
1982–83(Q)	23.8	20.3	49.1

(P) Provisional
(Q) 'Quick Estimates of National Income, etc.'
Sources: 'National Accounts Statistics', and 'Quick Estimates of National Income, etc.', Central Statistical Organization, Government of India

As pointed out earlier, in India public sector growth is not confined to any particular sphere of economic activity or sector of the economy, and covers almost all spheres or sectors. Table 20 shows how the public sector has been expanding in primary (consisting mainly of agriculture, forestry, fishing, mining, etc.), secondary (manufacture, construction, electricity, gas and water supply, etc.), transport, communications and trade (including railways) and other sectors of the economy, and its share in these sectors has been increasing over different plan periods. Over the period 1960–61 to 1981–82, the share of the public sector in GDCF increased from 31.5 per cent to 44.3 per cent in the 'Primary', 39.0 to 51.3 per cent in the 'Secondary', 45.8 to 50.0 per cent in 'Transport, communications and trade', and 44.5 to 47.7 per cent in 'Finance, community and personal services' sectors of the economy. On the whole, the public sector accounts for more than half the total capital formation in the economy.

Table 21 shows that, whereas GDCF as percentage of GDP in the

Table 19 Growth in the percentage share of the public sector in net domestic product and net domestic capital formation, 1970–71 to 1981–82 (at current prices)

	Percentage share of public sector	
	Net domestic product	Net domestic capital formation
1970–71	14.51	45.33
1971–72	15.25	44.06
1972–73	15.32	57.46
1973–74	14.24	49.08
1974–75	15.35	45.15
1975–76	18.25	55.21
1976–77	19.97	56.95
1977–78	19.19	46.22
1978–79	19.84	48.36
1979–80	20.93	52.50
1980–81	20.35	51.13
1981–82	21.42	55.38

Source: 'National Accounts Statistics', Central Statistical Organization, Government of India

Table 20 Growth in the share of the public sector in gross domestic capital formation, 1960–61 to 1981–82 (at 1970–71 prices)

	Percentage share of the public sector in the GDFC				
	Primary sector	Secondary sector	Transport, communication and trade	Finance community and personal services	Total
1960–61	31.5	39.0	45.8	44.5	40.4
1965–66	30.5	49.1	74.6	37.3	46.1
1968–69	32.9	54.5	73.2	20.5	41.6
1973–74	33.6	45.1	40.1	42.7	41.2
1978–79	36.9	44.5	42.9	36.0	40.8
1979–80	44.1	48.8	46.6	50.0	47.7
1981–82	44.3	51.3	50.0	47.7	48.9

Source: 'National Accounts Statistics', Central Statistical Organization, Government of India

Public enterprises in India   181

Table 21 *Growth of gross domestic capital formation as percentage of gross domestic product in public and private sectors over different plan periods*

	GDCF in the public sector as % of GDP in that sector	GDCF in the private sector as % of GDP in that sector	Total GDCF As % of total GDP
1960–61	73.9	11.2	18.1
1965–66	73.8	11.6	19.9
1968–69	50.2	11.3	16.7
1973–74	60.5	14.3	21.1
1978–79(P)	55.3	19.1	26.3
1979–80(P)	58.9	19.2	27.6
1982–83(Q)	57.4	18.6	27.9

(P) Provisional
(Q) 'Quick Estimates'
Sources: 'National Accounts Statistics' and 'Quick Estimates of National Income, etc.', Central Statistical Organization, Government of India

Table 22 *Annual compound growth rates of gross fixed capital formation in the public and private sectors over different plan periods (at current prices)*

	Public sector	Private sector	Total
1955–56/1950–51	18.9	0.1	5.8
1960–61/1955–56	14.6	8.1	10.9
1965–66/1960–61	14.2	13.6	13.9
1968–69/1965–66	1.0	16.1	9.2
1973–74/1968–69	13.7	9.0	10.9
1978–79/1973–74	16.1	15.6	15.8
1981–82/1978–79	19.8	13.6	16.4

Source: 'National Accounts Statistics', Central Statistical Organization, Government of India

public sector has varied between 50 and 74, the corresponding figures in the private sector have been 11 and 19, and in the economy as a whole, 17 and 29 (after rounding up the figures). This clearly indicates that most of the production in the public sector has been of capital goods for building up the capital base of the economy and thereby increasing the economy's capacity for sustained growth. This conclusion is supported by the fact that the growth rate of the gross fixed capital formation has been much higher in the public sector than in the private sector or in the economy as a whole. This is brought out in Table 22, which shows that, except for the period 1965–66 to 1968–69, the growth rate of gross fixed capital formation has been considerably higher in the public sector over different plan periods as compared to the private sector or the total economy. Owing to this higher growth rate, the share of the public sector in the gross fixed capital formation, particularly 'Construction' and 'Machinery and equipment', has been steadily increasing since the inception of planning in the post-independence period, as is revealed by Table 23.

Table 23 also shows that the public sector has roughly accounted

Table 23 *Growth in share of public sector in the gross fixed capital formation in India over different plan periods (at current prices)*

	Percentage share in total gross fixed capital formation		
	Construction	Machinery and equipment	Total
1950–51	23.18	22.82	23.09
1955–56	52.22	23.26	41.54
1960–61	50.56	46.28	48.93
1965–66	58.35	37.75	49.52
1968–69	38.94	39.80	39.27
1973–74	52.52	34.59	44.38
1978–79	49.88	38.97	44.93
1979–80	55.49	40.06	47.96
1981–82	55.88	41.42	48.93

Source: 'National Accounts Statistics', Central Statistical Organization, Government of India

Table 24 *Growth in the share of public enterprises in net domestic product and net domestic capital formation, 1970–71 to 1981–82 (at current prices)*

	Percentage share of public enterprises			
	Net domestic product (NDP)	NDP in public sector	Net domestic capital formation	NDCF in public sector
1970–71	7.5	50.0	34.0	75.0
1971–72	7.9	52.0	31.8	72.1
1972–73	8.1	52.8	34.1	66.4
1973–74	7.7	54.3	33.2	67.6
1974–75	9.0	56.6	35.3	78.2
1975–76	10.7	58.5	45.4	82.1
1976–77	12.3	61.3	47.1	82.6
1977–78	11.8	61.5	37.5	81.2
1978–79	12.2	61.6	37.8	78.2
1979–80	13.0	62.3	39.4	75.5
1980–81	12.4	61.1	37.9	74.1
1981–82	13.5	63.3	41.9	75.7

Source: 'National Accounts Statistics', Central Statistical Organization, Government of India

for more than 50 per cent of construction, about 40 per cent of machinery and equipment and nearly 49 per cent of the total fixed capital formation in India in recent years.

The public sector consists broadly of 'Administrative departments', 'Departmental enterprises' and 'Non-departmental enterprises', the latter two being generally referred to as 'Public enterprises'. Table 24 indicates the growth in the share of 'Public enterprises' in the NDP and NDCF. Public enterprises have accounted for more than 75 per cent of the NDCF of the public sector, nearly 40 per cent of the NDCF of the entire economy, more than 60 per cent of the NDP in the public sector and around 13 per cent of NDP in the entire economy in recent years; and these percentage shares have been growing over more than a decade.

Since the rate of fixed capital formation has been higher in the public sector (Table 22), and its share in total gross fixed capital formation has been increasing, and been nearly 50 per cent in recent years (Table 23), the total capital employed (fixed and working capital) in the public enterprises has also been growing rapidly. Table 25 brings out this position. Table 25 also shows that over the ten-year period 1973–74 to 1982–83, total capital employed increased by nearly five-and-a-half times (from Rs 5,256.40 crores to Rs 28,589.90 crores), capital employed in enterprises producing goods by nearly five times (from Rs 3,767.74 crores to Rs 17,948.41 crores), and capital employed in the enterprises rendering services by about six times (Rs 1,488.66 crores to Rs 8,605.49 crores). The increase in capital employed has also resulted in a considerable increase in capital employed per employee, and also in the productivity of both labour and capital, as reflected in value added per employee and the percentage of value added to capital employed. This is borne out by the figures in Table 26, which show that, over the four-year period 1978–79 to 1982–83, capital employed per employee nearly doubled, value added per employee more than doubled, and the

Table 25 *Capital employed in public enterprises, 1973–74 to 1982–83 (in Rs crores)*

	Enterprises producing goods	Enterprises rendering services	Total
1973–74	3,767.74	1,488.66	5,256.40
1974–75	4,634.84	1,992.31	6,627.15
1975–76	5,530.79	3,293.51	8,824.30
1976–77	6,472.41	4,389.00	10,861.41
1977–78	6,570.42	4,834.24	11,404.66
1978–79	7,175.71	5,653.20	12,828.91
1979–80	10,213.41	6,140.46	16,353.87
1980–81	12,100.95	6,106.28	18,207.23
1981–82	14,777.91	7,156.71	21,934.62
1982–83	17,948.41	8,605.49	28,589.90

Source: 'Public Enterprises Survey', Bureau of Public Enterprises, Government of India

Table 26 *Capital employed and value added in public enterprises producing and selling goods, 1978–79, 1981–82 and 1982–83 (in rupees)*

	Capital employed per employee	Value added per employee	Percentage of value added to capital employed
1978–79	54,030	20,066	37.1
1981–82	90,030	36,479	40.5
1982–83	101,743	47,207	46.4

Source: 'Public Enterprises Survey' — various issues, Bureau of Public Enterprises, Government of India

percentage of value added to capital employed also increased significantly (from 37.1 per cent to 46.4 per cent). Thus, increases in capital employed per employee have been enhancing the productivity of both capital and labour. There is, however, some empirical evidence that the public sector has been using more fixed capital relative to labour, and has also been having a higher capital value added ratio than the private sector, indicating higher and rising capital intensity. Table 27 brings out this position.

Table 27 *Fixed capital and value added in public and private sectors, 1973–74 to 1977–78 (in rupees)*

	Fixed capital per employee		Capital value added ratio	
	Public sector	Private sector	Public sector	Private sector
1973–74	47,392	8,678	6.09	1.09
1974–75	51,150	9,531	5.14	0.96
1975–76	54,311	10,860	4.83	1.13
1976–77	64,382	10,500	5.00	1.02
1977–78	74,590	11,188	5.81	1.01

Source: 'Annual Survey of Industries', Central Statistical Organization, Government of India

(a) Capital intensity in the sense of use of fixed capital relative to labour has been much higher and has also been increasing more rapidly in the public sector than in the private sector.
(b) The productivity of capital has been much lower in the public than in the private sector, as indicated by a much higher Capital value added ratio in the public sector.
(c) Although the productivity of capital has been rising somewhat in both the public and the private sectors, as reflected in slightly falling Capital value added ratio in both, there is as yet no such marked tendency.

A higher capital labour ratio or greater use of capital relative to labour (as reflected in higher and rising figures of fixed capital per employee) in the public sector has understandably resulted in diminishing returns to capital, causing a higher capital value added ratio. The somewhat declining Capital value added ratio in the public sector could possibly be accounted for by the fact that, with the increase in the Capital employed per employee, Value added per employee has also been increasing, as brought out in Table 26.

Rising capital intensity or greater use of fixed capital relative to labour is also reflected in the changes in the cost structure of public enterprises. Table 28 brings out the position in this regard and shows an increasing material content and slightly declining labour content in public enterprises in several sectors, such as steel, petroleum, transportation equipment, minerals and metals, chemicals, fertilizers and pharmaceuticals, and medium and light engineering industries.

Higher capital intensity in the public sector could possibly be explained by two factors. Firstly, as the figures in Table 21 show, GDCF has been between 50 and 74 per cent of GDP in the public sector, as against 11 and 19 per cent in the private sector, which shows that the public sector's output has consisted largely of capital goods which may require more capital to produce. These capital goods may have been produced by the use of imported technology involving greater use of fixed capital. A higher rate of fixed capital formation in the public sector (as shown in Table 22) and the fact that the public sector accounts for nearly half of the fixed capital formation in the economy (as brought out in Table 23) also help to explain higher capital intensity. The composition of output from the public sector itself has been such that relatively more capital has had

Table 28 *Changes in the cost structure of public enterprises producing goods*

	Percentage material content			Percentage labour content		
	1978–79	1981–82	1982–83	1978–79	1981–82	1982–83
Steel	36.2	56.4	54.5	15.5	13.4	13.2
Minerals and metals	24.6	27.9	24.6	18.2	18.1	17.5
Coal	9.9	15.3	15.4	54.0	56.4	46.0
Petroleum	34.9	88.0	86.3	1.1	0.9	1.0
Chemicals, fertilizers and pharmaceuticals	35.8	46.2	45.1	8.3	6.5	6.9
Heavy engineering	51.0	57.4	56.4	18.5	19.1	18.2
Medium and light engineering	51.2	55.0	55.6	23.6	21.8	22.9
Transportation equipment	44.7	56.0	57.7	28.6	22.4	17.9
Consumer goods	59.5	63.1	51.8	15.3	11.6	20.2
Agro-based products	13.1	48.0	46.1	22.2	25.4	27.1
Textiles	49.6	47.6	49.3	25.1	28.0	33.7

Source: 'Public Enterprises Survey', Bureau of Public Enterprises, Government of India

to be used to produce it. Secondly, the public sector has been expanding in the 'core' sector, such as in steel, fertilizers, heavy engineering, transportation equipment, petroleum, etc., and also creating infra-structural facilities required for industrial growth involving greater use of capital relative to other factors.

As pointed out earlier, the growth of the public sector is largely autonomous and not necessarily a consequence of the profitability and internal generation of resources required for growth. This is due to the absence of profit motive and the availability of funds required for expansion and growth from the budgetary resources of the government. Table 29 indicates the position regarding net profit/loss in public enterprises over the decade 1973–74 to 1982–83. Public enterprises had been earning very small profits (considering the investment made in the public sector, as shown in Table 15), or even incurring losses. The enterprises producing goods had actually been incurring losses continuously for four years — 1977–78 to 1980–81

Table 29 *Net profit/loss in public enterprises, 1973–74 to 1982–83 (in Rs crores)*

	Enterprises producing goods	Enterprises rendering services	Total
1973–74	25.54	38.88	64.42
1974–75	138.77	54.78	183.55
1975–76	209.19	96.46	305.65
1976–77	289.13	166.64	455.77
1977–78	−16.15	78.70	62.55
1978–79	−82.14	42.55	−40.09
1979–80	−78.51	4.23	−74.23
1980–81	−185.02	−17.95	−202.97
1981–82	381.33	64.59	445.92
1982–83	594.01	23.84	617.85

Source: 'Public Enterprises Survey' — various issues, Bureau of Public Enterprises, Government of India

— after which they recorded a small profit. Taking all public enterprises together also, the position is substantially the same. Table 30 shows the position relating to enterprises producing and selling goods, and it appears that, except for petroleum, medium and light engineering and agro-based products, public enterprises in all other industries have been continuously incurring losses.

Table 31 indicates the relative profitability of public and private enterprises over the period 1972–73 to 1978–79. Profitability (expressed in terms of net profit or percentage of net worth) in the private sector has been much higher than in the public sector. In the private sector it has ranged roughly between 8 and 14 per cent, while in the public sector the range has been between −2 and 6 per cent over the seven-year period 1972–73 to 1978–79. Whereas the public sector has been continuously incurring losses ranging between −23.49 and −2.06 per cent, the private sector (mining and quarrying) has been earning a small to reasonable profit, except for the year 1977–78, when it incurred losses. In the manufacturing and processing sector, public enterprises have earned a small profit in most of these years, as against continuous profits ranging between 7.54 and 13.25 per cent by the private enterprises.

Table 30 *Net profit as a percentage of net worth in enterprises producing and selling goods*

	1973–74	1978–79	1981–82	1982–83
Steel	L	1.8	L	L
Minerals and metals	L	0.1	L	L
Coal	n.a.	n.a.	5.97	L
Petroleum	9.8	16.6	30.44	32.7
Chemicals, fertilizers and pharmaceuticals	L	L	L	L
Heavy engineering	12.6	L	L	L
Medium and light engineering	8.1	7.5	13.74	14.9
Transportation equipment	7.9	L	L	L
Consumer goods	L	0.0	L	L
Agro-based products	13.9	L	10.29	4.8
Textiles	n.a.	n.a.	L	L

L — Losses
n.a. — Not available
Source: 'Public Enterprises Survey' — various issues, Bureau of Public Enterprises, Government of India

Table 31 *Profitability (net profit as a percentage of net worth) of public enterprises, 1972–73 and 1978–79*

	Mining and quarrying		Manufacturing and processing		Total	
	Public enterprises	Private enterprises	Public enterprises	Private enterprises	Public enterprises	Private enterprises
1972–73	−2.06	4.92	−3.27	10.65	−2.03	10.34
1973–74	−6.23	4.26	2.00	12.15	1.97	11.87
1974–75	−7.92	14.80	6.17	13.25	5.85	13.67
1975–76	−3.05	13.51	3.46	7.54	3.49	8.24
1976–77	−1.76	10.73	4.46	7.53	4.15	7.87
1977–78	−17.83	−8.52	−1.04	8.58	−2.43	8.78
1978–79	−23.49	2.56	1.05	12.80	−1.69	11.46

Source: Reserve Bank of India Bulletins

Table 32 *Changes in net worth as a percentage of capital employed*

	Enterprises producing goods	Enterprises rendering services	Total
1973–74	70.89	35.55	60.87
1974–75	67.12	33.50	57.01
1975–76	67.64	23.45	57.47
1976–77	69.44	21.01	49.87
1977–78	77.74	21.98	53.93
1978–79	77.55	20.36	52.35
1979–80	60.25	18.28	44.49
1980–81	60.95	22.33	47.20
1981–82	64.71	18.29	48.74
1982–83	64.41	16.40	47.63

Source: 'Public Enterprises Survey', Bureau of Public Enterprises, Government of India

Low and declining profitability in public enterprises is also reflected in low and falling net worth as a percentage of capital employed. Table 32 brings out this position. It can be seen that net worth as a percentage of capital employed has, on the whole, been declining over the decade 1973–74 to 1982–83, the fall being more

Table 33 *Internal resources as a percentage of total resources in public and private enterprises, 1972–73 to 1978–79*

	Mining and quarrying		Manufacturing and procesing		Total	
	Public enterprises	Private enterprises	Public enterprises	Private enterprises	Public enterprises	Private enterprises
1972–73	19.22	36.86	33.33	79.55	28.30	72.27
1973–74	10.36	56.00	25.81	55.37	24.75	51.14
1974–75	5.86	43.98	26.02	47.32	22.31	45.99
1975–76	n.a.	23.77	n.a.	45.27	n.a.	42.60
1976–77	17.37	11.51	33.42	44.07	31.71	44.14
1977–78	−11.44	3.29	25.81	42.89	16.08	41.62
1978–79	−19.88	88.95	17.96	45.87	12.82	42.96

n.a. — Not available
Source: Reserve Bank of India Bulletins

marked in the case of enterprises rendering services.

Because of low and declining profitability and net worth, the internal resources generated in the public sector have also been smaller, and declining relative to the private sector, as Table 33 indicates. Internal resources as a percentage of total resources have generally been at a much lower level and falling more steeply in the case of public enterprises than in private enterpises.

A low and declining level of internal resources (which is a direct consequence of generally low and falling profitability), coupled with relatively easier availability of financial accommodation from government and other sources is also reflected in rising 'Loans and deferred credit' as a percentage of net worth in the case of public enterprises. Table 34 reveals how the percentage has been rising rather steeply in the case of 'Enterprises rendering services'; but the percentage has on the whole been increasing in the case of 'Enterprises producing goods' as well; and the position is the same if all the public enterprises are considered together.

Another aspect on which the available statistical data throw some light in the rather steep increases in inventories in public enterprises in recent years, as Table 35 indicates. Total inventories in the public sector nearly doubled over the four-year period 1978–79 to 1982–83 (from Rs 726,941 lakhs to Rs 1,379,288), the largest increase being in

Table 34 *Loans and deferred credit as a percentage of net worth in public enterprises, 1973–74 to 1979–80*

Year	Enterprises producing goods	Enterprises rendering services	Total
1973–74	77.01	139.23	87.30
1974–75	80.57	137.45	90.62
1975–76	73.06	161.88	86.58
1976–77	91.41	158.49	102.83
1977–78	79.95	162.63	94.23
1978–79	72.89	182.02	91.59
1979–80	100.76	241.36	122.45

Source: 'Public Enterprises Survey', Bureau of Public Enterprises, Government of India

Table 35 Growth of inventories in public enterprises (Rs lakhs)

	Enterprises producing and selling			Enterprises rendering services			Total		
	Raw materials	Finished products	Total	Raw materials	Finished products	Total	Raw materials	Finished products	Total
1978–79	87,541	115,399	421,238	15,441	244,317	305,703	102,982	359,716	726,941
1981–82	207,166	266,173	852,843	11,125	277,859	372,197	218,291	544,032	1,225,040
1982–83	197,681	327,197	967,233	16,860	292,706	412,055	214,541	619,903	1,379,288

Source: 'Public Enterprises Survey', Bureau of Public Enterprises, Government of India

the case of 'Finished products', which increased nearly three times over this period (from Rs 115,399 lakhs to Rs 327,197 lakhs). This is a significant aspect of the working of public enterprises, since inability to sell, resulting in the growth of inventories of 'Finished products', could possibly be one of the causal factors responsible for their relatively low profitability.

As indicated above, the low profitability and low generation of internal resources in the public sector has not adversely affected the growth of the public sector. Obviously, funds for growing investment in public enterprises have come from the public exchequer, necessitating higher taxation. It is true that the need for higher taxation might have arisen as a result of several factors, including rising developmental expenditure; but the need to sustain the growth of an expanding public sector by autonomous investment and financial support may also have been an important factor in creating the need to raise more resources through taxation (see Table 35).

Table 36 shows that total tax revenue as a percentage of net domestic product at market price has gone up from about 14 per cent in 1974–75 to nearly 18 per cent in 1982–83, most of the increased revenue coming from indirect taxes (which increased from a little over 11 per cent to about 15 per cent over this period), the burden of which falls generally on the common man.

Table 36 *Growth of tax revenue as a percentage of net domestic product at market price, 1974–75 to 1982–83*

	Direct tax	Indirect tax	Total
1974–75	2.78	11.18	13.96
1975–76	3.56	12.41	15.97
1976–77	3.42	12.91	16.33
1977–78	3.16	12.47	15.63
1978–79	3.10	13.81	16.91
1979–80	3.08	14.53	17.61
1980–81	2.73	13.88	16.61
1981–82	2.98	14.40	17.38
1982–83	2.99	14.92	17.91

Source: Department of Economic Affairs, Ministry of Finance, Government of India

The tables in this chapter and the accompanying analysis contain empirical evidence of the following facts:

(a) Owing to the large autonomous investments made by the government, the public sector in India has been growing faster than the private sector and now accounts for nearly one-quarter of its GDP and half its GDCF. The share of public enterprises in the public sector has also been growing, and is nearly two-thirds of its output and three-quarters of its capital formation.

(b) GDCF in the public sector, as a percentage of GDP in that sector, which was about 74 per cent in the mid to late sixties, has now declined to nearly 60 per cent, the corresponding figures for the private sector being roughly 11 and 19 per cent. This indicates that the investment in the public sector has been mostly in building up the capital base or infrastructure required for the growth of the entire economy. This has also caused a higher rate of Gross fixed capital formation (GFCF) and an increasing share of the public sector in the GFCF of the entire economy — from less than one quarter in the early fifties, the share has increased to nearly half in recent years. This also explains the facts that the capital employed in public enterprises increased by nearly five-and-a-half times over the ten-year period 1973-74 to 1982-83, that capital employed per employee nearly doubled over the period 1978-79 to 1982-83 and that capital intensity (in the sense of fixed capital per employee) and capital value added ratio have been much higher in the public than in the private sector; and there is also some evidence of somewhat declining labour and rising material content in the cost structure of some of the public enterprises in recent years, for which data are available.

(c) The profitability of public enterprises has been very low, and they have generally been incurring losses. In some industries for which comparable data are available, profitability in public enterprises has been much lower than in private enterprises, and in some cases even negative as compared to positive and reasonably high levels of profit in the private sector. This is also reflected in comparatively much lower and declining internal resources as a percentage of total resources in the public as compared to the private sector in some industries for which comparable data are available; and also in declining net worth as

a percentage of capital employed and rising Loans and deferred credit as a percentage of net worth in public enterprises in recent years.
(d) Inventories of both raw materials and finished products have been growing rather rapidly in public enterprises, particularly of finished products, in recent years — involving the locking up of considerable funds.
(e) Large investments in the public sector, and their continued very low profitability and losses in several cases, could possibly have been an important contributory factor in compelling the government to resort to higher and higher taxation, particularly indirect taxation.

In any assessment or appraisal of the performance of public enterprises, and any analysis of the implications thereof, certain distinctive features of the public sector have to be kept in view. Firstly, the public sector has been playing the crucial role of creating a congenial climate and conditions for continuous and self-sustained growth, and acting as a catalyst for change, by creating the basic infrastructure and providing the critical inputs required for growth. Mere profitability may, therefore, not be an appropriate measure of the performance of public enterprises, and it may be necessary to consider their impact on the general industrial growth of the economy by removing the obstacles to growth and productivity. Secondly, in some sectors (for example steel and heavy engineering), the development of indigenous capability itself may be considered a significant achievement, although such ventures may not be profitable initially for a considerable time. Thirdly, in several cases, long gestation periods and low capacity utilization after commissioning owing to demand constraint, or scarce and sometimes irregular and somewhat uncertain supply of imported raw materials, spares, parts and components could lower profitability. Fourthly, many projects in the public sector have been based on imported technology developed in capital-rich countries, involving greater use of capital relative to labour and other factors, which raises capital intensity and does not, in the short run at least, generate more employment and make greater use of labour, which is generally an abundantly available resource in developing countries. The development of indigenous technology or the adaptation of imported technology to suit the factor endowment of a capital-poor country with vast reserves of unemployed or under-employed manpower is essentially a slow and long-term process.

One basic question which arises in regard to the performance of public enterprises is, what are the causal factors which could explain or account for the low profitability of public enterprises in India? The answer to this question could provide clues for remedial measures, or indicate the change in policy called for to improve the position. Another related question is, to what extent is the pricing policy relating to the products of public enterprises responsible for the losses they have been incurring, and what approach needs to be adopted in regard to the pricing of the products of the public enterprises?

Public enterprises may fall, broadly, into two categories, namely those producing price-controlled commodities and those engaged in the production or manufacture of non-price-controlled commodities. If the commodity produced by a public enterprise is under formal or informal price control, the controlled price can cause low profitability or even losses, depending on the extent to which it covers the average costs (including reasonable margins of profit) of the public enterprise producing it, irrespective of whether such an enterprise is in a competitive, monopolistic or oligopolistic situation. In cases where private enterprises are also producing such a commodity, and are able to break even or earn a profit, the failure of a public enterprise to make a profit or its actually incurring losses indicates its inefficiency, which could be due to a variety of reasons. But, in such cases, there could obviously be no question of any pricing policy of the public enterprises themselves having an adverse effect on their performance and profitability. This could not be said about the public enterprises producing or manufacturing non-price-controlled commodities. In the case of these public enterprises, their pricing policy (if they are allowed the freedom to fix the prices of their products), or the pricing policy and procedures relating to their products followed by the government (in cases where the government, formally or informally, fixes prices or requires public enterprises themselves to fix prices in accordance with certain rules, frames or guidelines issued by the government) may significantly affect their profitability. In India, several public enterprises come into this category, and pricing policy may have been, to some extent, responsible for their low profitability.

Given the price, profits are ultimately a function of the efficiency of an enterprise, which, operationally, implies the ability to

(a) minimize average cost by using the most cost-effective technology available, producing at the optimum level of output and capacity utilization, maintaining an optimum level of inventories of all kinds, minimizing overhead costs and transport, distribution and selling costs, etc; and

(b) maximize sales by sales promotion measures.

In a monopolistic or oligopolistic situation where the price is fixed by public enterprises themselves, by the government, or in the case of a price-controlled commodity, the level at which the price is fixed, the speed and degree of its responsiveness to changing costs, and the methods and procedures followed in initial setting as well as subsequent revision of the price, are important factors affecting the profitability of public enterprises. But in several cases, the real and more significant factors which account for low profitability or losses could sometimes be other than low price setting, or the inadequate or delayed response of price to cost increases, or dilatory, complicated and cumbersome procedures followed in the determination and administration of the prices of the products of public enterprises. The real factors in such cases may be managerial inefficiency, high capital cost, high overheads, low technology, the relatively higher cost of the feedstock or raw materials used, uneconomical scale of output, low capacity utilization, low sales etc., which could possibly be due to some unsound or unimaginative policies adopted in regard to public enterprises. The pricing of the final product may thus not be the only villain of the piece, and the causal factors need to be carefully identified in each case and remedial action taken accordingly.

Generally speaking, some of the causal factors responsible for the rather poor performance of public enterprises in India, as reflected in their continued low profits or losses, in some cases at least, appear to be low capacity utilization, high overheads, low operational efficiency and lack of an aggressive sales promotion drive, causing unsold stocks to pile up. Many public sector units have been in the core sector, requiring large investments and imported technology, involving high capital costs and high costs of production for a considerable length of time until they achieve reasonable levels of capacity utilization and scale of output. The overheads of these units may also have been quite high, though empirical evidence of this is not readily available. These units could perhaps, in course of time, start earning reasonable profits if the specific causes of their low profitability, in each individual case, are identified and the necessary remedial measures taken. But the same may not be true of some perpetually 'sick' units in the public sector (e.g. the textiles sector) whose sickness is not always entirely due to general industrial sickness or any recessionary tendencies in the industry or even managerial inefficiency, but to technological and other factors, for which no remedies can be found. Several of these units may initially have been in the private sector and have had to be taken over by the government in the public interest, but their 'sickness' has continued in the same or, in some cases, possibly in an aggravated form, in the post take-over phase also.

One point which needs to be made in this context relates to the general ethos or the motivating or driving force behind private and public enterprises. In the private corporate sector, where ownership and actual control and management have been almost completely separated, the driving force is still profit, which is taken to be the ultimate objective and the chief indicator of performance of an enterprise. The worth of the managerial personnel is also judged in terms of their contribution to the profitability of the enterprise, and generally they are remunerated and rewarded according to their worth in this sense. In public enterprises, although in the case of managerial personnel there is generally public accountability in a broad sense (as the performance of such enterprises could be a matter of public debate in various forums, including Parliament), managers of individual enterprises seem to have a somewhat protected and sheltered existence, as they can almost invariably explain and find reasons for the low profitability or losses of the enterprises they manage; and government may also find it necessary in some cases to defend their lack of performance or poor performance. Practically speaking, a certain indifference to results and an unresponsiveness or imperviousness to occasional criticism voiced within a system, which is rather slow to recognize and reward merit and good work, and perhaps slower and less inclined to detect lapses and shortcomings with a view to assessing responsibility and taking remedial action, seem to have considerably affected the concept of accountability in the case of public enterprises; and have tended to prolong or perpetuate the phase of their low profitability in several cases.

The basic problem relating to public enterprises in India is how to make them turn the corner and become efficient, profit-making concerns, generating and building up sufficient internal resources for their growth and development. This is not to imply that all public enterprises in India have been incurring losses, but there seems to be ample empirical evidence that, by and large, they have been performing rather poorly in terms of their profitability; and their continued growth has been largely the result of autonomous public investment and financial support from government rather than surpluses internally generated and ploughed back. While there may be certain causes peculiar to each individual enterprise which need to be studied and analysed, with a view to identifying them and taking suitable remedial measures, the following practical suggestions of a general nature could also be made in the light of the actual position which emerges from the empirical analysis and general observations made above:

(1) A realistic pricing policy needs to be adopted in regard to the pricing of public enterprises. By 'realistic policy' is meant a policy which recognizes the fundamental principle that a public enterprise is also a business enterprise which needs to be run, after a certain stage, on commercial lines, and not remain a perpetually loss-making concern. In the initial or promotional phase, when the cost of production may be high, possibly being in the trial stage, the capacity utilization gradually picking up, the economies of scale slowly accruing, and the market for the product getting gradually established, the price can perhaps be fixed at a level where the average cost is not fully covered, the difference being covered by government subsidy or else allowed to remain, causing actual loss. But the duration of this phase needs to be minimized, and the price fixed at a reasonable level as early as possible.

The implications of fixing the price at a remunerative level need to be spelt out. Broadly, it implies that the price fixed should cover the average cost fully, and also allow a reasonable margin of profit, or what is sometimes called 'normal profit', or else the profit earned by comparable private enterprises under fairly competitive conditions, or allowed by government price-fixing agencies to private enterprises in a monopolistic or oligopolistic position in the case of price-controlled commodities. In fact, the need for price setting would only arise in the case of public enterprises which were in a monopolistic or oligopolistic position producing a non-price-controlled commodity. Fixing the price of the products of such public enterprises in the manner indicated above also implies that there should be no subsidization of prices, which is a sound general principle which can only be relaxed in exceptional cases where subsidization is considered necessary to give protection to the vulnerable sections of the community to maintain their real incomes at a certain minimum level, or to some classes or categories of producers to enable them to get an essential input produced by a public enterprise at a reasonable price, to be able to survive in the market.

A question which arises in this context is whether public enterprises in a monopolistic situation need to make monopoly profits. There is, in fact, a range of output between the point of maximum profits (where marginal cost is equal to marginal revenue), and the break-even point (where price (average revenue), is equal to average cost (excluding profit)). A monopolist would normally fix his price at the point where his aggregate profits were maximized, i.e. where marginal revenue was equal to marginal cost. Assuming normal cost and demand functions (namely downward sloping demand or average revenue curve and a U-shaped average cost curve), the point of maximum profit would be that where price (average revenue) was higher than average cost, and the marginal cost lower than average cost. This implies that output at the point of maximum profits is lower than it would have been had it been pushed to the point where price is equal to average cost; and the average cost is also higher than it would have been, had production been allowed to increase to the point where the marginal cost became equal to average cost (the point of minimum average cost). It is thus clear that a monopolist could only maximize his profits by restricting output to a point where the marginal and average costs were still falling and the average cost was lower than the price. A monopolist might find that his profits were only maximized if he restricted output by not fully utilizing his production capacity, or by keeping it partly idle, which might not be in the public interest. In the case of public enterprises, where capacity is generally created by making large public investments, there would normally be no justification for keeping it idle in order to earn monopoly profit. Restriction of output by not fully utilizing installed capacity may defeat the very purpose of setting up public enterprises; and in the case of public enterprises producing capital goods or critical inputs, this pricing policy might even inhibit the overall industrial growth of the economy. Restriction of output and keeping capacity idle can only possibly be justified if it is found that, owing to incorrect demand projections, the capacity actually created is in excess of actual or projected demand; and that all the output at the level of full capacity utilization cannot possibly be sold. This may be a purely hypothetical situation, as in many cases even full capacity output may sometimes fall short of actual requirements.

It is argued that a public enterprise earning a monopolistic profit is analogous to levying a tax on a product, since they have the same effect, namely raising the price. Monopolistic pricing and taxation can in fact be considered as alternatives, the main difference being that whereas monopolistic pricing may increase the internal surpluses of the public enterprises concerned, taxation would directly increase the budgetary resources of the government. But, to the extent that the internal resources of the public enterprise are augmented, the need for financial support from government is reduced. However, monopolistic pricing cannot, in all cases, be advocated as a substitute for higher taxation: the deleterious effects such a pricing policy could conceivably have on the economy have to be kept in view.

The rationale of the view that the landed cost of comparable imported goods should be taken as the ceiling for the pricing of the products of public enterprises is also questionable. The landed cost of imported goods depends largely on the international conditions of demand and supply and the policies and practices followed by various countries in regard to their trade with other countries, and does not seem to have much relevance for the pricing of the products of public enterprises. While public enterprises must constantly endeavour to reduce their costs and prices, the prices of their products need not be pegged to the landed price of imported goods. A situation in which, despite the existence of indigenous capability to produce a commodity, that commodity is still being imported, would only arise if indigenous production is insufficient to meet domestic demand. The remedy in such cases lies not in artificially lowering the price of the product of a public enterprise to the level of the landed cost of its import (which may be lower than the average cost of the public enterprise owing to, among other things, different technological and other conditions under which it is produced in the countries it is imported from), but in adopting measures to sufficiently lower the costs to enable it to at least cover its average cost fully at that price. Landed costs of imports can thus only indicate the extent to which costs of indigenously produced goods need to be reduced, and need not be used to decide the levels at which the prices of products of public enterprises need to be fixed. Setting a lower price for the product of a public enterprise (in order to bring it down to the level of the landed cost of imports) may result in losses necessitating a subsidy or other financial support from government, and may not, therefore, be advisable.

Another basic question which arises is whether the prices of the products of public enterprises need to be fixed by government or whether any guidelines need to be given them regarding the manner in which they should fix their prices. While the basic considerations which should govern pricing decisions in a public enterprise (e.g. fuller utilization of installed capacity, availing of economies of scale as far as possible, meeting the existing or the projected demand as far as possible, generating enough surpluses to be able to pay loan and interest instalments and progressively reduce the need for subsidy of financial support from government, continuing R & D to evolve suitable technology or adapt existing technology to the needs and the factor endowment of the country, adopting measures to increase productivity and lower costs, etc.) can be spelt out, the actual price setting can be left to the management of the public enterprise itself. Pricing needs to be treated as a corporate management function, and management given full autonomy in fixing prices and made fully accountable for the performance of the enterprise. Apart from broadly indicating the general principles or considerations indicated above, there seems to be no need to give any instructions, guidelines or exhortations in particular cases; and the tendency of management in public enterprises to refer matters relating to pricing to the government for advice or approval also needs to be discouraged, so that no alibis or excuses are available to cover poor performance. Each public enterprise, or group of enterprises, can have a pricing cell consisting of economists, cost accountants and statisticians to collect and analyse the necessary data regarding costs and market conditions with a view either to initially determining the price or subsequently revising it, bearing in mind the broad principles indicated by government. All price decisions can be taken by the board of directors or by a subcommittee of them appointed by the board on the basis of the report of this cell. In the case of industries where a few public sector units produce the bulk of output (e.g. steel in India), there could be a common arrangement; and decisions could be taken by a joint committee consisting of representatives of each unit. This system might be more conducive to the health and growth of the public enterprises than government fixing prices and making subsequent adjustments to them to make them move in line with changing costs, sometimes in a possibly somewhat *ad hoc* manner with inevitable procedural delays, lagged and inadequate adjustments, and the consequent adverse effects on the profitability of the public enterprises concerned, and on the relative price strucutre of the economy.

(2) As a general rule, subsidization of the products of public enterprises needs to be minimized or avoided altogether. Besides being a drain on the budgetary resources of government, subsidies can also result in inequities, as their benefit may accrue in greater

measure to those who have more money to buy the subsidized products and who can subsequently even make illegitimate gains by reselling them. Cross-subsidization in the sense of one public enterprise subsidizing another (e.g. the supply of steel or any other critical input by one public enterprise to another) needs to be avoided, as it may cause a more liberal use of the subsidized input or product than warranted by its actual cost, and may distort the cost structure of those public enterprises using it. Wherever subsidies are considered necessary, they should be made directly available only to identified groups of consumers or users, so that their exact financial burden is known. Indirect or concealed subsidy in the form of fixing an unremunerative price could sometimes be of unintentional benefit to those classes or categories of consumers or users who do not need it; and its exact financial implications may not be properly assessed or appreciated. Moreover, any government subsidy scheme needs to be accompanied by a conscious policy and programme to eliminate the causes which necessitated it; and the subsidy tapered off over a specified period of time. Public enterprises need not (as a rule, with exceptions only in exceptionally deserving cases) be given concessionary finance, or such financial accommodation as the rescheduling of debts, conversion of debts into equity, or moratorium on recovery of loans, inasmuch as they constitute an outgoing of government funds, or a reduction therein. There seems to be no special advantage in this indirect subsidy as opposed to giving direct financial assistance as required, which is directly reflected in the government budget. These concealed subsidies may also, to some extent, conceal the real performance of the public enterprises which are the beneficiary *vis-à-vis* those enterprises in the public sector itself or in the private sector which are not their beneficiary. The availability of cheaper, long-term credit could possibly cause more liberal use of scarce financial resources, and also render cost estimates unrealistic inasmuch as they do not reflect the real costs to the economy.

(3) Profitability is ultimately a function of productivity. Increase in productivity or cost reduction is thus the ultimate remedy for the low profitability of public enterprises. Productivity depends on

several factors, such as availability of infra-structural facilities, state of technology, scale of output, managerial efficiency, labour/management relations and the overall industrial climate in the country. Technology is one of the most important factors affecting productivity. Relatively easy access to foreign technology which is suited to the factor endowment of the country may in some cases result in high costs, necessitating constant R & D efforts to adapt it to suit local needs and resources as much as possible; and to improve it, so as to make it more cost-effective. Technology and scale of output are generally interrelated, and capacity utilization and output may have to be kept at a certain minimum level to take full advantage of the technology adopted and the economies of scale. Managerial efficiency is the key factor in the functioning of an enterprise and a key input which affects the productivity of all other inputs. Proper selection of managerial personnel is necessary to ensure operational efficiency and a proper labour/management relationship, without which no industrial unit can run smoothly and profitably.

(4) Unlike the private sector, where competition may eliminate inefficient and high-cost units, these units may continue to survive in the public sector. Sometimes government pricing policy itself (e.g. setting of different cost-based retention prices for different units whose average costs are different owing to differences in technology and feedstocks, or any other factor) can enable high-cost units to survive over long periods without effecting any cost reduction to narrow the gap between their costs and the costs of other units. Government can sometimes take over a high-cost or sick unit in the private sector which may be on the verge of closure or liquidation owing to low profitability or losses, and continue running it as a losing concern. A positive policy, therefore, needs to be adopted by government in order to:

(i) identify high-cost or uneconomical units in the public sector whose costs cannot be reduced because of technological or other factors, and gradually phase them out;

(ii) abolish the system of different cost-based retention prices, phased over a reasonable period of time, so that those units which cannot even break even at a uniform price fixed on the basis of certain productivity and efficiency norms (which need to be suitably revised from time to time in the light of changing conditions of production), give way to the more efficient existing ones (which can expand), or the new ones (which can come up); and

(iii) diagnose the causes of the 'sickness' of individual units with a view to determining whether they could either be removed or restored to health, and take the necessary remedial measures, and generally refrain from taking over such units as are found to be incurably 'sick'.

(5) Since the driving force of the profit motive is virtually absent in the public sector, an organized and effective system of accountability at different technical and managerial levels should be characterized by:

(i) assignment of specific tasks, responsibilities and targets with the necessary delegation of powers to individuals manning the technical and managerial posts at different levels;

(ii) appraisal of their performance in objective terms with reference to the tasks, responsibilities and targets assigned, with a view to adequately rewarding good performance and penalizing those whose performance has been below expectations; and

(iii) offering incentives and opportunities for development and updating of managerial and technical skills in deserving cases.

(6) In some cases (where, for instance, inventories of finished products or stocks of unsold goods have been piling up) there also seems to be a need for active demand management consisting of:

(i) realistic assessment of the size and pattern of market demand with a view to adjusting production plans as far as possible;

(ii) dissemination of relevant information relating to the use, standard and quality of the goods produced, so that there is no lack of demand caused by ignorance on the part of the present or prospective consumers or users of such goods; and

(iii) an aggressive sales drive, wherever necessary.

(7) It is essential for the ministries concerned to review the

performance of the public enterprises under their control, to ascertain whether they are being managed properly, and whether the broad principles indicated are being followed in the pricing of their products. The aspects which need particular attention and close monitoring at government level are production, capacity utilization, inventories, overhead costs and internal resource generation. Various cost-efficiency and inventory norms, etc. also need to be adhered to. This would enable the government to properly evaluate the functioning of public enterprises and to issue such directions (e.g. setting production targets) as may be considered necessary to ensure the efficient functioning of the units. Further it would deal with the bottlenecks which need to be removed, and those difficulties which can be sorted out by co-ordination at government level. Any directives or instructions issued need to be based on a careful analysis of the facts of each case, and have to be kept to the minimum. It is also essential that specific written directives are issued (not mere exhortations, informal advice or suggestions) wherever necessary, after discussion with management, so that their views can be taken into consideration.

Notes

1. Ragner Nurkse, *Problems of Capital Formation in Under-developed Countries*, Oxford, Blackwell, 1957, p.4.
2. Ibid.
3. Ibid., p.5.
4. Ibid.

11 Price control: some conclusions

It may be worthwhile drawing together the main conclusions which emerge from the discussion in earlier chapters, as they could be of interest and relevance of those concerned with the formulation and implementation of price control measures, particularly in the developing or Third World countries. This is an attempt at a recapitulation and summary restatement of the salient points brought out by this study.

The case for price control, which implies various forms of interference in the free functioning of the market mechanism, rests essentially on the imperfections of the market which cause distortions in the allocation of scarce resources, in the resultant pattern of national output and its growth, and also in income distribution. As has been observed, in a dynamic world, especially in the case of developing countries, the real problem is not that of maximization of 'efficiency' or 'welfare' under given conditions, but of growth and equity or social justice, which necessitate an active interference in the free play of market forces and a large-scale mobilization and allocation of resources according to a predetermined plan for the achievement of certain economic and non-economic objectives, determined by a country on the basis of certain value judgements.

In operational terms, price control is an instrument or measure of economic policy for correcting distortions in the relative price structure, resource allocation and income distribution caused by market imperfections. In a developing country which has chosen the path of planned development, it could also help in achieving a pattern of resource allocation and resource mobilization in accordance with plan priorities, and in promoting stability and correcting inequities which might arise in the process of development. The proper formulation and effective implementation of any system of price control would require the adoption of a definite 'pricing policy', which is a wider term implying, *inter alia*, a clear perception of the objectives to be achieved, the nature, extent, timing and duration of the control called for; and also the legal, administrative and procedural framework and the institutional set-up needed to operate any set of price-control and related measures.

The existing body of economic theory (of which price theory is a part) explains the factors and compulsions which give rise to the need for price control. There is, therefore, no need to develop any separate theory of price control; nor could such a theory possibly be developed, since this is the realm of economic policy which may be based on political ideology or value judgements and, as such, is not amenable to being systematized or formalized into a theory.

'Pricing policy' is, in fact, a part of the economic policy which is a comprehensive expression for the entire set of principles and measures governing the management of the economy, and it has to be formulated and implemented within the broad framework of the general economic policy being pursued, and not work at cross purposes to it. Any particular situation may call for a combination of various measures — monetary, fiscal and other measures, including price control — and all these measures have to be so conceived, formulated and implemented that they support, sustain and reinforce each other for the achievement of certain objectives. In a planned economy (as most of the developing countries are), pricing policy has to be so evolved as to be consistent with the objectives, priorities and programmes envisaged in the plan, and also with the entire packge of other policies adopted for the achievement of plan targets.

Price control measures are generally resorted to in situations of shortage or scarcity. Shortages may be real, created by excess demand and inelasticity of supply in the short run. They can also be artificial, caused by the hoarding or holding back of stocks by traders, or the monopolistic restriction of output by producers. Since pricing policy has to remedy such a situation, it may involve both demand and supply management through rationing, public distribution and a package of measures designed to increase production and productivity. In some cases, price control may have to be extended to substitutes and related products, as well as to inputs as part of total demand and supply management. Any rational system of price control has, however, to aim not at perpetuating itself or unnecessarily increasing its coverage but at creating conditions where the basic cause of control, namely scarcity of the commodity subjected to price control, is removed, so that the control (which is always irksome and involves administrative cost) can be lifted as quickly as possible. The argument that price controls have a natural tendency to escalate and envelope the entire economy and are, therefore, not consistent with the capitalist system, is neither theoretically valid nor borne out historically by actual experience. Price controls have in fact been used in both developed and developing market economies to achieve certain objectives without transforming them from capitalist to socialist economies. Both purely capitalist and purely socialist economies are conceptual models, the actual economies being mixed in varying degrees, having features of both. With the emergence of the concept of the 'welfare state', most modern states have pursued policies designed to achieve certain objectives in accordance with their value systems, priorities and aspirations, without any doctrinaire adherence to the ideology of capitalism or socialism, and without eschewing measures which may be termed 'capitalist' or 'socialist', if they are found to be necessary to achieve those objectives.

Price control measures differ from other economic measures (e.g. monetary and fiscal measures) in two important respects. Firstly, whereas other policy measures mostly operate indirectly by creating a set of incentives and disincentives, price control is a direct measure, and pricing policy seeks to control prices, and in many cases also, production and distribution of the controlled commodity. Secondly, while other policy measures operate through the market mechanism by providing the necessary incentives and disincentives, price control measures interfere with the free play of the market mechanism itself; and are in effect a declaration of lack of faith in the market mechanism to deliver the goods. There could be situations unamenable to monetary or fiscal measures alone. For instance, monetary measures may only be effective in limited areas in a primarily agricultural economy consisting mostly of rural areas not covered by banks or financial institutions or where monetary transactions have not fully replaced the barter transactions prevalent in a primitive economy. Similarly, the erosion in real incomes caused by a rise in the general price level (and also the price of wage-goods (and also the price of wage-goods or essential consumer goods), owing to massive investments in long-term capital projects in the initial stages of planned development in a developing economy, may necessitate resorting to price control measures to provide the necessary protection to the weaker sections of the community and to prevent distortions in cost structures caused by the rise in input costs. Fiscal measures such as subsidies on the required scale may not always be feasible, owing to limited government resources. Tax concessions (which in any case would not provide any relief to those whose incomes are not taxable, and who generally do not consume taxable consumer goods, as is the case with the majority of the rural population in a developing economy like India) may not always be passed on to consumers in the form of lower prices.

The objectives of pricing policy can broadly be categorized under the headings Efficiency, Welfare, Full Employment, Equity, Growth and Stability. These can be said to be the objectives of economic policy as such, of which pricing policy forms a part. In actual fact, there is a good deal of overlapping and complementarity in the objectives of different economic policies; and all economic policy measures are necessarily interrelated and interdependent to achieve certain common objectives. As indicated above, pricing policy may be more effective in some situations than others operating through the free market. These objectives may also be given varying priorities and importance under different conditions and in economies at different stages of development. In developing economies, Growth, Stability and Equity may be given relatively greater importance. While pricing policy could be used for resource generation and resource mobilization, in the developing economies it may be found more useful in ensuring certain minimum levels of consumption (through control of prices and distribution of essential consumer goods) by the poor, and preventing steep drops in their real incomes; and also in maintaining agricultural incomes at a reasonable level (through support price operations). In the developed economies, price controls have been found useful in peacetime for maintaining prices and availability at reasonable levels; and in wartime for restricting civilian consumption, mobilizing resources and achieving a 'militarily optimum allocation of resources'.

The objectives of pricing policy may not always be in harmony with each other. There is an obvious conflict between the objectives of economic growth and equity. Price controls which may keep the prices of controlled commodities sufficiently low to make them affordable by the vulnerable sections of the community may not be conducive to the growth of the industries producing them. To achieve a high rate of economic growth, greater sacrifice of present consumption or further tightening of belts may be necessary, even beyond what might be considered desirable from the equity angle. Policy-makers may, therefore, have to make a compromise or strike some kind of balance between conflicting objectives based on various economic and non-economic considertions.

The criteria for the selection of commodities for price control would depend largely on the nature of the situation being tackled. In an inflationary situation, for instance, it is necessary to identify the commodities primarily responsible for or contributing most to the rise in the general price level, the fall in the real incomes of vulnerable sections of the community, the distortions in cost structures or the mis-allocation of resources or their diversion to inessential or non-priority sectors, or those where monopolistic restriction of output results in under-utilization of available industrial capacities. Once they have been identified, they can be brought under some kind of price discipline. Other relevant criteria might be relatively inelastic demand (owing either to the essential nature of the commodity as an item of consumption or to it being an essential industrial input, with no substitutes), and an ascertainable demand (so that, if need be, both production and distribution could also be controlled). From the administrative angle, the homogeneity of the product, and the requirement of a relatively small number of inputs or components, could be some additional criteria.

Price control may take various forms, such as the setting of a ceiling price; or the freezing of the market price at a level obtaining on a particular date; or imposing a ceiling on the profit margin at the production, sale or distribution stage; or fixing a 'minimum', 'floor' or 'support' price (e.g. in the case of agricultural produce like food grains, sugar-cane or cotton); or setting a 'retention price' on the basis of 'standard' or approved cost norms. In the EEC countries, price controls have taken the form of a 'price framework' (a system of working out the maximum price on the basis of a number of predetermined factors); 'stability contracts' with business enterprises (which envisage freedom to vary certain prices provided that they undertake not to increase the overall price level of their production programme); 'programme contracts' ('accession' to which gives enterprises freedom to increase their prices within the growth rates specified in the Plan); prescribing rules for costing; requiring compulsory reporting or display of prices; and prohibition of resale price maintenance, discriminatory practices, or 'overcharging'. In India, there is a statutory control of 'monopolistic', 'restrictive' and 'unfair' trade practices, which is also a form of price control in a broader sense.

There could in fact be no standard price control measure for dealing with any particular market situation. Even situations apparently the same or similar in two different economies may have some distinctive or unique features of their own, calling for some subtle, but significant, variations in the details of ostensibly the same measure adopted in each economy. However, in any economy, different situations will prevail in different markets or sectors of the economy which may call for different measures. An economy might, at any time, therefore, need, not one, but a package of suitably devised measures according to its own particular requirements.

Price control measures need not necessarily have a statutory basis or legal sanctions. Prices can also be regulated on the basis of an informal understanding or arrangement with the industry (as in the case of certain varieties of paper, *vanaspati* and tractors in India). But a statutory basis makes enforcement easier. Statutory controls may be unavoidable, if price control is coupled with a compulsory 'levy' and procurement (as in the case of food grains, cotton, cement etc., in India). Legal provisions may also become necessary to prohibit unhelpful practices on the part of producers or traders.

Price control can be total or partial. Total control involves setting the price of the entire quantity produced or available, and administering and enforcing it by a public distribution system and several 'control' orders. There may be situations which call for this total control, for example in time of war when the entire production and productive capacity has to be geared to sustain the war effort; or in the case of an essential item of mass consumption or an essential industrial input whose supply is inelastic in the short run. But where there is no such extreme situation or crisis, and only certain identifiable groups of consumers or users need protection, partial control in the form of 'dual pricing' may be a better alternative. Dual pricing involves:

(a) determining a certain proportion of the output of a commodity to be procured by the government at the 'levy rate';
(b) setting the price at which procurement is to be made — the 'procurement' or 'levy price';
(c) arranging distribution of the quantity procured to specified categories of consumers or users, or for specified purposes, at a price often referred to as the 'issue price'; and
(d) leaving the remaining quantity to be sold on the open market, sometimes called 'free sale quantity' at the price determined by the free play of market forces.

Dual pricing could be easier and less expensive to administer. By allowing the sale of a certain portion of the output at the price it could command in the open market, the main cause of black marketeering is eliminated; and the industry is also able substantially to make good the loss it may have incurred by its obligation to sell part of its production at the procurement price fixed by the government. The surpluses or resources so generated internally could remain with the industry for further investment and growth, instead of being appropriated by traders and middlemen, who thrive on the black market. It might also mean a relatively smaller drain into subsidization on the limited budgetary resources of the government. A system of differential levy rates could, in some cases, also be used to encourage the setting up of new units, or to correct regional imbalances in industrial growth.

An important problem in administering 'dual pricing' is that of leakages, which invariably arise if the difference between the 'issue price' and the open market price becomes too wide. This problem can be tackled by strict enforcement and efficient distribution arrangements; ensuring that the same dealers are not allowed to sell the controlled commodity both at the controlled price and in free sale; and wherever feasible, setting up government-run shops exclusively to sell controlled commodities.

Price control, whether total or partial, and whether intended to protect the consumer or the producer, may involve the setting of a controlled price. As a general rule, the controlled price has to be cost-based. To enable the price setting body to collect reliable cost data, it is necessary to have separate statutory costing rules for different industry groups; and legal provisions are also necessary to enable it to ensure the observance of those rules by the industry groups and the availability of the cost data required for any price-setting exercise, whenever needed.

In many cases, the number of industrial units in the price-controlled industry may be so large that the controlled price may have to be based on the average cost worked out on the basis of the cost data of a sample of units. These units could be so selected that the weighted average of their costs roughly represents the average cost of the relatively more efficient units accounting for two-thirds of the output of the industry; and the price fixed on the basis of either such an average or the average cost of the unit at the cut-off point where two-thirds of the output is accounted for. The latter alternative is preferable as it may enable a larger number of units to cover their costs fully.

Average cost pricing is preferable to marginal cost pricing for several reasons. The case for marginal cost pricing rests essentially on the static equilibrium theory of price formation, and is of little relevance in a dynamic world where cost functions are constantly changing because of competition or the policies pursued by the government. If marginal cost pricing is used there is the problem of subsidizing decreasing cost industries, and the almost insuperable practical difficulties of working out the marginal cost. Average cost is relatively simpler to work out. It also highlights the need to adopt a conscious policy in the case of price-controlled industries of constantly changing the cost functions themselves in accordance with technological improvements, modernization, etc., so that the average cost can be lowered at the same level of output; and of simultaneously expanding output by fuller utilization of the existing capacities up to the point where the average cost is minimized (the point where it equals marginal cost).

Any exercise to set a controlled price has to be based on a study of the industry producing that commodity, covering all relevant aspects, such as the regional and overall demand and supply position, the causes of shortages and the remedial measures necessary. The price should be fixed so that it provides incentives for efficiency and growth. Some of the important points which need to be kept in view in this exercise are as follows:

(a) As a general rule, the controlled price has to cover all costs, fixed and variable, fully; and also allow a reasonable margin of profit so that the industry can build up its own internal resources and substantially meet its requirements for funds for expansion and modernization. It should also be considered whether an element of contribution to the development of the price-controlled industry needs to be built into the controlled price itself, to create a separate development fund. Alternatively, such a fund could be created by levy of a cess (rate) on the value of goods produced, by making the necessary legal provisions.

(b) The controlled price could, in some cases, justifiably be fixed at a level where it does not cover costs fully, for example in the case of essential consumer goods of mass consumption whose price may have to be kept low enough to be affordable by the class of consumers who are to be protected; or essential inputs in short supply brought under price and distribution control to protect the enterprises using them. In some cases, subsidization can take the form of direct cash subsidies or tax concessions to enable the producers to export their products at competitive international prices, or sell them profitably within the country (e.g. in the case of producers in the cottage or small-scale sector) in competition with other producers whose costs may be lower because of mechanized, large-scale production. Government may sometimes give a capital investment subsidy to new units set up in backward areas to enable them initially (when their costs are generally high) to survive and effectively compete in the market. Direct cash subsidies may sometimes be preferable to concealed subsidies in the form of the setting of a lower 'controlled price' or tax concessions, as their exact burden on the public exchequer is known. Measures designed to increase production and productivity need to be taken simultaneously so that the subsidies, which may involve a considerable financial drain on the government, are minimized, tapered off and phased out as quickly as possible.

(c) It is necessary to provide sufficient incentives for the substantial expansion of the existing units and the setting up of new units in the price-controlled industry. There are practical difficulties in implementing a scheme allowing a higher price for the product of a new unit or for additional production owing to the substantial expansion of an existing unit. It may, therefore, be advisable to consider some non-price incentives such as liberal licensing and import of machinery and technology, tax concessions, concessional finance, more and cheaper infrastructural facilities (e.g. land, transport, fuel, power, water, etc.).

(d) Although a uniform price is more conducive to efficiency, as it leaves a larger margin of profit to more efficient and lower-cost units, it may be necessary to fix different 'retention prices' in the case of units in an industry (e.g. the fertilizer industry in India) whose costs of production are different due to differences in feedstock and technology. Such a system is operated through a pooling arrangement to maintain a uniform consumer price, involving subsidization of high-cost units by low-cost ones. Alternatively, a uniform price could be fixed and the high-cost units directly subsidized to the extent required for their survival, from the budgetary resources of the government (so that the financial burden of the subsidy is not borne by the relatively more efficient units). The uniform price needs to be fixed on the basis of certain cost norms, which have to be suitably revised from time to time; and the direct subsidy to less efficient units made to taper off over time, so that they are urged to progressively adopt cost reduction measures as far as possible.

(e) Transport costs, namely the cost of transport of raw materials and other inputs from their source to the factory/plant site, and that of finished product from there to consumption centres, should both be reckoned as costs. A system of freight equalization which equalizes the transport cost from production sites to consumption centres for all units through the operation of a freight equalization pool has several deleterious effects. Some of these are: rendering the units near the consumption centres (set up prior to the introduction of such a scheme) virtually 'sick', setting up of new units at sub-optimal locations;

clustering of production units near sources of raw materials (thus preventing their dispersal and giving rise to or accentuating regional disparities); and avoidable transport costs to the economy. This system, wherever prevalent, therefore, should gradually be phased out.

(f) A system should be evolved that makes the short-run adjustment of prices to changing costs automatic. The price-setting bodies also need to make a comprehensive review of costs and prices of price-controlled industries periodically. The purpose of the review, *inter alia*, should be to ascertain whether the controlled price has been moving in line with costs without unduly long time-lags to cause distortions, whether the industry has been maintaining the desired rate of growth, and whether the other objectives of price control are also being achieved, with a view to identifying the areas of success and failure, the causal factors, and the remedial measures.

(g) After the initial setting of the controlled price, in the course of every subsequent price revision exercise, the general level of efficiency of production in the industry should be examined. If it is found that some units have enhanced their profit margins by technological improvements, modernization or fuller utilization of installed capacities, thereby bringing down the average cost of the industry (which would form the basis of the revised controlled price), the price needs to be revised so that the benefits of cost reduction or gains in efficiency are shared equitably between the industry and the consumer. This is achieved by allowing a reduction in price which is less than proportionate to the reduction in costs, in order to preserve the motivation for greater efficiency and also benefit the consumer.

Since the controlled price has to allow a reasonable margin of profit over costs, there is a range of problems relating to the rate of return to be tackled in any exercise setting a controlled price. Two basic questions arise: to what should the margin of profit or the rate of return be related (i.e. how is it to be based), and what should that rate be? A combination of the two (the base and the rate) has to be chosen which yields a price which is both adequately remunerative to the producer and sufficiently low to be affordable by the consumer — it is essentially a problem of reconciling these two seemingly conflicting (at least in the short run) interests. The alternative bases could be 'capital employed' (fixed plus working capital), 'net worth' (paid-up capital plus reserves), 'turnover' (total sale proceeds of the goods sold), 'value of output', and the 'value added' in the process of production. But whichever of these bases is adopted, the rate of return is always translatable into the rate per unit of capital invested. Available empirical evidence relating to India shows that, of the three bases, 'capital employed', 'net worth' and 'turnover', 'net worth' is generally the smallest and 'turnover' the largest base. The rate will have to be higher if a smaller base is chosen, and vice versa.

There is no validity in the argument that 'net worth' as a base is neutral to the contribution of borrowed capital to total investment and, therefore, discourages borrowed capital and encourages the use of equity capital. The contentions that net worth encourages greater use of fixed capital or increases capital intensity, and discourages investment in the lines of production where the use of fixed capital per unit of output is very low (e.g. industries primarily involving assembly jobs) or where the depreciated value of the old capital stock is very low (e.g. coastal shipping), also have to validity. But 'net worth', as an accounting concept, is amenable to manipulation by the accounting procedures followed, and would also depend on the policy regarding depreciation and other reserves and payment of dividends, and the taxation policy of the government. Adoption of 'net worth' as a base could possibly encourage the use of equity capital resulting in an increase in the average 'net worth' of the industry only in monopolistic or 'oligopolistic' situations where one or two producers could, by their own individual action or in combination with others, hope to increase the average 'net worth' of the industry to take advantage of it in the subsequent revision of the controlled price. Moreover, allocation of 'net worth' to each firm might be difficult in the case of multi-product firms; and may also pose practical problems in the case of enterprises whose 'net worth' may have been considerably eroded by losses.

Although 'net worth' is a function of the efficiency of production and profitability of an enterprise (which generate internal surpluses and build up 'net worth'), the other three bases — 'turnover', 'value of production' and 'value added' — are directly related to production and productivity. The adoption of any of these three bases could directly encourage production and productive efficiency, as the units which achieve a higher rate of 'turnover', 'production' or 'value added' per unit of capital invested than the rate assumed in the price-fixing exercise would get a larger margin of profit. Operationally also, these three bases have the advantage of being easily ascertainable and much less susceptible to manipulation by accounting procedures, etc., and do not pose any problems in the case of multi-product firms or of enterprises that incur losses.

The institutional set-up needed for the proper formulation, implementation, enforcement and monitoring of price control measures may consist of the following type of bodies:

(i) A broad-based institution or body of a national character such as the National Prices Committee in France, the Prices Commission in Belgium or the erstwhile Prices and Incomes Board in Britain, giving due representation to agriculture, industry, trade and different political viewpoints set up to consider major policy questions relating to price control, and to advise the government either generally or on specific issues referred to it by the government.

(ii) A central organization consisting mainly of professional economists and statisticians with the necessary field staff for collecting, processing and analysing data relating to the relevant variables such as costs, prices, availability and the distribution of essential agricultural and industrial commodities (including raw materials and inputs); for monitoring their behaviour with a view to identifying significant distortions necessitating some kind of price control; and for ascertaining the effects of specific price control measures. This monitoring would enable the government to decide which commodities need to be brought under price discipline and the nature and timing of the control measures needed, and would allow the government to take timely remedial action to ensure proper implementation of the measures taken.

(iii) A price-setting body consisting mainly of experts (economists, statisticians, cost accountants, etc.), with the necessary statutory powers to collect the cost data required for any exercise in setting or revising the controlled price, and also to ensure proper maintenance of the necessary cost accounts by the individual industrial units according to such costing rules as may be notified by the government.

(iv) A statutory body of quasi-judicial or judicial character (such as the Monopolies and Restrictive Trade Practices Commission in India) consisting of legal experts, professional economists and those with expert knowledge of industry and trade to enquire into complaints regarding contravention of the legal provisions relating to 'monopolistic', 'restrictive' or 'unfair' trade practices, or 'price discrimination', 'overcharging', or 'resale price maintenance', etc.

There is also a need to streamline or evolve suitable administrative procedures — both in the internal procedures governing the institutions connected with the formulation, implementation and enforcement of price control measures and in the procedures within the government ministries or departments concerned — so as to minimize the time taken at each stage of collection and processing of data/information/facts and decision-making. This is necessary to minimize delays and corruption at various levels, and at the various stages of the implementation of the pricing policy and enforcement of the price control measures.

Several significant conclusions could be drawn from the Indian experience of price control. The available empirical evidence regarding the relative performance of certain price-controlled and non-price-controlled industries in India seems to suggest, broadly, that the controlled prices have moved more or less in line with the general price level; growth in capacity, production and capacity utilization has, on the whole, not been slower in the controlled as compared to the non-controlled industries; and profitability and internal resource generation in the controlled sector have also not been lower than in the non-controlled sector. These statistical data do not substantiate the view that price controls keep the prices of controlled commodities unduly depressed, thereby adversely affecting the profitability and growth of the price-controlled industries.

The Indian experience also highlights the need to simplify the system of statutory price controls; build-up an efficient monitoring system; abolish the multiplicity of price-fixing bodies; build up a powerful consumer movement and create voluntary organizations at the grass-roots level to ensure the proper functioning of the public distribution system; make the entire system of price controls productivity- and efficiency-orientated; adopt a conscious policy to minimize the burden of subsidies and to taper them off over time; examine whether some more liberal and innovative forms of price controls such as 'stability contracts', 'programme contracts' or 'a price framework', as tried in the EEC countries, could be tried in India in some suitable cases; merge the concepts of 'monopolistic' and 'restrictive' trade practices by suitably amending the relevant legal provisions; and decentralize the administration of the legal provisions relating to 'unfair trade practices' by suitable legislation or legislative amendment.

As regards the pricing of the products of public enterprises (which occupy a prominent place in the Indian economy), there is sufficient empirical evidence that their profitability has been very low, and that they have generally been incurring losses. The situation could be gradually remedied by measures such as setting the prices of the products of public enterprises at a remunerative level (except perhaps in the initial promotional phase); treating pricing as a corporate management function and giving full autonomy to management to set prices, and making them fully accountable for the performance of the enterprise; avoiding government subsidies, or cross-subsidization by one public enterprise of other enterprises; taking all possible measures to increase productivity; identifying high-cost or uneconomical units whose costs cannot be reduced because of technological and other factors, and gradually phasing them out; diagnosing the causes of the 'sickness' of individual units with a view to taking remedial measures, and generally refraining from taking over or nationalizing incurably 'sick' units in the private sector; evolving an effective system of accountability at different technical and managerial levels; active demand management; and regular periodic review of performance by the administrative ministries or departments concerned.

Appendix

Table of products or groups of products covered by stability contracts (as at 27 June 1966) in France

1. Talcum
2. Cast-iron sanitary ware, central heating boilers and radiators
3. Malleable cast-iron joints
4. Motor and hand pumps
5. Industrial and commercial refrigerating plant
6. Machine tools
7. Electrical and pneumatic hand tools
8. Woodworking machinery
9. Agricultural tractors and motor-cultivators
10. Agricultural winches
11. Land preparation and drainage equipment, sowers, sprays
12. Harvesting and haymaking equipment
13. Threshing and pressing equipment
14. Other equipment for sorting and packing after harvest
15. Dairy and cheese-making equipment
16. Miscellaneous agricultural implements
17. Sewing machines
18. Agricultural, domestic and industrial hand tools
19. Ironmongery
20. Galvanized and tinned articles
21. Cutlery
22. Safes
23. Industrial and commercial metal furniture
24. Metal beds and mattresses
25. Hospital furniture
26. Metal kitchen furniture
27. Metal garden furniture, miscellaneous metal seats, metal indoor and outdoor furniture, mechanical steps and ladders

28. Spare parts and accessories for motor cars
29. Spare parts and accessories for cycles and motorcycles
30. Radio and television receivers, record players and tape recorders
31. Incandescent electric lamps
32. Clocks and clockwork
33. Watches and chronometers
34. Compasses and drawing instruments
35. Surgical, medical and veterinary instruments
36. Blown and semi-automatic glassware
37. Sanitary ceramics
38. Stoneware
39. Pottery or stone facing tiles
40. Clay and enamel powders
41. Asbestos cement products
42. Concrete products
43. Sulphuric acid
44. Hydrochloric acid
45. Carbon disulphide
46. Caustic soda
47. Metal salts and oxides
48. Nitrate
49. Methanol
50. Synthetic rubber and elastomers
51. Sulphamides, vitamins, hormones
52. Iodine and salts of iodine
53. Detergents
54. Grinding wheels and compound abrasives
55. Wood board and fibres
56. Man-made continuous fibres and yarn
57. Preserved vegetables
58. Preserved fish

Index

(Note: *passim* means that the subject so annotated is referred to in scattered passages throughout these pages of tect. 'T' indicates a table and 'n' that the reference is in note form.)

Acts
    Companies 71, 72–3
    Essential Commodities 141, 146, 147
    Industrial (Development and Regulation) 71–2, 73, 78, 146
    Monopolistic and Restrictive Trade Practices (MRTP) 152, 153, 156
    MRTP Amendment Act 153
    Prices and incomes 58
    see also control, orders
advertising 6, 19
advertisements 7, 11
Agricultural Prices Commission (APC) (India) 61, 137, 149, 157, 158
agricultural
    economy 30
    holdings 24
    incomes 27, 48
    price level 19, 23, 38–9, 48, 133, 150
    produce 50–1, 60
    production 22, 138
    sector 48
    tractors 119
agriculture
    failure of 123
    Indian 151
    predominance of 21
    price operations for 16,
    price protection for 18, 38–9

    yields in 9–10, 137
aluminium 86, 148–9
Annual Compound Growth Rates (ACGR) 160–1, 177
anti-inflationary measures 18, 28, 47
armed forces 19
assumptions about a phenomenon 33
authority, price controlling 32 *see also* government, price fixing body
Average Annual Growth Rate (AAGR) 160
averaging costs 74–5 *see also* costs, average
averaging output 74–5

base(s) 104–7 *passim*, 108, 110, 115–19T *passim*, 220
behaviour, human 33
behaviour, of variables 33
Belgium 59, 71
benefits
    accruing 56
    'marginal private' 6
    'marginal social' 6
Bergson, A. 16n
Bombay 149
borowed funds 105–6, 108
Bureau of Industrial Costs and Prices (BICP) (India) 61, 71–2, 73–4, 146, 149, 157, 158
business units 6
butter 146
buyer(s)

buyers (*continued*)
   categories of 51
   and equilibrium price 35–6
   prices offered by 57
   as price takers 3, 5

capacity 164
capital
   assets 76, 110
   borrowed 105–6, 110, 116, 219
   costs 66, 76, 130, 147
   depreciation 72
   employed 110, 184–5T, 190T, 219
   equipment, age of 76, 130
   equity 106, 110, 115, 219
   fixed 103, 114, 185T, 219
   formation 183–4, 194
   intensity 108–9, 110–11, 113, 115, 118, 186, 194, 195, 219
   investment 6, 108–9, 118, 166T–7, 219
   /labour ratio 113, 114, 186
   lack of 175
   productivity of 186
   and rate of return 105
   resources 22
   value added ratio 186, 194
   variable 103
capitalism 2, 35, 39, 40
capitalist
   countries 18
   economy 2, 4–5, 20–1, 44, 210
   system 2–3, 35, 210
cement 122, 127, 128, 130–1T, 149, 151–2, 158, 161–2, 168
cement, freight equalization of 84
Cement
   Development Fund (India) 77
   Industry, Committee on the Development of 79, 128
Central Statistical Organisation 166
cereal production 138T, 150
cess (tax) 78
change, structural 24, 90, 195
chemicals 167
citizen's councils 160

cloth 122
coal 158
'cobweb theory' 36
Committee on Controls and Subsidies 136–7, 149, 151, 169
commodity
   agricultural 220
   controlled 96, 131, 134–5
   distribution of controlled 210, 214
   essential 140
   government regulation of 122
   identification of 127–8
   industrial 220
   informal 145
   non-price controlled 196
   price controlled 91, 161, 196, 202, 212
   price discipline for 44, 47, 171
   pricing of 36–7, 43, 48
   scarcity of 123, 210
   selection of 212
   significance of 31
   'worth' 92, 93, 95
   see also goods
community, the
   best interests of 37
   deserving sections 126
   households in 4
   and prices 94–5
   sections of 12, 22, 23, 27, 29, 125, 211, 212
   welfare of 8, 15
competition
   between large- and small-scale industries 88
   effects of 37, 93, 216
   imperfect 5, 94, 97, 170
   international 65
   perfect 3, 5, 8–9, 14–15, 17, 34–6 *passim*, 40, 75, 93, 94
   restraint on 55
concept
   of average cost 100
   of equilibrium 12, 35–6
   of marginal cost 96–8
   normative 7, 11, 15

subjective 20
  of welfare 7-8, 9, 11, 15
  of the welfare state 39-40
  see also net worth
conclusions, about price control 208-22
conflict between economic growth and equity 27
construction 182, 183
consumer(s)
  actions of 9
  and affordable commodities 78, 96
  association 154
  as buyers 3
  category of 88, 129
  classes of 127
  demand 176
  incomes of 15
  and economic distortions 46
  influence of seller on 6
  legitimate interests of 153
  movements 160
  needs of 18
  preference 7
  price index 124
  and prices 109, 204, 218
  protection of 102, 123
  and rationing 80
  sovereignty of 4, 7, 25
  welfare 20
consumption
  areas of 84
  centres of 84, 85, 151, 217
  levels of 211
  standards of 11, 13
contracts
  government 73
  individual 156
  programme 52-3, 213, 222
  public 71
  stability 52, 213, 222, 223-4T
control(s)
  direct 26
  false 34, 36, 37
  measures 137, 159, 220
  orders 142, 143, 146, 147, 155, 213
  price ix, 1-16, 26-7, 29, 32-43, 44-5, 47-9, 52, 55, 56, 59-60, 64-91, 92-101, 102-20, 121, 125, 140-73, 176, 196, 208-22
  of production and distribution 47, 49
  of rebates 55
  statutory 142, 213
  system of 121, 159
  true 34, 36, 37
  of wages 41
  see also rationing
core (industries) sector 187, 198
Cost Audit Report Rules 72
cost(s)
  'absolute figure' 104
  accounts 70, 221
  agricultural 60
  assessment 73
  auditor 72
  average 69, 73-4, 80, 98, 99-100, 102, 104, 110, 115, 197, 200, 215, 218
  -based pricing 65-6, 69-70, 215
  covering of 102, 131
  curve 93, 95, 96, 97
  data 60, 69, 73-5, 91, 102
  defining 53, 68-9
  differentials 86
  differing 67
  effectiveness 205
  element 117
  historical 68, 69
  increased 103, 130
  industrial 60
  items 72
  long-term marginal 79
  manufacturing 148
  marginal 79, 80, 96-7, 200, 215
  'marginal private' 6
  'marginal social' 6
  normative 68, 69

costs (*continued*)
   operating 76
   plus formula 107, 108–9, 114–15
   and price controls 38, 56
   pricing, marginal vs average 92–101
   projected 68, 69
   reduction in 70, 85, 96, 218
   standard 51, 68
   structure 28, 131, 186–7T, 204
   total 90
   transport 67
   unit 51, 68
cotton 144, 150, 164 *see also* textiles
countries
   developing ix, 208 *see also* Third World countries
   underdeveloped 9, 10, 82, 123, 175
Courts 61
crop failure 132

data
   analysis of 60, 70, 73, 76, 99, 159, 168, 220
   available 118, 164–5, 191
   classifying and converting 159–60
   collection of 70, 136, 215
   empirical 140
   of industrial costs 69, 71–2, 99, 194, 203
   statistically 160, 221
debt/equity ratio 106–7, 111, 126, 167–8T
decision-making 62, 221
decontrol 136, 147, 162
defence
   of India Rules (DIR) 141
   theoretical, of the free functioning of the market mechanism 35
demand
   actual 210
   constraint 195
   created by supply 10

curve, elastic 3, 6, 92–3, 97, 135
elasticity of 36, 90, 92, 134
excess 35, 38, 41, 125
functions 200
increase in 31, 34
inelastic 48, 212
management 29, 38, 42, 222 *see also* rationing
pattern 7, 28
projected 202
and supply 28, 78
Department of Economic Affairs 59
Department of Petroleum and Fertilizers 148
Departmental Prices Committee 58
developed countries *see* capitalist countries
developing countries, economies of ix, 24, 27, 97, 211, 208
development
   fund 77–8, 84, 216
   industrial 66, 77
   planned 22–3, 27, 44
   process of 208
diesel oil 83
digopoly in production 6
discriminatory practices 54–5, 57, 152
disincentives 25, 144, 152 *see also* incentives
display of retail prices, compulsory, 54, 57
distortions in economics 45–6, 59, 84, 218, 220
dominant position 55
donation voluntary 78
drugs 166, 167
dual pricing 121–39, 146, 170, 214

economic
   activity, control of 39
   effects 83
   forces 10
   growth 10, 27, 44, 175
   judgement 47, 50

measures 42, 144
order 4
policy 14, 17, 22, 29, 43, 92, 96, 138
problem 9, 15
progress 13
resources 4, 10, 152
system 7, 17, 90
theorists 92
theory 209
variables 12, 15
Economic Administration Reforms Commission (India) ix
economics
applied 43
'normative' 17
'welfare' 7
economists 10, 220
economy, the
agrarian 21, 210
backward 10
categories of 2
changing 12-13
competitive 5
developing 24, 27, 97, 211
free market 18, 39, 40, 104
growth in 11, 195
Indian 158, 182, 194
influence on 11
management of 17
national 56
planned 59, 65
price controls and 213
primitive 210
of scale 88
underdeveloped 45
efficiency
greater 87
maximum 95
maximization 19-20, 94
norms 86
objective 19
elasticity of price 90
employment
desirability of full 13

full 19, 24
levels of 10
local 88
objective 115
entrepreneurs 83, 85, 103-6 *passim*, 112, 114-15, 119, 176
Enquiry, Commission for 154
enterprises
departmental 183
non-departmental 183
private 174-5, 182
public ix, 174-207
equilibrium
attainment of 8, 9, 12, 17
of a firm 75, 96
general 31
price 34-5, 50-1, 92, 95
stable 10, 15
European Economic Community (EEC)
control measures of 51, 71
countries 57, 71, 140, 152, 156, 170, 222
price controls in 43n, 57, 212-13
expansion of industrial units 67, 77, 81, 82
export subsidy 90
external
agency 12, 35
diseconomy 6
economy 6

factors
causal 196, 197
complicating 56
determining 8, 33
disequilibrating 12-13, 15
economic 106, 108
endowment of 82, 196, 203
of production 4, 5-6, 69, 76, 82, 222
fair price shops 88, 142, 160
false representation 153
farmers
fall in income of 19

farmers (continued)
  producing food grains 150
  in underdeveloped countries 9–10, 21
  low holding capacity of 39
feedstocks 147, 217
fertilizer(s)
  demand for 9–10, 162–3
  Industry Co-ordinating Committee (FICC) 147, 158
  manufacturing plants 10, 217
  Pool Equalization Charge 148
  Prices Committee 148
  retention prices for 86
  statutory control of 146, 147
  subsidy 90
  transportation cost of 85
financial institutions 116
finance
  of companies 164
  concessionary 204
  raising of 77
flour milling 142
Food Corporation of India (FCI) 142
food
  grains 88, 123, 132–3, 136–7, 138, 142, 149, 150–1
  subsidy 90
  supply 137
foreign exchange 65, 88
framework
  of economic policies 40
  or parameters of action 51
  price 51–2, 222
  procedural 209
France 51–2, 54, 58, 59, 71, 170, 223–4T
free-on-rail (f.o.r.) price 151
free sale quantity 214
freedom
  controlled 51, 53
  to fix prices 53, 54
freight equalization pool 84–5, 146–7, 151, 152, 217
funds for development 77

Galbraith, J.K. 33, 40–3
garages and compulsory display of prices 54
GDP (gross domestic product) 177–8, 179T, 181T, 186, 194
generalizations see hypotheses
Germany, Federal Republic of (FDR) 54, 55, 71, 140
ghee 146
goods
  availability of 82
  capital 21, 182, 186
  changes in 6
  consumer 7, 10, 18, 21, 22, 25, 27, 37, 56, 87, 88, 124, 176–7, 211, 216
  deterioration in 46
  essential 18
  imported 201–2
  inventory of 117
  lack of demand for 9
  prices for 4, 37
  production and distribution of 49, 67
  and restrictive practices 155, 156–7
  and services 156
  small-scale sector 47
  substandard 46
  taxable 30
government
  budget 87, 204
  budgetary resources 84, 87
  departments 59 see also institutions
  dependence on 66
  distribution system 123
  expenditure 89–90
  financial burdens of 27
  food subsides 134
  French 52–3
  interference in the market mechanism 64–5, 124
  intervention 35, 60, 95, 97, 105, 203
  price fixing body 61, 70–2, 73,

74, 83, 91, 108, 117, 118, 158, 169, 200, 215, 218, 220
  pricing 121
  procurement 129–31
  regulation 81, 121
  restrictions by 50
  -run shops 135
  see also state
gross domestic savings (GDS) 177–8T
gross domestic capital formation (GDCF) 177–8, 179–81T, 186, 194
gross fixed capital formation (GFCF) 181T, 182, 184, 194
groundnuts 149
growth
  accelerating 13
  in capacity 163T
  and equity 29, 131
  industrial 79, 81, 103, 144, 162, 218
  objective 19
  of output 81
  performance and pricing 174, 213
  and the public sector 195
  in productivity 79, 162
  rate of 120, 177, 178T
  and stability 13, 15, 53
  of subsidies in India 89T
Gujarat 149

harmony of interests, theory of 6, 11
high-cost firms 70
high-cost units 87, 222
hypotheses, set of 33, 40

ideology
  economic 14
  political 14, 209
imports 202
imprisonment 156
incentives
  and disincentives 25, 210
  provision of 67, 217
  to reduce costs 65

schemes of 144
  towards efficiency 69, 86, 103, 125, 216
  towards expansion 81
income
  of consumers 7
  of the community 23, 30
  distribution of 8, 9, 15, 18, 44, 47, 144
  erosion of 210
  fall in 46, 212
  low levels of 175
  minimum level of 11–12, 13–14
  national 13, 14
  real 125
  relative 134
  spending of 10, 27
India
  agricultural population of 30
  burden of growth 89
  Constitution of 145
  cost accounting in 71–4, 105, 107
  development funds 77, 78
  dual pricing in 127–8, 135
  economy of ix, 118, 132, 219, 222
  fair price shops in 88
  and freight equalization 84–5
  Government of ix–x, 74, 118, 127, 130, 136, 141
  and Monsoons 123
  price controls in 57, 68, 111, 118–19, 122, 130, 136, 137, 140–73, 213, 217, 221
  pricing policy organizations 61–2, 83
  procurement and distribution 133T
  public enterprice in 174–207
  see also defence
Indian Union 145
individual
  as best judge 11
  firms 96
  households 8
  mistaken ideas of 11

individual (*continued*)
  self-interest of 20
  unit cost 102
  welfare of 4, 7, 11
industrial
  capacity 96, 212
  competitive 113
  growth 26, 82, 83
  inputs 37
  marginal costs of 96–7
  modernization/expansion 66
  sickness 198, 222
  units 5, 6, 17–18, 27, 38, 47, 48, 51, 64–6, 72, 74–7, 79, 86, 88, 112, 116, 198, 205, 215, 217, 221
  units, dispersal of 82
  units, giant 82
industry
  categories of 119
  competitive 75, 134
  core 176, 187
  development fund for 77–8
  government aid for 88–9
  and government regulation 121–39
  non-controlled 163–4, 221
  price-controlled 102–20, 215 16, 218, 221
  priority 120
  profitability of 160
  restrictions on 46
  sick 198, 206, 217, 222
  study of 215–16
  textile 141
inflation 28, 125
inflationary
  pressures 23, 28
  situation 28, 212
  spiral 41, 46
information 60, 71–2
infrastructure, basic
  creation of 45, 176, 194, 195
  facilities 175–6
  lack of 10, 22, 27
  necessary 96

inputs
  agricultural 28
  control of prices of 45, 147
  costs 52, 59
  essential 88, 200, 216
  industrial 23, 28, 83, 214
  key 205
  prices 60
  production 31
  scarce 127
institutions
  Agricultural Prices Commission (India) 61
  Bureau of Industrial Costs and Prices (India) 61
  Department of Economic Affairs (UK) 59
  financial 77
  Ministry of Economic Affairs (Belgium) 58
  Ministry of Economic Affairs & Finance (France) 58
  Monopolistic & Restrictive Trade Practices Com (India) 61
  national 59
  National Board of Prices & Incomes (UK) 50, 59
  National Prices Committee (France) 58, 59, 157, 220
  Price Commission (Belgium) 59, 220
  Prices and Income Board (UK) 157, 220
instrument, policy
  economic 40, 44
  effective 24
  of resource mobilization 41
  suitable 29
interest rate of 10, 105, 113
interpretation of price control 40
inventories 105, 197, 206
inventory management 96
Investigation and Registration (India), Director-General of 62, 154, 157

investment
  in agriculture 39
  discouraged 107, 219
  in the economy 13, 45
  government 184, 216
  growth 177T
  inducement for 175
  in industry 103, 111, 129
  'lumpiness' of 94
  planned 169
  programme 45
  public sector 195, 199, 201
  resources for 27
  by the state 11, 24
  subsidy 89
  in underdeveloped countries 10
iron 127, 152
issue price 56, 134
issues, general policy
  and problems relating to
    determination of controlled
    prices 64–91
  relating to pricing policy 44–63

Joint Plant Committee (JPC) 128, 158
justification for price control 48
jute 164

Kaldor, N 16n

labour
  abundant 82
  costs 71, 107
  declining demands for 194
  greater use of 195
  -intensive 114, 117–18
  direct 71
  waged 108
laissez-faire, policy of 8, 9,
Law
  courts of 140, 156
  EEC 54–5
  for setting up development funds 78
  of Diminishing Returns 3, 93
  of Diminishing Utility 3
  and restrictive practices 154, 171
  need for systemized 72–3
leakages 134–5
legal provisions 57, 72–3, 152–3, 213, 222
levy price/rate 121, 128, 129–31, 131–9, 213, 214
licensing of dealers 142
limestone 151–2
loans 166T–7, 191T, 195, 202, 204
locational advantage 88
Luxembourg 54, 71

machinery and equipment 182, 183
management 96, 116, 197, 203, 209, 222
'*mandi*' 150
manufactures 1, 5, 47, 54
margin of tolerance 41, 42
marginal analysis 92
marginal conditions 94–5
marginal cost pricing versus average
    cost pricing 92–101
market
  black 24, 29, 34, 38, 124–6, 214
  conditions 75
  consumer goods sector of 2
  control of 17–19
  domestic 65
  economies ix, 10, 28
  establishing a 199
  export 88
  forces 1, 2–3, 8, 19, 22, 35, 50, 123
  free 28, 30, 122, 211
  government intervention in 1, 5, 9, 14–16, 46–7, 64–5
  imperfections 9, 18, 44
  international 65, 87
  mechanism 1–4 *passim*, 10, 12, 14, 17, 20–1, 25, 37, 44, 48, 50, 58, 150, 208, 210
  oligopolistic 40, 42
  open 51, 80, 125–6, 129, 132, 214

market (*continued*)
  price 5, 6, 7, 75, 92, 93, 94, 121, 134, 149
  situations 55, 112, 176
Marshall, Alfred 119
mass consumption 127, 140, 213, 216
materials, raw 83, 90, 149, 162, 195, 217, 218
measures
  of economic policy 208, 210
  effectiveness of 62
  emergency 44
  fiscal 26, 29, 45–7, 211
  for increased production 216
  monetary 26, 29, 30, 45–7, 210
  package 49, 56
  of price control 32, 37, 51, 209, 213, 220
  prohibiting certain practices 53–5
  remedial 135, 196, 218, 222
mills 143
Minister of Economic Affairs and Finance (France) 58
Ministerial Order 71
Ministry of Finance (India) 145
mixed economy 2
model(s)
  conceptual 2, 31, 35, 210
  of competitive economy 5, 6, 19
  efficiency 205–6
  of perfect competition 7, 8–9, 15, 20
  theoretical 39
  see also capitalism, socialism
modernization 77
money
  black 24, 124
  demand 41
  erosion in value of 46
  votes 4, 7, 9
  utility of 8
monopoly(ies)
  emergence of 18
  marginal costs of 99
  in production 6, 75
  profits 200, 201
  of supply 34, 37
monopolist 200
Monopolistic and Restrictive Trade Practices Commission (MRTPC) (India) 61–2, 153–7, 170–1, 221
monopolistic
  practices 170–1, 219, 222
  position 56, 200
  pricing 201
multi-product firms 116, 118, 219, 220

nationalized
  enterprises 23
  industries 92
  see also public sector
National Board for Prices and Incomes (UK) 58
National Prices Committee 58, 59, 220
nature and objectives of pricing policy 17–32
needs, real 29, 77
net domestic capital formation (NDCF) 178T, 183T
net domestic product (NDP) 177–8T, 180T, 183T, 193T
net profit/loss 187–8T, 189T
net worth 105–6; 108, 110–12, 113, 115–16, 164, 189T, 190T, 191T, 195, 219
normative
  cost 87
  economics 17
norms
  capital investment 108
  of consumption 102, 148
  cost 217
  efficiency 86, 96
  industrial 76, 86, 109
  ratio 118
  of utilization 145–6
Nurkse, Ragner 175

objectives
  basic 49–50, 136, 143
  economic 81, 211
  of pricing policy 17–32, 40, 43, 209, 211–12
  variety of 56
  oil hydrogenated 167
oil-seeds 149
oligopolies 18, 73, 75 see also market
oligopolistic
  industries 51, 99
  market 40, 42
  position 56, 200, 219
  units 73
orders see control, orders
organization(s)
  central research 59
  voluntary 222
  see also institutions
output
  aggregate 41
  composition of 7
  for free sale 214
  industrial 51, 80, 94
  level of 93, 96, 97, 100
  and marginal costs 215–16
  national 7, 24
  restriction of 9, 19, 26, 46, 64, 124, 201
  total 18
  unit of 98–9
  valve of 116, 117, 219
over-capitalization 107
overheads 71
Oxford, University of ix–x

package
  of economic policies 26
  of measures 27, 38, 56
  of policies 96
paper 122, 160, 168
penalties 55
perspective
  dynamic 96
  economic 82
  long-term 81
pharmaceutical products 71
phenomena
  causal factors in 33
  elimination of 34
  of price control of 39
Pigou, Prof. A.C. 98
Plan, Fifth Economic and Social Development 53
Planning Commission 160
plant, industrial 80, 83, 84
policy
  change in 196
  conclusion 42
  economic 2, 13, 14, 25, 209
  federal 145
  instruments 15
  of *laissez-faire* 8, 9
  lending 107
  long-term 67
  package of 26
  realistic 199
  pricing ix. 1–16, 17–32, 37, 44–63, 92–101, 112
  of reducing subsidies 145
  state 40
policy-makers 25, 36, 50, 55, 56, 58, 124, 160, 212
population
  agricultural 30
  of underdeveloped countries 24
  rural 211
post-costing 103–4
poverty, vicious circle of 21
power 72, 82, 220
price(s)
  adjustment to changing costs 218
  average 80, 131
  bracket 51, 64, 121
  ceiling 50, 64, 212
  competitive 87, 216
  compulsory reporting of 53–4
  consumer 83, 217
  control of 1–16, 26–7, 29, 30, 32, 33–43, 44–5, 47–9, 52, 55, 56,

236 Index

prices (*continued*)
    59–60, 64–91, 102–20, 121, 125, 140–73, 176, 196, 208–22; partial 121, 124, 215; total 121–2, 124, 125–6, 215
  determination 65
  discrimination 54, 221
  equalizing of 98
  fixed 23
  fixing 28, 51, 70, 76, 98, 102, 105, 109, 115, 121, 196, 220
  fixing body 61, 70–2, 73, 74, 79, 83, 91, 108, 117, 118, 158, 169, 200, 215, 218, 220
  floor 30, 48, 50, 64, 146, 150–1, 212
  formation 57
  freezing 50, 51, 52, 212
  givers 5
  gross 55
  and incomes 59
  issue 122, 132, 214
  market 5, 7, 36, 42, 212
  market-clearing 36
  mechanism 17, 60
  parameters 52
  procurement 80–1, 90, 121, 151
  and production, equilibrium of 4
  reform 21
  regulation 17, 31, 59
  relative 18
  retention 51, 86, 147, 212
  review 79, 218
  rise in 25
  setting exercise 215
  signals 4, 5, 8, 9, 11–12, 14
  stabilization 18, 19, 41–2
  standard 86–7
  structure 27, 47, 50, 65, 158
  support *see* floor
  system 12, 14, 30
  takers 3, 5
  theory 33, 96
  uniform 217
  wholesale, changes in 161T, 162T

pricing policy
  dual 80, 121–39
  explanation of term 1, 209
  general issues relating to 44–63
  government 205
  implementation of 221
  in India 140–73, 174–209, 221
  marginal cost 215
  monitoring of 58, 158–9, 160
  nature and objectives of 17–32
  and price controls ix, 1–16, 33–43
  in the public sector 196, 199, 202
  see also government, price controls
principles, basic, for pricing controls 1–2, 57
priority, national 26
private sector 174–5, 182, 185T, 186, 190T, 194, 196, 198, 205
problem(s)
  of allocating resources 13
  of ensuring a rate of return 56
  and issues relating to the determination of controlled prices 64–91
  of pricing, efficiency and output 97
  of rate of return in relation to price-controlled industries 102–20
process 82
procurement 121–9 *passim*, 142, 151, 213, 214
producer(s)
  categories of 18, 87, 88, 219
  control over market place 5
  failure of 6
  incomes of 16
  and pricing 51, 91, 95, 119, 132
  rate of return 56
  as seller 3, 6
  of tractors 145
production
  capital 175, 220
  of consumer goods 27
  controls 40
  costs of 83, 86, 88, 98–9, 199

distortion in structure of 36
efficiency of 93, 115, 116, 218
factors of 4, 5–6, 70
growth 129
investment in 103
large scale 94
pattern of 18, 29, 44
and productivity 184, 204–5, 220
quotas of 25
scale of 80
surplus 86
units 20, 99, 147
value of 117
products
  covered by stability contracts 223–4T
  distribution of 122, 212
  export of 65
  finished 83, 193, 195, 206, 217
  homogeneity of 5–6
  inputs for 30, 147
  intermediate 147
  price-controlled 31
  price setting for 91, 222
  range of 5
  sale of 87
  subsidies for 88
profitability of public enterprises 188–9T, 191–7 *passim*, 203, 205, 222
profits
  after tax 164, 165T
  aggregate 104–5
  control of 64, 66, 212
  and controlled costs 102
  earning 82, 174
  excess 76–7, 135
  excessive 26
  for growth 27
  low 97
  margin of 29, 38, 68, 70, 86, 87, 93, 103–4, 109, 114, 118, 196, 200, 216, 217, 218, 220
  maximization of 4, 19, 75, 92, 93, 97, 104, 200
  motive 206
  normal 119
  for old/new units 80
  private sector 194
  producer's 5
  public enterprise 188
  smaller 95
prohibition
  of discriminatory practices 54
  on overchanging 55, 57
  of resale price maintenance 54
propositions 33–4, 40–1
public
  distribution system 116, 123, 133, 134, 138, 150–1, 213
  enterprises ix, 174, 207, 222
  interest 154–6, 201
  sector 129, 169, 176, 177, 179–80T, 182T–4, 186–7, 188T
  utilities 92, 100

quantum 104, 106, 107
Queen Elizabeth House ix

railway wagons 164
Raj, Dr. K.M. 127
rate of return in relation to price-controlled industries 102–20, 218–19
rationing 34–5, 41, 42, 49, 80, 122, 142
RBI *see* Reserve Bank of India
real life situation 94
real world 8, 9, 15, 19, 39
rebates 55, 57
recommendation 74
refusal to sell 54
regional disparities 218
regulation *see* control
regulatory action 77
regulatory mechanism, 73
remedial measures 77, 199
resale price maintenance 54, 57, 152, 156, 157, 213, 221

238 Index

researchers, academic 160
research and development (R&D) 66, 113, 202–3, 205
Reserve Bank of India (RBI) 118, 164
reserves, building up of 107
resources
    allocation of 5, 7, 8, 9, 13, 44, 46
    diversion of 103
    diversion of economic 46, 113
    employment of 10–11, 24
    financial 26, 126
    generation of 77, 78
    government 211, 217
    human 13
    internal 165T, 190T, 191, 193, 194, 210, 214, 216
    misallocation of 36
    mobilization of 18–19, 23, 27, 41, 45, 144, 208
    scarce 65, 83
    total 190T
    underutilization of 9, 18
    utilization 15, 20
responsiveness 197
restrictive practices 61–2, 154–6 *passim*, 170, 213, 221, 222
restrictions 81
retention prices 64
revenue
    average 94
    curve 93–4, 95
    for firms 93
    government 23–4, 26
    marginal 93, 97
revision of controlled prices 68, 81, 218, 219
rice 133, 142
rules
    Cost Audit Report, 72
    for costing 53, 71, 215, 216
    framing of 73
    standard 72–3
sales 117, 126–7, 130, 132, 197
sales below cost price 53

sales promotion drive 6, 206
savings 23, 24, 41
scarcity *see* shortages
seller(s)
    and equilibrium price 36
    informal control over demand 40
    and net prices 55
    as price takers 3, 5
shortage(s) 26, 28, 49, 55, 116, 123, 127, 209–10
Smith, Adam (1723–90) 16n
social
    benefit, marginal 98
    cost, marginal 98
    security 12
socialism 3, 35, 39, 40
socialist
    economy 2, 20, 21, 210
    system 3, 35
society
    changes in 20
    classes of 60
    effects on 7
stability
    contracts 57
    and growth 27
    objective 19
State
    and the consumer 20
    intervention 1, 5, 9, 10, 11, 34, 45, 47
    monopolies 100
    Planning Boards 160
    Trading Corporation 146
    welfare 11, 20
statutory
    basis for controls 42, 57
    body 61
    minimum prices 150
    price controls 169
steel 77, 78, 127–8, 149, 152, 158, 204
Steel Development Fund 77, 78
Steel Authority of India Limited (SAIL) 128, 158

Index 239

stocks, buffer 132, 133, 134, 142, 150
structure
  cost 80
  of input and output prices, 30
  of relative prices 31, 46, 59
subsidies 47, 64–5, 68, 84–7, 88–9, 100, 126, 133, 135, 145, 170, 203–4, 214, 216–17, 222
substitute commodities 38, 45, 50
sugar 31, 77, 122, 127, 128, 135T, 136–7, 149–50, 161, 168
Sugar Development Fund 77
suppliers
  failure of 6
  of goods 1, 156
supply
  elasticity of 36
  of essential inputs 29
  excess 35, 39
  of goods and services 41, 156
  inadequacy of 116
  inelasticity in 22, 23, 214
  management 29, 42
  position 34
support price operations 30, 150
surpluses 112–13, 174
system
  of determination 65
  of Disequilibrium 41–2
  distribution 222 *see also* transport
  dual pricing 51
  of freight equalization 83
  monitoring 50, 90, 136
  of monitoring production 32
  perfectly competitive 8, 10
  price 12
  of price controls 57, 141
  public distribution 56

Tariff Commission (India) 146
tax
  concessions 26, 65, 89, 211, 216
  element 78, 117
  revenue 23–4, 89, 103, 124, 193T

taxation 30, 105, 107, 112, 125, 193, 195, 201, 219
taxpayer 87, 125
technology
  development of 195–6, 205
  existing 203
  foreign 205
  improved 5, 79
  imported 198
  industrial 69, 70, 82, 108, 217
  labour absorbing 114
  labour intensive 115
  outdated 76
  type of 115
technological
  advances 17
  change 6, 69, 95
  improvement 90
  transformation 81
tenders 73
textile(s) 90, 142–3, 198
theory
  'cobweb' 36
  of harmony of interests 6
  of a market economy 10
  of imperfect competition 8, 12
  of price control 33–43, 209
  of price formation 95
  of static equilibrium of price formation 215
  of Von Mises 34–5, 39
  of welfare optimum 11
Third World countries 18, 21, 44, 208
tractors 145, 213
trade
  margins 54, 56
  methods of 119
  traditions of 119
  practices 152–3, 154, 170, 221
traders 151, 153, 209
traffic, road 83
transport
  costs 67, 83, 84, 107, 151, 217–18
  and storage 133

transport (*continued*)
  subsidy 84–5T
turnover 107, 116–17, 118, 219–20

uneconomic units 64 *see also* subsidization
unemployment 24, 196
unfair practices 46, 153, 222
United Kingdom 54, 58
United States, price control in 41
unrest, social and political 18, 46
urea 147, 148

valuation 76
valued added 117, 219–20
vanaspati 74, 146, 213
value judgement(s) 1, 7, 8, 11, 13, 15, 17, 20, 21
variables 33
vegetable oils 146
vicious circles of poverty 21
Von Mises, Ludwig 33–40 *passim*, 42–3

wage(s)
  control of 41, 42
  increases 52
  level of 22
  price spiral 19, 46
  rate 108, 113
war
  effort, effects of 123, 213
  Second World 40, 41, 42, 137, 140
wartime 18, 19, 44, 211
weaving capacity 143
welfare
  economics 7
  of the individual 4, 7
  maximization of 8–12 *passim*, 19–20, 92, 94, 96
  objective 19
  optimum 7, 10, 11, 15, 19–20, 92, 93, 94–5
  state 11, 39–40, 210